A TREASURY OF MOM, POP & KIDS HUMOR

**Edited by
James E. Myers, Sr.**

THE LINCOLN-HERNDON PRESS, INC.
818 S. Dirksen Parkway
Springfield, Illinois 62703

A Treasury of Mom, Pop & Kids' Humor

Published by

The Lincoln-Herndon Press, Inc.
818 South Dirksen Parkway
Springfield, Illinois 62703
(217) 522-2732

Printed in the United States of America.

Library of Congress Cataloguing-in-Publication Data
ISBN 0-942936-29-9
Library of Congress Catalogue Card Number 97-071785
First Printing

Typography by Communication Design, Rochester, IL

TABLE OF CONTENTS

INTRODUCTION

America's strength is based on, and continued by, the family unit known as: "MOM, POP AND THE KIDS." True—it's serious business—this matter of marriage and kids, but it does have its humorous, funny side as any mother or father can attest. This collection of jokes, stories and cartoons reflects that humorous side and, indirectly, its serious side as well.

But let's reflect here on the humorous side of family life. Every family could write a book on the funny events, discussions, accidents, "boners" that occur at home. The humor between husbands and wives is legendary as is the humor of kids-with-kids and with teachers and advisors in and out of school.

This collection offers a humorous view of family life with many of the jokes, sayings, stories, being true to life—actual happenings.

So...if you love family life or have grown a bit bored with it, the stories and cartoons in this collection will amuse and stimulate you to see not only the serious, earn-a-living, get-along-with-her/him side of marriage, but the joyous fun side of it, also.

CHAPTER I

Kids in School

The teacher took the first grade class to the Chicago Museum of Natural History. That evening, after the kids had come back from the museum and gone home, one father asked his son what they had done in school that day. The lad replied: "Well, Daddy, our class went to see a dead circus."

———————— 🧑‍🤝‍🧑 ————————

The minister's family was seated around the dinner table, quietly eating, when father spoke: "Curiosity. It's a blessing and a curse. Can any of you children tell me where we'd be today if no one had been curious?"

"I can Daddy," his ten-year-old responded. "We'd be in the Garden of Eden!"

———————— 🧑‍🤝‍🧑 ————————

Describing his teacher to his mother, Jimmy called her "mean but fair!"

"Just what do you mean by that?" his mother asked.

"She's mean to everybody," he replied.

———————— 🧑‍🤝‍🧑 ————————

The sixth grade class was giving imitations of various animal sounds. Very good imitations were given of a dog, a cat and so on until the question of the sound of a wolf came up. One young man gave a low, drawn-out whistle!

———————— 🧑‍🤝‍🧑 ————————

The eighth grade class was studying the reaction of the body to hot and cold water. The teacher asked: "What is the reaction of the body when it is in the bathtub and covered with hot water?"

One student replied: "I'm not sure of the reaction but I am sure the telephone will ring."

———————— 🧑‍🤝‍🧑 ————————

"Mama," the little boy said, "In school today, my teacher asked if I had any brothers and sisters, and I said I was just an only child."

"What did the teacher say to that?" asked his mother.
"Well, she said...she said...thank goodness!"

The little boy had undergone a circumcision rather late in life. In class he was having a terrible time, squirming and fidgeting and sighing so that, at last, the teacher asked: "Albert, what in the world is wrong with you?" So the little guy tells her of his circumcision.

"Now I understand," said the teacher. "You go to the principal's office and see if he can't give you some help, some advice that'll let you cope with the pain."

The boy walked slowly to the principal's office and soon came back. His fly was open and his little you-know-what was just hanging out. The teacher said, "Albert, why on earth did you come back to class in this disgusting way?" And the boy replied: "Well, the principal said if I could just stick it out till noon, he'd let me go home."

Teacher: "Class, can anyone tell me why the Middle Ages were called the Dark Ages?"
Student: "I suppose it's because there were so many knights."

The fifth grade class was asked to use the word "jubilant" in a sentence. One lad held up his hand and the teacher nodded to him. "That Bobby is a terrible boy...he's a jubilant delinquent."

In the high school French class, the teacher asked if anyone knew the meaning of *mal de mare*?"
One boy held up his hand, was recognized, and said: "It means you can't take it with you."

A teacher at my son's grade school announced that she was engaged and the entire school was delighted. Everybody liked this particular teacher. One boy wrote her a note:

8

Dear Mrs. Albright:
I sure do hope you have a happy and sexfull life.
Your student and friend,
Howard Viel

Isn't it amazing how customs change. Remember the time when you couldn't go to school wearing pants with a hole in them? Now kids refuse to go if they don't have those holes.

The ten-year-old walked up to his teacher and said, "Have you heard of the Unfinished Symphony?" The teacher nodded. The lad handed her his homework. "Well, I want you to know that this is my Unfinished Homework!"

One happy first grader came to school and ran up to his teacher to announce that he had a new sister. The teacher said, "Wonderful...and how much did she weigh?" The lad replied: "It's not important because she didn't cost anything. My Mom laid her."

Some kids are born with modern know-how. Here's an example. The lad slipped in the school yard and skinned his elbow. "Now remember," the school yard monitor told him, "Big boys don't cry!"

"Cry!" the boy responded, "who's gonna cry. Not me! I'm suing the school!"

"How come school was so bad for you today?" her Mom asked six-year-old Susan.

"Because of what the teacher lied to me about," said Susan. "She said, 'Susan...now you go sit in that chair in the corner for the present.' And then she didn't give me no present!"

Teacher: "Emil...why are you coming into my classroom on your hands and knees?"

Emil: "Because yesterday you told me not to *walk* into your class late."

Little Tommy was in the first grade. One day, he came home and his mother asked: "Well, Tommy, what did you learn in school today?"

"In arithmetic, I learned that three and three make seven."

"But that's not correct," his mother said.

"Well, then, I guess I didn't learn anything."

The teacher asked, "What biblical story had a man swallowed by a whale? Eddie Johnson?"

"No...ah..."

"That's right. Now, tell me what is used to conduct electricity?"

"W-w-why...er..."

"Once more you're right. Now, tell me, what is the unit of electrical power?"

"The what?"

"Just right, young man. Now, class, you see what study can do for you!"

On our vacation in Wisconsin last summer, I saw fireflies for the first time. I thought they were mosquitoes coming after us with flashlights.

Boy, the food was awful at summer camp this year. My first day there, I threw mine in the lake and darned if the fish didn't throw it back!

Little boy on the meaning of conscience: "Something you tell your Mother before your sister does."

Teacher: "If your father earned $42,000 a month and gave your mother half, what would she have?"

Student: "Heart failure or maybe a stroke!"

Teacher: "In the alphabet, what comes after 'O'?"
Student: "Yeah."

————————  ————————

Student: "Mrs. Ames, would you punish one of your students if he didn't do something?"
Teacher: "Of course not. Why do you ask?"
Student: "Well, I didn't do my homework!"

" SEVEN TIMES 4 IS 36. NOW DON'T BOTHER MOTHER WHILE SHE'S BALANCING HER CHECK BOOK."

Teacher: "How many fingers do you have on your right hand?"
Student: "Five."
Teacher: "And if you lost two of them, what would you have?"
Student: "No more piano lessons."

Teacher: "If I had ten apples in this one hand and twelve oranges in the other hand, what would I have?"
Student: "The world's biggest hands!"

───────── 🏃 ─────────

"Attention class! First off, who can name a deadly poison?"
"I can, teacher," Charlie said. "Aviation. One drop and you're dead."

───────── 🏃 ─────────

Teacher: "I'd like to go an entire day without scolding you!"
Student: "Well, teacher, you certainly have my permission."

───────── 🏃 ─────────

"It's no wonder you are such an awful wimp," said the lad to the little neighbor girl, "your daddy and mom were married by a Justice of the Peace."

"Nuts to you!" retorted little Susie. "From the noise and hollerin' I hear comin' from your house, I know your Dad and Mom musta been married by the Secretary of War!"

───────── 🏃 ─────────

"Can you tell me how long Franklin Roosevelt lived?"
"All his life."

───────── 🏃 ─────────

"Can anyone tell me the benefit to humanity of gravity?"
"I can. It's a lot easier to clean up a bowl of spilled soup from the floor than from the ceiling."

───────── 🏃 ─────────

"Can anyone in the class tell me what is H_2O?"
"Water."
"Correct. Now can anyone tell me what is H_2O_4?"
"Drinking."

───────── 🏃 ─────────

"Hey, Eddie. How did you do in your chemistry exam?"
"I don't know. The teacher ain't come down yet."

"Gerald, please use a sentence with the word 'deceit' in it."

"OK, Mr. Brown. Here goes. I prefer to sit down only because my pants have got a hole in 'deceit'."

I got an "E" in English this year. That dern teacher of mine said I didn't deserve an "F."

Student: "Mrs. Norman, could you tell me if there's really and truly life after death?"

Mrs. Norman: "Why do you need to ask such a question?"

Student: "Because I'm sure gonna need it to do all the homework you've given us."

My Dad always says, "what you don't know won't hurt you." Well, he's wrong! How do I know that? I'll tell you...I took a test in science last week and the grade from that hurt like heck!"

Eddie: "Sorry, teacher, but I don't have a pen or pencil."

Teacher: "Where's your head, your brains. How could you forget to take a pen and pencil?"

Eddie: "Easy. I took the bus."

A little fellow in second grade remarked: "I ain't got no pencil, teacher."

The teacher groaned and said to him, "It's I *don't* have a pencil—*you* don't have a pencil—*we* don't have any pencils—*they* don't have any pencils. Now, do you understand that?"

"Not really," the kid replied. "Tell me...what happened to all them pencils?"

A little boy had been handling the greeting card stock for quite a while. The manager came over to him and asked, "What is it you're looking for, son? Birthday greeting? Anniversary card for your folks' anniversary? Card for somebody sick?"

The little fellow shook his head. "No, that's not it. I wonder if you've got any blank report cards."

———————— 🧑‍🤝‍🧑 ————————

Teacher: "Just how did this window get broken?"
Student: "I was cleaning my slingshot and it went off."

———————— 🧑‍🤝‍🧑 ————————

The first grade teacher had her class make zeroes on their notebook paper. But little Amy wasn't working at it. The teacher asked her why she wasn't writing.

"I was afraid they might roll off," she said.

———————— 🧑‍🤝‍🧑 ————————

These quotations supposedly came from an expensive private school in California:

1. The name of a former ruler in Ethiopia is Hail Silly Assy.
2. Gothic architecture is easy to find because of its use of flying buttocks.
3. The safest kinda girl to have a date with is one who wears glasses and that's because if you blow your breath on her...she can't see what you're doing.

———————— 🧑‍🤝‍🧑 ————————

The class was discussing the story of Noah and the flood and the teacher asked Bobby to tell the story, Bobby began, "Well, God spoke to Noah and told him it was gonna rain like crazy and that he'd better begin to build himself a yacht."

———————— 🧑‍🤝‍🧑 ————————

The new teacher seemed to have succeeded in taking charge of the fourth grade class in a ritzy Los Angeles suburb. Then, a little girl walked up to her desk, handed her a note, and waited for her to read it. The teacher began to read: "I think you're gonna be a fine teacher, Miss Edward. I like you a lot, but the girl who sits next to me thinks you're a fat slob."

14

Teacher: "Class, there will be an eclipse of the moon this evening. Be sure and ask your parents if you can stay up and watch it."
Student: "Tell us, Ma'am...what channel is it on?"

Teacher: "Class, can anyone tell me what is the highest form of animal life?"
Pupil: "I'm not sure, Ma'am, but it's either the elephant or the giraffe."

Teacher: "Dudley, can you tell me what the four seasons are?"
Dudley: "Salt, pepper, mustard and vinegar."

It was a snowy day outside and the kindergarten teacher was helping the kids put on their raincoats and boots before she sent them home. But she had a real tough time with little Jim's. The boots just didn't fit him at all. Finally, she got one on him and it took almost five more minutes to get the other one on.

When she was done, Jim stood up and said, "You know, Mrs. Wright, these really aren't my boots."

"What! They aren't? Oh my goodness," said the teacher and then began to take them off the boy.

Finished with their removal, she asked: "So, tell me...whose boots are they?"

The lad replied: "They're my brother's. He wore 'em all last year but they got too small and now my Mom makes me wear them!"

Teacher: "Tell me, Albert Jefferies, if your mother gave you five cookies and asked you to split them with your brother, how would you do it?"
Albert: "Depends on whether it was my big brother or the little one."

Teacher: "Don't worry about the date on your examination paper, Eddie. I'm only interested in what you've written."
Eddie: "Well, I was anxious to have at least one thing right on my paper."

"WITH SEX EDUCATION, SELF-ESTEEM, MULTICULTURALISM, SELF AWARENESS, COMPUTER STUDIES, AND TOUCHY FEELY, I'M NOT GOING TO HAVE TIME FOR READING, WRITING AND ARITHMETIC. THAT'S WHERE YOU, AS PARENTS, COME IN ..."

From what five-letter word can you take away two letters and have just one left?

Alone.

Joe: "Doc, come quick, my wife broke her leg."
Doc: "Sorry, can't help you, I'm a doctor of music."
Joe: "Good. Perfect. It's the piano leg."

A teacher was explaining to her fourth grade class the importance of penmanship: "Class, it's terribly important that you write well. If you don't learn how to write, you'll have to pay cash for everything."

The teacher was explaining to her second grade class the various animals in the world. She was using a video and having the kids try to identify them. They got along fine with lions, tigers, and elephants but no one could identify a deer.

"If your father was gone for a few days and then came home, what would your mother call him?"

"Oh," one little boy piped up. "So that's what a *!#*! is!"

"Seven is truly an odd number. Does anyone in class know how to make it even?"

One lad raised his hand. "Yes?" said the teacher.

"Take away the 's'," was his reply.

Kids are a paradox...hard to figure out. They easily learn to operate a computer but never learn how to use a clothes hanger!

Kids can be very adept at improvisation. Consider this true case. A Sangamon County, Illinois teacher was discussing the proper use of "setting" and "sitting" with her fifth grade class. She asked a student to create a sentence with the word "setting" in it.

A boy raised his hand, was recognized, then said, "A man is setting in the chair."

"Not correct," said the teacher. "Living things sit. Things without life set. So give me another sentence using the word setting."

The lad thought a minute, then grinned in triumph. He had it! "The dead man is setting in the chair."

The teacher had a call to the telephone, picked it up and said, "Yes?"

"I just want to tell you that Adam Elpot won't be in school today."

"And who is this speaking?" she asked.

"This is my father," was the reply.

Teacher: "Can anyone tell me the difference between hay and straw?"

Student: "I can. You can't sip a coke through hay."

"I'll be late getting my report card back to you," the student told his teacher. "You gave me an A in arithmetic and my Mom is still mailing the report card to all of her relatives."

17

Teacher: "What did Caesar say when Brutus stabbed him?"
Pupil: "Ouch!"

On the east side of New York, a student was asked to make a sentence with the word "bewitches" in it. He thought a moment, then said, "I'll bewitches in a minute."

Teacher: "Class, can anyone tell what a reindeer is?"
Student: "I've always thought it was a horse with a TV antenna."

Teacher: "Tommy, why did you write that George Washington was a spendthrift?"
Tommy: "That's exactly what a man is when he goes around throwing a dollar across a river."

Which is proper to say—3 plus 5 *is* 7 or 3 plus 5 *are* 7?
Neither. 3 plus 5 are 8.

The third grade teacher wrote several everyday words on the blackboard. Then she asked the class to make shorter words from each.
"I especially want you to consider this word," she said, writing the word "kitten" on the blackboard. "Tell me how many words you can see in the word 'kitten'."
A little girl raised her hand. "I've got the word 'itten'," she said.
"Very interesting," said the teacher. "Please use it in a sentence."
"My goodness, but 'itten this a lovely day."

The teacher was trying to have the students get accustomed to knowing and writing certain words. So she asked the class to tell about their favorite TV program. "And if you want help in spelling a word, just come to me and I'll help you."

Soon a youngster tip-toed his way to her desk and asked:
"Superman." She spelled it for him but very soon the lad was back to ask,
"How do I spell egg?"

"Why on earth do you need to spell 'egg'?"

"It's part of my sentence," the boy said. "Superman has an
egg-splosion."

"Daddy," the little boy asked, "why do I have to go to school?"

Very sensibly the father answered, "Because the school won't come
to you."

When the sixth grader was asked to give an example of a collective
noun, he replied: "I've got a magnet at home and it sure is a collective
noun."

"Tell me, Charlie," his daddy asked, "what grade did you get on your
history test today?"

"Not a good one, Pop," the boy replied. "But the test was not fair.
Why, they asked me about stuff that happened before I was born!"

Little Mort was just beginning the first grade. He got along fine that
first day when he took the school bus to school. But he had to walk home
because, as he explained to his parents, "You guys would think I really
took it home...and would make me give it back."

Little Bob was asked who shot Lincoln and he answered: "I ain't tellin'.
I ain't no stool pigeon."

An English teacher was talking about the short stories of a nineteenth-
century famous writer who wrote, "I keep writing and writing, always

19

hoping that I'll get paid enough to keep the wolf away from the door."
"Can anyone explain what this writer meant by the phrase 'keeping the wolf away from the door'?"

A boy raised his hand. "I'd guess that the lady just didn't want the gent bothering her anymore."

When the librarian questioned the little boy's book choice, *Advice to Young Mothers*, he explained, "I'm collecting moths."

The second grade was learning how to write and were studying the letters of the alphabet. "What letter comes after the letter T?" asked the teacher.

A little girl promptly replied, "V."

A little guy was on his way to school in the school bus. He said to his seat mate, "I woke up this morning with a headache, a stomach ache and pains in my chest...but it didn't work!"

Teacher: "Class, can anyone tell me what are the three most used words in grades one through eight?"
Student: "I don't know."
Teacher: "Correct!"

Just before Thanksgiving, a second-grade teacher asked her class what, in their coming prayers, they would say they were thankful for.
One student replied: "I'm sure as heck thankful I'm not a turkey!"

"Hey, Mom, I nearly got all hundreds at school today."
"Wonderful! Please tell me about it."
"Well, I got all zeroes."

**"PLEASE, MISS CRUMP, ALL SECOND GRADE TEACHERS
HAVE THEIR BAD DAYS."**

I teach freshman history, and one day I asked my students to write a letter as if they were an historic personage during his lifetime. One lad wrote: "Dear Josephine: I am awful sorry to inform you that I did not make out so well at Waterloo. Your friend, Napoleon."

A school specialist was working with a first grade girl who seldom showed any reaction to subject learning. He read her this rhyme: "There was a little girl, who had a little curl, right in the middle of her forehead. When she was good, she was very, very good. But when she was bad, she was horrid." So, the following day, he asked the same little girl if she'd enjoy hearing the poem again. "OK," said the child, "but this time leave out the bad news!"

Teacher: "Class, could any of you tell me their judgment of the most useful animal in the world?"

Pupil: "I'd pick the chicken 'cause you can eat 'em before they're born and after they're dead."

A Minneapolis, Minnesota high school teacher, hung this sign under the clock in her classroom: "Time will pass...will you?"

It was a great May day, and four high school boys decided to heck with school...they'd rather go fishing. So, in the morning, they did go fishing. But they returned to school after lunch. They explained to the teacher that they'd had a flat tire on the way to school.

"Tough luck about that flat tire, boys," said their teacher, "because this morning we had a most important test. So now, take seats on all four sides of the room...one in front, one in back, one on the right side and one on the left...then get out paper and a pen."

"My first question," began the teacher, "is...which tire was flat?"

Aaron: "Teacher, I don't think I deserved a zero on this test."

Teacher: "Neither do I...but it's the lowest grade I can give you."

Teacher: "What are clinics?"

Student: "A brand of facial tissue that pops up one at a time."

An elderly woman ignored the red light and walked out into the street. A cop tried to stop her, held up his hand, then, when she still walked on, ran over to her. "Lady!" he roared, "don't you know what it means when I hold up my hand?"

"I ought to," she snapped back at him. "I've been a school teacher for thirty years!"

There was one boy in my class who had a tendency to monopolize our classroom discussions. He got so much on my nerves that I wrote a letter to his father: "Tom is a good student but, quit simply, he talks too much."

The father returned the note with a P.S. on the bottom: "You should meet his mother."

In an American history class, a lad answered one of the questions on the semester's final test as follows: "The principle export of the United States is money."

Here is a well-observed definition of "adult" written by an eighth grade student:
"An adult is a person who has stopped growing except in the middle."

The teacher picked up the chalk and wrote on the blackboard, "I ain't had no fun all summer." Then she turned to the class and asked, "Now tell me, class, what is wrong? What should I do to correct it?"
A boy raised his hand. "Yes?" said the teacher nodding to him.
"Maybe, just maybe, you should get a boyfriend."

Teacher: "Eddie, do you use paper or cloth napkins at home?"
Eddie: "Neither. We lick."

It really was nobody's fault that the teacher set him on fire. If it was anybody's fault, it was the kid's because he had a box of matches in his back pocket!

"I'd like to apply for that job as a riveter," the woman said to the foreman.
"Good. Tell me your experience."
"Well, I just quit my job as a riveter at the shipyard."
"I've got to tell you, Ma'am, this job is on a skyscraper, over 80 stories up. For this job, you've got to have nerves of iron, strength of six guys, unfailing sense of balance, stamina and, above all, patience."

"I've got all that," said the woman. "Y'see, before I worked at the shipyard, I drove a school bus!"

My school teacher is a really funny man. He's as bowlegged as a possum and his ears are just perfect for tucking in a pencil.

It was back in the 1920s and the little boy came home from his east side New York school. His father asked what subject he liked best, and the lad said, "Me? I sure do like Gozinter best, Papa."

"Gozinter? What kind of subject is that?"

"Well, Papa, I kin best esplain it by tellin' what we do. Gozinter. Well, 2 gozinter 4 twict. And 4 gozinter 12 three times. Understand now?"

In school at that same east side New York location, a teacher asked her class: "Children, does anyone know the meaning of 'stoic'?"

A little girl raised her hand. "Yes, Rebecca...tell us," the teacher said.

"A stoic is a boid what brings kids to yer mudder."

The student was asked to define abstract and then concrete. He stood and said: "Abstract, you can't see, but concrete, you can."

"Very good," the teacher said. "Now give me an example of each."

"My pants...they're concrete 'cause you can see 'em. But, your pants, Ma'am, are abstract!"

A little girl asked her mother what the word "fornication" meant. Mother was flabbergasted to hear such a word from the little girl and asked where she had learned that word.

The little girl responded: "Well, our teacher said the principal would visit our class tomorrow and that it was important that we be well-dressed fornication like that."

"Good news! I'm nearing the top of the under-achiever list."

I was teaching my first class...in English...since I graduated in Education. And I was emphasizing that women can do anything that a man can do. Then, just kidding a bit, I said, "There is one thing women can do that is impossible for men...have a baby."

One student in the back of the room quipped, "Not without us, you can't."

My son came home complaining about his new male teacher. "When he paddles us kids, he uses a paddle with a hole in it."

"Really?" I asked. "But why would he need a hole in the paddle?"

"To let the smoke out!"

25

Bloopers & Boners from Kids' Essays

Polite people don't break their bread and roll in their soup.

When Elmer Jenkins died, it turned out to be the turning point in his life.

Abstinence is very necessary but only when used in moderation.

Adolescence is that time in the life of a young person between puberty and adultery.

The Eskimos are God's frozen people.

A spinster is a bachelor's wife.

A census taker is a man who goes from house to house increasing population.

Owing to a lack of demand, there came about a slut on the market.

Faith is that quality of mankind that lets us believe what we know isn't true.

Excuses at School (and Other Unbelievables)

My son must go to the doctor today and should not take Physical Education. Please execute him.

Please permit our son, Tom, to miss school today. He's got diarrhea and what's more, his boots leak.

Dear Teach: Kindly eckuse our son, John, for not being there on Jan. 28, 29, 30, 31, 32 and also 33.

Mary won't be in school a week from Thursday because then we got to go to a funeral.

Please don't punish Tod for being absent last Wednesday. He had awfully loose vowels.

Please excuse Maybelle's lateness at getting to school. I forgot to wake her and didn't discover her at all until I began to make the beds.

Paul and I beg you to excuse Morrie for being. It was his Daddy's fault.

The Crazy Things Kids Write on Tests

Acrimony is what a divorced man gives his wife.

Queen Victoria was the very special queen who sat on a thorn for sixty-three years.

The difference between a king and a president is that a king is the son of his father, but a president isn't.

A mountain range is a stove that they use at high altitudes.

Abraham Lincoln was born and lived his boyhood in a log cabin he built with his own hands.

The most important contribution the Phoenicians made to civilization was the invention of blinds.

During the Napoleonic Wars, crowned heads were trembling in their shoes.

There would have been no Civil War if Abraham Lincoln hadn't signed the Emasculation Proclamation.

The plural of "forget-me-not" is, obviously, "forget-us-not."

Definitions from the Third Grade

Deceit: My mom makes me wear pants with patches on *deceit*.

Terrorize: If Susie doesn't stop pulling my hair, I'll *terrorize* outa her head.

Archaic: We can't have *archaic* and eat it too.

Arrears: My mom makes us wash in back of *arrears*.

Antidotes: My uncle thinks I'm just fine and my *antidotes* on me, too.

Justify: My daddy promised me a buck *justify* take a bath.

Lilac: He's a mighty sweet boy except he can sure *lilac anything*.

Falsify: If I put a plate on my head it falsify make a move.

Explain: Don't give me ham for breakfast, I like my explain.

Teacher: "The rule is to eat a good, hearty breakfast so that you'll grow up quicker and stronger."

Student: "Not me, teacher. Because if I grow up quicker, I'll get old sooner and, naturally, die younger."

Teacher: "What is the use, the purpose, of taxes?"

Student: "So that if your car doesn't start, you can call for one."

Teacher: "Why are you running?"

Boy: "I'm running to stop a fight."

Teacher: "Between whom?"

Boy: "Between me and the guy who's chasing me!"

Billy: "I wish I had been born a thousand years ago."
Mike: "Why?"
Billy: "Just think of all the history I wouldn't have to study!"

———————— 👫 ————————

Pat: "Why weren't you in school today?"
Jeff: "I had a toothache so I went to the dentist."
Pat: "Does your tooth still ache?"
Jeff: "I don't know. The dentist kept it!"

———————— 👫 ————————

Kids who watch television day and night will go down in history—not to mention mathematics, science and grammar.

———————— 👫 ————————

A lot of students have a certain spark of genius...but seem to have ignition trouble.

———————— 👫 ————————

The greatest aid to education of an adult is the child.

———————— 👫 ————————

"When I asked who was involved in the cafeteria food fight, George, why didn't you answer?"
"I didn't hear you, Miss Elkins, my ears were full of tomato sauce."

———————— 👫 ————————

Teacher: "Do you have any idea, Sid, how many times you've been late for school this semester?"
Sid: "This is just a guess, Miss Thomas, but I think it's not been more than once a day."

———————— 👫 ————————

Teacher: "Can anyone tell me what side of a tree moss grows on?"
Student: "The outside."

"SURELY YOU'VE HEARD OF INFLATION?"

Tell me this...If teachers are so darn smart, why is it that their book is the only one that has the answers printed in it?

If I don't lead a long life, I'm in trouble. Why? Because that's the only way I can possibly get caught up on my homework.

"So you tell me that your dog gobbled up your homework?"
"Yep, teacher, he sure did."
"And where is your dog now?"
"He ran away from home 'cause he doesn't like math any better than I do."

I get done with my homework in about three hours. Four, if my Dad helps me.

My Dad always says, 'What you don't know won't hurt you.' Well, he was sure wrong yesterday. That's when I took a math test!"

―――――――― 🤸 ――――――――

"How come your history grades are so bad? When I was a kid, I always got A's in history."

"That could be, Dad. But you got to remember there's been a lot more history since then."

―――――――― 🤸 ――――――――

Teacher: "Can you tell me, Myrtle, how long Henry Ford lived?"
Myrtle: "All his life."

―――――――― 🤸 ――――――――

I got to tell you, Mom, the food in our school cafeteria is just awful. Y'know, they serve roast beef once a week and all the kids take their portion home and use them for knee patches.

―――――――― 🤸 ――――――――

Not only is the roast beef bad, it is really tough. Last Wednesday, when we had roast beef, they kept half the class after school so they could finish chewing it.

―――――――― 🤸 ――――――――

"This Thursday, they served meatloaf in the school cafeteria."
"Really! And what did it taste like?"
"Like it should have been served last Monday."

―――――――― 🤸 ――――――――

"Tell me, Susie, what method do they use to keep flies out of your school cafeteria?"
"They let the flies taste the stuff."

―――――――― 🤸 ――――――――

"This stuff they're serving today looks like spaghetti and meatballs."
"Gee, I'm glad you told me. I thought it was shoelaces and hockey pucks."

Teacher: "Stanley, if I were ten minutes late for school every day, like you are, how would you like that?"

Stanley: "I'd like it a lot. Then we could walk to school together."

My daddy has a swell way to get me out of bed in the morning. He puts me to sleep with both dogs in my bed. Then, in the morning, when it's time to get up, he puts the cat in the bed!

I'm never late getting out of bed because I figure the sooner I get to school, the sooner I can get back to sleep.

In my dream last night, I dreamt that I was eating a humongous marshmallow. Well, when I woke up, I found that most of my pillow was gone!

Teacher: "Charles, you are the worst, the truly worst, trouble-maker in class."

Charles: "Wonderful, Miss Perry. Now I'm really happy because my folks told me I'd never amount to anything."

There's one girl in our class who has brought her parents to class—at teacher's request—so many times that they have a better attendance record than she has.

At the school street crossing, there was posted a sign that read: "SCHOOL. GO SLOW...DON'T KILL A CHILD."

Below the words a student had scrawled: "Wait for a teacher."

It had been a tough week, so, after school, the two teachers went to the teachers' lounge and had a cup of coffee. One said to the other: "I'm glad I believe in reincarnation because when I come back after death, I want to come back as a childhood disease!"

Teacher: "Emil, give me the formula for water, just...plain...water."
Emil: "I,J,K,L,M,N,O."
Teacher: "Emil! You know that's not right!"
Emil: "I was certain that it was. Didn't you say the formula was H...to...O?"

Teacher: "Class, consider what you would do if you were in the bathroom and a boy had a bat and was breaking toilets, doors, lights, etc. What would you do?"
Mary Sue raised her hand: "Mrs. Smothers, I think I'd get out of there real fast because I was in the wrong bathroom."

Kids Sure Do Write Odd Answers in School

The witness was told not to purge himself.
Opium is the religion of the people.
In Christianity, a man is allowed only one wife. This is called Monotony.
Capital punishment should be used only rarely in schools.
A horse divided against itself can't stand.
The greatest miracle in the Bible is when Joshua told his son to stand still and he obeyed him.
A shintoist is an Oriental shin and toe dancer.
Each morning, my father exercises by stretching his abominable muscles.

Teacher: "Albert, every last one of your answers on the math homework was wrong. Wrong! Wrong! Wrong!"
Student: "Don't let my Dad hear what you said! He says his best subject in school was math."

Teacher: "Well, Mr. Shubert, there's one thing I can tell you about your son that's encouraging. With grades like his...he couldn't be cheating."

Teacher: "Tell me, Edgar...what do you expect to be when you get out of school?"
Student: "A very, very old man."

———————— 👫 ————————

Bobby: "I won't be walking to school tomorrow with you. I'll be home sick."
Jonesy: "How can you tell today you'll be sick tomorrow?"
Bobby: "Tomorrow my Mom sees my report card. Then I'll be sick!"

———————— 👫 ————————

Teacher: "Who can tell me what follows the letters A, B, C, D, E, F, G?"
Student: "Hm-m-m...the letter G? I know! Whiz!"

———————— 👫 ————————

Teacher: "Class, can anyone tell me why an empty purse is always the same?"
Student: "I'd guess it's because there's not any change in it."

———————— 👫 ————————

Teacher: "If you have five candy bars and I ask you to give me one, how many will you have left?"
Student: "Five!"

———————— 👫 ————————

Teacher: "Can anyone tell me what an atom is?"
Student: "Wasn't he the guy who was the husband of Eve?"

———————— 👫 ————————

Mother: "What does this "F" on your report card mean?"
Son: "Fantastic?"

———————— 👫 ————————

Teacher: "This is the fourth time you've been so bad that I've had to punish you...this week. What do you care to say about your actions?"
Student: "Thank God it's Friday!"

"MIND BOGGLING, ISN'T IT?"

Teacher: "Paul, I suspect you have something to tell me. Go ahead."
Student: "I don't think so."
Teacher: "But you missed school yesterday!"
Student: "I didn't miss it at all. I had lotsa fun!"

————————— 🧒👧 —————————

Teacher: "Richard told me you threw a stone through my classroom window."
Student: "It was all Richard's fault."
Teacher: "Please explain how and why it was Richard's fault!"
Student: "Y'see…I threw it at Richard…but he ducked."

————————— 🧒👧 —————————

Teacher: "What did Ben Franklin say when he discovered electricity?"
Student: "E-E-Ow-W-ch!"

34

A teacher asked that her students make a list of the ten greatest Americans.

"And are you finished yet, James? Everybody else is."

"Almost," said James. "I'm having a tough time thinking of a quarterback."

———————— 🙆 ————————

Question: 'Who knows what an echo is?"
Answer: "Could you repeat the question?"

———————— 🙆 ————————

Question: "What did George Washington, Abraham Lincoln and Christopher Columbus have in common?"
Answer: "Each was born on a holiday."

———————— 🙆 ————————

Teacher: "Suppose you were in the African jungles and came upon an alligator, a leopard and a tiger. Which one would you get fur from?"
Donny: "I'd get as fur from *all* of them as I could get!"

———————— 🙆 ————————

Manny: "My Boy Scout buddies had to carry an old lady across the intersection yesterday."
Teacher: "Why did you have to carry her?"
Manny: "Because she didn't want to go!"

———————— 🙆 ————————

Question: "When did Columbus discover America?"
Answer: "It was Columbus Day!"

———————— 🙆 ————————

Teacher: "Stanley, every day since school began you have been late. Why?"
Stanley: "It's not my fault! There's a sign at almost every crossing that says, 'GO SLOW'!"

Teacher: "Can you define the word *dogma?*"
Pupil: "Dogma is a puppy's mother."

———————— 🧒 ————————

The teacher handed out the report cards. Paul took his, saying, "I don't want to scare you, Miss Applebaum, but my Daddy said that if I didn't get a good report card, somebody was sure as heck gonna get a good spanking."

———————— 🧒 ————————

Teacher: "Sally Ann, you aren't paying attention! Is it because you are having trouble hearing?"
Sally Ann: "No, that's not it. But I am having trouble listening."

———————— 🧒 ————————

Teacher: "Morton, do you know Lincoln's Gettysburg Address?"
Morton: "Nope! Y'see, I thought he lived in the White House."

———————— 🧒 ————————

Teacher: "Charles, you failed to wash your face this morning. Why, I can see the eggs on your face."
Charles: "That was yesterday's b reakfast. Today I had cereal."

———————— 🧒 ————————

Teacher: "Class, can anyone tell me something about Buddha?"
Pupil: "I can. It's what we used to have at meals. Now we use margarine."

———————— 🧒 ————————

Jim's Mother: "Jimmy told me he got 100 on his test yesterday."
Jim's Teacher: "He did! He got 50 in spelling and 50 in arithmetic."

———————— 🧒 ————————

The grade school class went to the local museum. They stopped before a glass case with a sign: "500 BC" The teacher asked, "Class, can anyone give me the meaning of the sign?" A student replied: "That's the number of the license plate that hit him."

Teacher: "If you saved a dollar a day for an entire year, what would you have?"
Student: "A new bicycle."

———————— 🕺 ————————

Patty brought her report card home the first day after Christmas vacation. Her mother was furious. "So tell me, Patty, how come you got a 55 on your math test?"
Patty replied: "Oh, you know how it is after Christmas. The teacher always marks things down then!"

———————— 🕺 ————————

Teacher: "When you think of Greece, what comes to your mind?"
Student: "Burgers and french fries."

———————— 🕺 ————————

Jerry: "I'm not getting out of bed today and I'm sure not going to school."
Mother: "Don't be ridiculous, Jerry. Of course, you're going to school. And it's late now! Get up! After all, you're the principal."

———————— 🕺 ————————

Perry: "Summer vacation. Wow! I plan to do nothing for the next three months."
Teacher: "That should be easy, Perry. You've been practicing for nine months!"

———————— 🕺 ————————

Albert: "I'm going to spend my vacation reviewing all that I learned in school this year."
Sally: "You don't say! But what are you going to do the second day?"

———————— 🕺 ————————

Readin', 'Ritin' and 'Rithmatic.
Nine months o' that'll make you real sick.

What did I learn?
I don't remember.
And I ain't gonna try
Till next September!

———————— 🧑‍🤝‍🧑 ————————

Roses are red,
Violets are blue.
It's the end of school,
Toodle-oo to you.

———————— 🧑‍🤝‍🧑 ————————

Wacky Exam Answers!

Heredity means that...if your grandpa didn't have any children, then your daddy probably wouldn't have had any, and neither would you, probably.

SOS is a term used in music. It means the same only softer.

Trigonometry occurs when a lady marries three men at the very same time.

A tantrum is merely a two-seated bike.

Milton wrote "Paradise Lost." After that his wife up and died and he wrote "Paradise Regained."

Martin Luther died an awful death. He was excommunicated by a bull.

The King of England is known as a limited mockery.

———————— 🧑‍🤝‍🧑 ————————

Mother: "So tell me how'd you do in your chemistry experiment?"
Son: "I don't know yet...the teacher ain't come down."

———————— 🧑‍🤝‍🧑 ————————

Teacher: "Why is it incorrect to use the word 'ain't'?"
Elmer: "Because it ain't correct."

———————— 🧑‍🤝‍🧑 ————————

My grades are so darned low that I had to get down on my knees to read my report card.

I flunked every test I took this year. At least I was...consistent!

───────── 🏃 ─────────

Sarah: "How many books to do you figure you've read in your lifetime?"
Sam: "I don't know since I ain't dead yet."

───────── 🏃 ─────────

Teacher: "John, tell me who your favorite author is."
John: "George Washington."
Teacher: "But George Washington never wrote any books."
John: "You got it!"

───────── 🏃 ─────────

Tommy: "Dad, my teacher says I should have an encyclopedia."
Dad: "Ridiculous. You'll walk to school just like I did."

───────── 🏃 ─────────

Teacher: "Can anyone tell me why the law of gravity is so sensible?"
Pupil: "Because if you drop a plate of spaghetti on the floor, it's much easier to get it off the floor than the ceiling."

───────── 🏃 ─────────

Teacher: "What category of animal life does the bat belong to?"
Student: "It's a mouse who attended pilot training school."

───────── 🏃 ─────────

The teacher was taking her class through the modern art museum and the class paused before an exhibit of abstract art. In a few minutes, the teacher felt a tug on her blouse, turned and said, "Yes?"

"Mrs. Briggs," the boy replied, "don't you think we'd better be leaving here before they accuse us of doing this?"

"YOUR GOING TO MAKE A GREAT GOLFER SOMEDAY."

Teacher: "Peter, can you give me an antonym for 'upright?'"
Peter: "Sure. 'Downright'."

——————— 🧒🧒 ———————

"Now, Peter, can you give me an antonym for 'woe'?"
"Sure can. 'Giddyup'!"

——————— 🧒🧒 ———————

Teacher: "Can anyone give me the plural of 'radium'?"
Student: "I can.'Radius'."

——————— 🧒🧒 ———————

Teacher: "Please write a story in the first person."
Student: "Does that mean to write it just like Adam woulda done?"

40

Question: How do you spell *hard water* with only three letters?
Answer: *I-c-e.*

————— 🕺 —————

Question: How do you spell dry grass with only three letters?
Answer: *H-a-y.*

————— 🕺 —————

Here's an old joke from the 1890s: What's the difference between the Prince of Wales, a papa gorilla and a bald head?
    Answer: The first is an heir apparent, the second is a hairy parent, and the third is no hair apparent.

————— 🕺 —————

Italians are the people who write in Italics.

————— 🕺 —————

You can study compounds either in chemistry or sentences.

————— 🕺 —————

When asked the proper use of "can" and "may," the little girl responded: "Can means we can do whatever we want to and nobody can say we're wrong. But may means that it might be better to ask anyway."

————— 🕺 —————

Teacher: "John Jones, I want you to spell Tennessee."
John Jones: "Sure, teacher. Here goes:

One-sy	Six-sy
Two-sy	Seven-sy
Three-sy	Eight-sy
Four-sy	Nine-sy
Five-sy	Ten-sy

————— 🕺 —————

Some Doo-Doos, Curioustakes and Malaprops

My sister is suffering from indolent fever.
Thanksgiving is a swell time of happiness for every child, adult and adultress.

One of the strange things about my family is that my cousin, Adolph, just happens to be the son of my father's brother.

Medieval cathedrals were held erect by flying buttocks.

Abraham Lincoln wrote the Gettysburg Address while going from Washington to Gettysburg on the back of an envelope.

"Mother told me to use plenty of milk in the eggs if I wanted to make a good omen."

"Can anyone tell me the cause of the 1929 stock market crash?"

"I been told it's because people kept on puttin' their money in socks instead of savings accounts."

Teacher: "Class, what is a surtax?"
Student: "It's a tax put on English gentlemen."

"Teacher: "Class, can anyone give me an example of government waste?"

Student: "Well, just think about the post office way of canceling stamps so that we can't ever use them again. Now that's waste!"

Teacher: "Can anyone tell me about the secretaries the president appoints?"

Student: "All I know is that he keeps them in a cabinet."

Teacher: "Please add any needed punctuation marks to this sentence: May was swimming but suddenly lost her swim suit!

Student: "I think I'd make a dash after May!"

"Is it correct to state that the human race comes from dust?"

"I think so because under my sister's bed, there's enough to be the birth of a nation."

Teacher: "Give me the plural of *mouse.*"
Pupil: "Mice."
Teacher: "Correct! And now give me the plural of *baby.*"
Pupil: "Twins."

Teacher: "Jane, do you know the meaning of 'trickle'?"
Jane: "To run slowly."
Teacher: "That's right. Now tell me the meaning of 'anecdote'."
Jane: "That's a short funny tale."
Teacher: "Very good. Now give me a sentence with both those words in it."
Jane: "Our dog...let's see now...our dog trickled down the street and...and...he was wagging his anecdote."

How do you communicate with a fish?
Just drop him a line.

Harry: "What is the very hottest letter of the alphabet?"
Mary: "B."
Harry: "Why?"
Mary: "Because it makes oil boil."

Teacher: "Andy, what is 'can't' the short form of?"
Andy: "Cannot."
Teacher: "Very good. Now Carol, what is 'don't' the short for?"
Carol: "Doughnut."

Teacher: "Tell the class what your father said when he fell off the ladder."
Pupil: "Should I leave out the bad words?"
Teacher: "Of course."
Pupil: "Absolutely nothing."

Mary came running into her third grade classroom and went up to the teacher. "Miss English," she cried, "Paul said a terrible word in the hall!"
"Really. Well, can you tell me what the word was?"
"Yes. He said 'quap'!"

Teacher: "Class, can anyone tell me about French syntax?"
Student: "It's real odd that they had to pay for it!"

**"The title of my composition is
'More Pay for Teachers'!"**

A mother wished to enter her five-year-old in the classiest kindergarten in town, but the child was only five whereas the entrance age was six. "I do think my Janet can pass the six-year-old exam," she said.

"We'll test her and see," said the entrance teacher. "Now, dear, just say a few words that come to your mind."

"Mama?" asked the child, "does he want carefully contrived sentences or merely odds and ends of words?"

The teacher asked little Ernie if he knew where the Declaration of Independence was signed. "I sure do," he replied, "on the bottom!"

Little Fulton took his report card home to his parents and said, "I think I better explain what it all means. *A* means excellent. *B* means you did real good. *C* is just a fair grade and *D* is what I got."

The teacher began: "Can anyone in class tell us the meaning of axis?"

"I can, Sir. Here goes: The axis of the earth is an imaginary line that passes from one pole to the other and on which the earth revolves."

"Very good," the teacher said, "but could you hang clothes on that line?"

"Yep! You sure could," the student replied.

"Is that so?" the teacher said. "And just what kind of clothes would you hang on that imaginary line?"

"Imaginary clothes, Teacher."

The absolute stupidity of some kids is simply astounding. There was this one boy, Johnny Penny, who was late to school every day for an entire month. The reason? He kept trying to put his pants on over his head.

We have one kid in our class who gets into a fight every day, sometimes for a month at a time. Asked why, he said, "It keeps me out of trouble."

More Wacky Exam Answers!

The Kodak is the Bible of the Mohammedans.

A martyr is a load of wood on fire with a man on top.

They gave William IV a great funeral. It took eight men to carry the bier.

Magna Carta said that the King was not allowed to order taxis with the consent of Parliament.

The Duke of Marlborough was a great general who always commenced his battles with a fixed determination in his mind to win or lose.

"Miss Sebastian, how can I possibly get into college with the bad grades you've given me?"

"Why don't you apply for janitor?"

I tell you our school library is so dern quiet that I can hear my eyebrows grow!

Unknown author of this statement found on a fifth grade blackboard: "If God had wanted us to take schoolbooks home from school, He would have put wheels on them!"

The teacher asked: "What was the name of the person in Greek mythology who was half man and half animal?"

Paul raised his hand. "Yes?" the teacher nodded.

"Buffalo Bill!"

Teacher: "And now, class, can anyone tell me the whereabouts of the Andes?"

Student: "They're at the end of your wristies."

Teacher: "George, what's a Hindu?"
George: "It lays eggs."

———————— 🧍🧍 ————————

"Eddie, why are you so late getting home from school today?"
"The teacher kept me after school because I didn't know where the Himalayas were."
"Shame on you. You must remember where you put those things!"

———————— 🧍🧍 ————————

Mr. Clemenceau posted a sign in the classroom stating: "Due to a conference, Mr. Clemenceau will not teach his classes tomorrow."
One of his smart-alecky pupils erased the "c" in "classes."
Up to such student shenanigans, Mr. Clemenceau erased the "l".

———————— 🧍🧍 ————————

Dear Teacher: Please excuse Janet for her absence from school Wednesday. She had a very high fever and so I had her shot.

———————— 🧍🧍 ————————

The class was having a bad time with the subject of SUBTRACTION. The teacher kept at it, asking questions. "Children, can anyone tell me the result if I have ten fingers and then have three fewer. What would I have?"
"No more violin lessons," one student answered.

———————— 🧍🧍 ————————

And here are some of our favorite books from the school library. together with their authors:
Swimming the Channel by Francis Near.
At the North Pole by I.C. Blast.
At the South Pole by Ann Arctic.
The Bullfighter by Matt Adore.
Rice Growing by Paddy Fields.
Aches and Pains by Arthur Ritis.

———————— 🧍🧍 ————————

Teacher: "Emma, give me a sentence with the word *gruesome*."
Emma: "My father didn't shave for a week and he sure grew some whiskers."

47

"The subject we shall take up first is lying," said the teacher. "How many of you have read Chapter 17 in the text?"

Every hand was raised.

"Let that be a lesson to you, lesson number one. There is no Chapter 17!"

Time and its uses was the subject of the class for the day. "Can anyone give me an example of a waste of time?" the teacher asked.

Edith raised her hand: "What about telling a hair-raising story to a bald-headed man?"

In Springfield, Illinois, music in high school is of enormous importance and concerts are frequent. All concerts are critically reported in the Illinois State Journal, the local paper. The review of a recent concert said: "The orchestra played Wagner. Wagner lost."

"What did you think of the ventriloquist?" the teacher asked the sixth grader, after the show in the auditorium.

"He was kinda simple, even dumb," replied the student. "But that little fellow on his knee, my oh my, he was super!"

On his first day at school, six-year-old Tommy was asked, "Do you know your alphabet?"

"Yep. Sure do," Tommy replied.

"Good. Now give me the letter that comes after 'A'."

"All of them," Tommy responded.

The teacher of torts in law school banged his desk and yelled: "Order! Order please!"

From the back of the class came a sleepy voice: "I'll have a hamburger and a coke."

Teacher: "Johnnie, please don't burst out laughing in my class."

Johnnie: "Honest, Mrs. Lloyd, I didn't mean to. I was just smiling but my smile busted!"

The high school English teacher was emphasizing the importance of increasing one's vocabulary. "Use a word ten times and you'll never forget it. It'll be yours forever."

Students Kathy Freund began repeating: "Jim, Jim, Jim, Jim, Jim, Jim, Jim, Jim, Jim."

© 1996 Jonny Hawkins

"I slanted my writing because I heard you graded on a curve."

A mother came to the prep school to register her son. "I want my boy to have the best education possible," she said. "I want him to study Latin."

"Very good, Madam," said the head scholar. "But you must know that Latin is a dead language."

"Yes, I know that," said the mother. "But Cecil is going to be a funeral director."

Adam's mother happened to meet the school band director on the street. "Tell me," she asked him, "how is my son getting along playing the clarinet?"

"Very good," replied the teacher. "He's been making quite good music."

"Thanks a lot. That makes me feel better. I was beginning to feel that I was just getting used to it."

"Tell me, Peter, how are you doing in history?"

"I got an 'A' this morning, Dad."

"Wonderful. And history used to be your weakest subject. How'd you turn things around like that?"

"Well, today, the teacher asked the class to pronounce the name of the Polish General, Kosciusko. Nobody knew it. Then I sneezed and the teacher smile, applauded and gave me an A."

Miss Mandel was disturbed by scuffling and noises in the back of her overcrowded room.

"Listen, back there," she called. "Quit all that fussing around and answer this question: What was the date of the attack on Pearl Harbor?"

"I don't know," was the reply.

"Then tell me the date of World War II's ending."

"I don't know that, either."

"You are a dunce," she called out angrily. "Last night's assignment was all about Pearl Harbor and World War II. And just what were you doing last night?"

"I went to a party and didn't get home till 4 a.m."

"Then how do you expect ever to pass this course?"

"I don't know, lady. I'm here just to replace the light bulb."

After the concert, the student approached his teacher and asked: "The soprano was awful. Who the heck was she?"

"My wife!" the teacher replied.

The student gasped, blushed, then said, "Actually, her voice wasn't the problem. It was the song. I wonder who wrote it?"

"I did!" replied the teacher.

"Name two days of the week beginning with the letter T," the teacher asked.

Elmer raised his hand. "Yes?" responded the teacher.

"Today and tomorrow!"

The teacher asked: "Class, I want to know something about Red China. Can any of you tell me something about it?"

Sally raised her hand. "Yes?" said the teacher, nodding to Sally.
"It looks just fine on a white tablecloth," said Sally.

The principal of a girl's school noticed that her students were not
crossing the street at the corners but in the middle of the block. She could
not get them to change their ways until she put up a sign in the middle of
the block that said, "CATTLE CROSSING!"

"Johnny is doing just great in school," the private school principal
wrote. "His only trouble is that he can't keep his mind off the girls."
Johnny's mother wrote back. "His father has the same problem. If
you have a solution, let me know."

With the first game only a few days away, the baseball coach lit into
the team.
"Can't you guys ever learn how to hit the ball?" he growled, grabbing
a bat.
"Throw me a few," he yelled to the pitcher.
The pitcher pitched him ten pitches, and ten times the coach swung
and hit nary a ball.
"Y'see that!" he yelled at the team. "That's what you guys looked
like!"

Mr. Carlyle took his eighth grade class to a large farm to show them
something about agriculture. As they walked down the long, beautiful rows
of corn, Mr. Carlyle looked forward, backward and sideways to make sure
nobody was looking, then snapped of an ear of corn to take home.
"Mr. Carlyle," said one student. "I think you forgot to look up!"

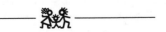

The music teacher took her class to its first grand opera. The lights
dimmed and the conductor began waving his baton while the soprano
started to sing.
After a while, a student asked his teacher, "Why is the conductor waving his stick at that woman?"

51

"Oh, don't worry, he won't hit her," the teacher assured him.
"Then why is she screaming?"

The school offered a prize to the student who could sell the most tickets to the benefit concert.

Sandra sold more than any other student and won the prize. She was asked how she managed to sell so many tickets.

"It was easy," she replied. "I asked every prospect what they were doing on the 25th. If they said they were busy then, but could come any other night, I had 'em cold! That's when I sold them tickets for our show on the 26th."

Teacher: "Daniel, you must not use 'a' before a plural noun. Say 'cow' not 'a cows'."
Daniel: "But Teacher, my preacher always says 'amen'."

The teacher asked Eli: "Do you believe in life after death?"
Eli replied: "I sure do, yes Ma'am."
"I thought you did. Because after you had gone to your grandfather's funeral, he dropped by to see me."

Teacher: "There are many words that begin with 'dog', such as dog-rose, dog fennel and there's a plant called dog's tooth. Can anyone give me another word that relates to dog?"
Albert: "I know one, Teacher. How about collie-flowers?"

The class was studying early American history and the teacher called upon Jonas to describe who the Pilgrims were.

"The Pilgrims," Jonas said, "were early settlers of America and a musical people."

"Now wait a minute," the teacher said. "What gave you the idea they were musically inclined?"

"My textbook says it plainly," Jonas replied. "It says right here— 'A band of Pilgrims came over on the Mayflower'."

A sixth-grader came rushing into class nearly ten minutes late. "Why so late?" his teacher asked.

"I squeezed the toothpaste too hard this morning and it took me near an hour to stuff it back in the tube."

As the fifth grade class was taking a tour through the zoo, the staff member showing them around told them how the zoo fed the animals when they were sick. "Y'know, people feed the wrong things to our animals and often they get sick. Do you know what we give elephants when they get diarrhea?"

One lad held up his hand. The guide nodded to him. "Plenty of room!"

"Albert," said his teacher, "it was so nice of your mother to send me that delicious apple strudel. I must thank her for it."

"When you do, Teacher, please thank her for two, will you?"

"I'M NOT CRYING BECAUSE SHE'S GOING TO KINDERGARTEN. I'M CRYING BECAUSE I HAVE TO GO BACK TO WORK."

Tommy was not very bright, nor was he self-confidant. So when he was called to the head of the class to make a three-minute talk on ancestors, he walked to the front of the room, turned, wiped his brow and said. "Class, let's now observe three minutes of silence in memory of our illustrious ancestors."

The class was studying the Native American and the teacher said, "We know that the wives were called squaws. Can anyone tell me what Indian babies were named?"

"Squawkers," was the single response.

Still More Wacky Exam Answers!

He was dressed in the garbage of a monk.
Geometry teaches us how to bisex angels.
An axiom is a thing that is so visible that it is not necessary to see it.
A prime milk cow can be told by her rudder.
Herbert Hoover was President of the United States, and is best known as inventor of the vacuum cleaner.
Certainly the pleasures of youth are many, but the pleasures of adultery are many more.
You can stop a nosebleed by standing on your head till your heart stops beating.
Often when people are drown, you can revive them by pounding them in the belly, but not too hard. This is called resurrection.

The dance instructor noticed that one of the beginners in her class simply could not keep step with the rhythm.

"Can't you hear the beat of the music?" she asked.

"Oh sure," said the student. "But I don't let it bother me."

"Elmer, our school principal made a speech to the teachers today," the teacher remarked to her husband.

"Was it any good? What'd he say?"

"He spoke straight from the shoulder. I could discern nothing from a higher origin."

Teacher: "Can anyone tell me why the Middle Ages are called 'dark'?"
Pupil: "Because they had so many knights."

Kitty Collins was the new teacher in the small-town school. On her first day of class, she asked one little boy, "What's your name?"
"Jule."
"No! No! Don't use contractions you your name. You are Julius."
Ms. Collins turned to the next lad and asked: "What's your name?"
The lad replied, "Bilious."

The teacher had her class at the zoo. She pointed to a deer and asked: "George, what is that?"
George replied: "I don't know."
Teacher: "What does your mother call your father at home?"
George: "Don't tell me that's a louse!"

In first grade, the teacher was offering the class questions about the alphabet. "Can anyone tell me what comes after 'O'?
"I know," a little girl replied, holding up her hand.
"Very good," said the teacher. "Tell the class."
"'Yeah' comes after 'O'" was the reply.

Teacher: "Class, can you tell me the name of the ruler of the Kingdom of Russia?"
In unison, the class said, "Tzar."
"Correct," the teacher said. "And now what was the designation of his wife?"
"Tzarina," came the reply.
"Very good," said the teacher. "Now, please, what were the children called?"
There was a long pause followed by one lone voice saying, "Tzardines?"

The teacher was complaining to the school principal about George Tolan. "He's without doubt the worst-behaved, devilish, absolutely irremediably mischievous boy in this school. And to make things worse he's got a perfect attendance record!"

Teacher: "Can anyone in the class tell me what is a cannibal?"

Not a pupil raised a hand. "Come on, now, the teacher prodded, "surely somebody knows. Let me put it this way. What would you be if you cooked and ate your Mommy and Daddy?"

Little Elmer raised his hand. "If I did that, I'd be an orphan!"

The teacher was truly vexed with the regular tardiness of William at school. "You've got to do something about this, William, or I shall report it to the principal and he just might expel you."

William vowed to correct things, went home, had a good night's sleep, a good breakfast and reported to school. "I'm on time today, Teacher," William said.

"You sure are," the teacher replied. "But where were you yesterday?"

Elmer Chiantry had eight daughters and then, at last, he had a son. Man-oh-man was he proud! A friend asked, "And does the lad look like you?"

"We don't know." Elmer answered. "We haven't looked at his face yet!"

Teacher: "Can anyone tell me the meaning of anatomy?"

Jack: "It's something that everyone has but it looks a heckuva lot better on females."

Teacher: "Can anyone tell me the difference between night and day?"

Pupil: "Night falls but doesn't break. Day breaks but doesn't fall."

On his final exam, Emmett was stumped. He didn't know any...not one...answer. Finally he wrote: "God alone knows the answers to these questions."

He got his report back. On the report was written: "God gets an A. You get an F."

GASPIRTZ

IT'S SUPPOSED TO BE "SHOW AND TELL", NOT "SHOCK AND YELL"

The school employs a doctor to teach the children about body parts. One day, the doctor came to school, assembled the class and pointed to his nose. "Is this my ear?" he asked.

Little Johnny walked to the teacher and whispered: "I think we better get a new doctor."

In class, the arithmetic teacher asked: "What's the difference between two thousand fifty four and four thousand a hundred and sixty?"

"I agree," Eddie said. "What's the difference!"

They're telling a story at school about a kid who drank eight bottles of Coca Cola and threw Seven-Up!

Teacher: "What do you call a person who puts you in touch with spirits?"

Chick: "A bartender."

Teacher: "What is it that goes in like a lion and comes out like a lamb?"
Eddie: "My father."

Teacher: "Now, class, can anyone tell me the name of the greatest inventor in America?"
Student: "I can, Teacher - PAT PENDING!"

They were having a sex education class at school. The boy said to his sweetie sitting next to him: "Let's play Adam and Eve. You tempt me with the apple and I'll give in."

Teacher: "Now, class, give me a sentence using the word denial."
Student: "Cleopatra lived on denial."

Teacher: "What can you tell me about nitrates?"
Pupil: "They're sure a lot cheaper than day rates."

Kids' Minds work in Strange Ways!

Almost at the very bottom of Lake Michigan is Chicago.
The Orpheum was the business end of Venus.
A bust is something a lady wears above her stomach.
Well's history is really a millstone on the road to learning.
Don't let your actions belie your word.
A virgin forest is a bunch of trees where the hand of man hasn't set foot.

At a class reunion, one guy said, "My teacher once said to our fifth grade class, 'Just show me a boy who swears, fights and constantly interrupts me and I'll show you a genuine pain in the class!'"

School bus drivers have had a material effect in the declining birth rate in this country because they've taken a secret pledge to remain single!

———————— 🚶🚶 ————————

Teacher: "What's a millennium?"
Student: "It's just like a centipede only it's got more legs."

———————— 🚶🚶 ————————

Dad: "Were you a good boy at school today?"
Son: "How could I be anything else...standing in the corner all day!"

———————— 🚶🚶 ————————

Little Emma came home from school one day to find a large sign posted on the TV set: 'THIS PICTURE HAS BEEN DISCONTINUED BECAUSE OF HOMEWORK!"

———————— 🚶🚶 ————————

Class hatred is quite common in grade school. Some kids really hate going to class!

———————— 🚶🚶 ————————

The teacher announced to her class that Billy the Kid had killed twenty people before he was twenty-one years old.
A boy held up his hand and asked: "What kinda car was he drivin'?"

———————— 🚶🚶 ————————

Teacher: "Today is the day for learning a thing or two about first aid. Elmer, what would you do first if you broke your arm in two places?"
Elmer: "You can be darned sure I wouldn't go to those places ever again!"

———————— 🚶🚶 ————————

Teacher: "Can anyone in this class tell me what important event happened in the year 1809?"
Student: "That was the year Abraham Lincoln was born."
Teacher: "Correct! Now can anyone tell me what important event took place in 1813?"
Student: "Abraham Lincoln had his fourth birthday."

Pupil: "Teacher, what part of the body is the fray?"

Teacher: "I'm not sure I understood you. Did you say fray?"

Pupil: "Yes, Ma'am. It says here in the textbook that General Eldridge was shot right in the thick of the fray."

Teacher: "Paul, I'm anxious to know about something you wrote in your essay."

Paul: "What was it?"

Teacher: "You say that the citizens of New York are famous for their stupidity."

Paul: "Well, the encyclopedia says that the New York City population is extremely dense."

Students at a Chicago grade school christened their drinking fountain..."OLD FACEFUL."

The teacher asked: "Can anyone tell me whether George Washington was a great general or an admiral?"

"I don't know if he was a great general," the little guy replied, "but I do know he sure wasn't an admiral."

"And just how can you be so sure of that?" the teacher asked.

"Because no admiral, wise or dumb, would be caught standing up in a moving boat!"

The teacher asked the boy to create a sentence beginning with I.

The lad began: "I is..."

"No!" the teacher interrupted. "Not 'I is' but 'I am'...is correct."

"I got it," the boy replied. "Here goes: 'I...am the ninth letter in the alphabet."

Hilarious Replies to Exam Questions

The mother of Achilles washed him in the River Stinx until he was intolerable.

Gladstone was important in the British Government and was Queen Victoria's Lord of the Privy.

Malays are happy people, generally, and inhabit Malaria.

Science is material. Religion is very immaterial.

The people of Japan go about in jigsaws.

A permanent set of teeth consists of 6 canines, 6 cuspids, 2 molars and 7 cuspidors.

The United States are populated entirely by people.

The class was on a tour of the local art museum and the teacher stopped before a reproduction of a DaVinci painting. "Class, this man was a genius. With just one, single stroke he could change a smiling face into a pained, sorrowful one."

A little boy raised his hand. "Question, Elmer?" the teacher asked.

"I just want to tell you that my Mom can do the same thing."

The teacher asked: "Edgar, if your father borrows twenty dollars from me and pays me back at two dollars a month, after six months, how much will he owe me?"

"Twenty dollars," was the reply.

"You don't know much about arithmetic, Edgar."

"Maybe so. But for sure you don't know much about my father."

Teacher: "James, why are you late for school?"

James: "Well, y'see, I was dreaming about a football game and it went into overtime. So, y'see, I had to...had to...stay asleep to see the finish."

After the third day of school, the six-year-old came running home from school crying and sobbing. She ran into the house and up to her mother, sobbing: "M-mom, how long does it take a little girl to finally graduate?"

The kid let loose with a four-letter word, and the teacher was horrified. "You shouldn't use a word like that in class or anywhere else! Why, you don't even know what it means!"

"I sure do," the lad replied, "it means the car won't start!"

The teacher announced: "If any of you need to go to the bathroom, raise your hand."

One little guy asked: "How's that going to stop it?"

An observer of today's education remarked: "There are no more 'Little Red Schoolhouses'...but there are bushels of little-read youngsters."

Teacher: "Can anyone define or tell me the meaning of prayer?"

Pupil: "Sure! I can. It's a message sent to God on nights and Sundays when rates are cheaper."

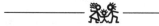

One kid identified a 'Granny' better than the teacher thought possible. The lad said, "Granny is the old lady who gets between your parents and you when they want to beat you up."

Condensation was the topic in the third grade science class. The next morning, standing at the back door, our third grader watched the fog slowly rising.

The lad turned to me and asked, "Mom, do you know what causes all that wet stuff out there on the grass?"

"No, but perhaps you'll tell me the cause of it."

In his most serious, professor-like manner, he replied: "Constipation."

History teacher: "Charles, would you rather be right than President?"

Charles: "I can't say about that. Y'see...I've never met Mr. Wright."

It was the first day of kindergarten and Jimmy Jones was very uneasy. And he was a shy kid. His teacher asked if his name was Jimmy Jones but he shook his head. So the teacher asked: "Tell me, what does your mother call you?"

Jimmy swallowed, then said, "She always says: Jimmy don't!"

It was in 1946 and the teacher was discussing rural life. She asked: "Can anyone tell me what R.F.D. stands for?"

One lad held up his hand. The teacher nodded to him and he said, "R.F.D. means Ranklin Felano Doosevelt."

Eddie Watson was the son of a baker who specialized in baking pretzels. One day, Eddie brought his favorite teacher a sack of his father's product and the teacher tasted one, saying, "Eddie, these are just too salty for me."

The next day, Eddie brought in another sack of pretzels to school and the teacher ate one. "These are great, Eddie," she said, "but I do hope your father didn't go to a lot of trouble to make unsalted ones for me."

"He didn't go to no trouble at all. I did it. I just licked the salt off the pretzels I gave you yesterday."

Mrs. Spiro, teacher of the sixth grade was having trouble with one of her pupils, Richie. She told the principal about him and the principal suggested that the next time there was trouble with Richie, she should send him to the office. This she did.

When Richie walked into the principal's office, he said, "Mrs. Spiro sent me to get a spa..." The principal grabbed him, put him over his knee and gave him a tough spanking.

"Now, what have you got to say for yourself!" demanded the principal.

"Nothing...much...all I was going to say was that Mrs. Spiro sent me down for a Spanish book she left in your office."

"Sure, maybe I'm an under-achiever.
But did you ever stop to think
maybe you're an over-demander?"

Certain that their teacher would be gone at least fifteen minutes, one boy hurried to the blackboard and sketched a wonderfully clever caricature of the teacher. When the master returned to the schoolroom, he noticed the drawing and turned to demand angrily, "And just who is responsible for this atrocity?"

A week, disguised voice came from the back of the room, "Your parents, Sir!"

Kids Sure Come up with Odd Answers!

An illiterate child has parents who aren't married.

Robert Louis Stevenson got married and went on his honeymoon. After that, he wrote Travels with a Donkey.

A burning glance froze him tight to the spot.

An active verb shows action while a passive verb shows passion.

A proper Boy Scout obeys all duly constipated authority.

To avoid auto-infection, place slip covers on the seats and change them weekly, and then drive with the windows wide open.

CHAPTER II

Children Talk to Children

"There's a word you don't hear much any more."

Brother: "I think we have company downstairs."
Sister: "How do you know?"
Brother: "I just heard Mom laugh at one of Dad's jokes."

———————— 🧒 ————————

A 12-year-old boy was leading a milk cow down the road. A neighbor woman driving on the road stopped beside the boy. She rolled down her window and said, "Hi, Petey, what are you doing?"
Petey replied, "I'm taking ol' Buttercup down to Mr. Moore's bull."
"Shouldn't your daddy be doing that?" asked the woman.
"Oh no," said Petey. "That's a job for the bull."

Two little urchins grinned expectantly when the fat lady hauled herself up onto the scale. They craned their necks when the penny tinkled down into the mechanism. But the scale apparently was on strike for it registered only 82 lbs.

The boys looked at each other in astonishment, then one said: "Well, what do you know. She's hollow."

While taking my two children for a treat at the local restaurant, I asked them what they were going to order. Pat said, "I'll have a chocolate shake," and Emma replied, "I'll have a hot-fudge."

Her brother looked at her and said, "You mean sundae?"

She looked puzzled for a moment and then indignantly replied, "No, silly, I want it today."

My mother feeds me chicken,
But chicken makes me cough.
I wish that when she cooked it,
She'd take the feathers off!

A young child explaining the use of a stethoscope to his friend: "It's a spyglass that big people use to look into kids' chests with their ears."

One Cub Scout to another: "The best way I know to make a fire by rubbing two sticks together is to be sure one of them is a match."

A small boy ridiculed the talk about a painless dentist in his neighborhood. "He's not painless at all," said the lad. "He put his finger in my mouth and I bit it and he yelled just like anybody would."

There's a flood in a little Illinois town, and a little girl and a small boy are sitting on top of a house.

As they sit there watching different articles floating by, they notice a derby hat floating past them. Pretty soon the hat turns and comes back and then turns again and goes downstream. After it goes a hundred feet or so, it turns around and comes back.

So the little girl says, "Wow! Did you see that derby? First it goes downstream. And then it turns and comes back."

The little boy says, "Oh, that's my daddy. This morning he said come hell or high water, he was going to cut the grass today!"

Small boy to small girl: "Are you the opposite sex, or am I?"

"Watch!"

"What do you plan to be when you grow up?"
"Nothing, because I don't plan on growing up."
"But...why not?"
"Because of all the bills you got to pay at the end of the month."
"Would you like to be head of Walmart Department Stores?"
"Nope. Sure wouldn't."

"How about Governor of our State?"

"Nope. Not a chance."

"Then would you like to be mayor of this city?"

"No! No! No!"

"Why not?"

"Because the mayor's a girl horse."

Two small boys were sightseeing in a museum. They stood in front of a mummy having a descriptive sign that read: "2549 BC" One lad said, "I wonder what that means?"

The other kid nodded, saying, "I think I know...it's probably the license number of the car that hit him."

Two little sisters were watching a British television documentary about the royal family. Betty, age seven, was puzzled by one of the scenes.

"I wonder how Queen Elizabeth knew she was gonna have a baby," she asked.

Her nine-year-old sister, Susie, was disgusted with such a display of juvenile ignorance.

"Everybody knows that," said Susie loftily. "She read it in the papers."

The boy of ten was sipping his favorite strawberry soda at McDonalds when his pal strolled in. The boy looked up from the drink and said, "Thought you were over at Jenny's house."

"I'm through with girls," the other said, "after all, they're a dime a dozen."

"You mean it?" The boy again halted his sipping. "A dime a dozen? Gee whiz. And all this time, I've been spending my money on sodas."

The little girl, aged five, had heard several times that Christmas was "just around the corner".

One afternoon, as she and her four-year-old brother were watching the falling snow, she told him all about Christmas, ending with: "And you know, Jimmy, Christmas is only two blocks away!"

"Better not wait for me today, Charley.
I've hooked into a real doozey."

Pete: "This match won't light."
Bob: "What's the matter with it?"
Pete: "I don't really know—it lit before."

Two small kids were talking about the latest addition to their family.
"I heard daddy say that a new baby costs almost three thousand dollars," said the little sister in a hushed voice.
"So what?" replied her brother. "They last an awful long time!"

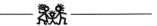

George: "I lost my dog."
Ed: "Why don't you put an ad in the paper?"
George: "That wouldn't do any good! He can't read."

"That little girl over there looks like Helen Red."
"You oughta see her in green!"

Eight-year-old Johnny told his nextdoor friend that his Aunt Clara had just had a baby. He added, "And I think my mom is coming down with it, too!"

Bob: "Last night, I put my tooth under my pillow. This morning I found a dime there instead."
Pete: "When I put mine under my pillow, I got a dollar."
Bob: "That's because you have buck teeth."

Sister: "How's it going at school, Tommy?"
Tommy: "I've been working awful hard to get ahead."
Sister: "Well! You sure as heck could use one."

Teen-age girl to boyfriend: "I would never have realized by dating you that the American teen-ager spends ten billion dollars a year!"

Two kids were playing cowboys and Indians and they agreed to walk into an imaginary saloon for a drink. The first kid walks to the "bar" and says, "Hey, Buddy, I'll have a shot of rye."
The second kid swallows hard, thinks a bit, then announces, "Make mine a whole wheat!"

"Did you know that Johnny's father is an optician?"
"I sure didn't. Maybe that explains why he keeps on making a *spectacle* of himself."

"What did your Dad say to your Mom when they were married?"
"He told her that marriage and a career just don't mix! Since then, he's never worked."

"Susie told me that your sister is awfully shy."
"Susie told you the truth. Why my sister Aimee is so shy, she covers the birdcage when she undresses at night."

Elmer: "So, your Pop collects fleas, eh...what does your Mom do?"
Peter: "She scratches."

"What is big at the bottom, little at the top, and has ears?"
Answer: A mountain.
"But what about the ears?" asks the chump.
 "Didn't you ever hear of mountaineers?"

What goes "ninety-nine clump?"
A centipede with a wooden leg.

New kid: "Where do you live?"
Old kid: "On Tough Street. The farther you go, the tougher you get. I live in the last house!"

Hay is for horses,
Straw is for cows.
Milk is for babies
For crying out loud.

It was a wonderfully deep snow and the little boy stood at the top of a hill readying his sled for a slide downhill. Another boy came up to him and asked: "Can I share your sled?"
"Sure," the owner of the sled said. "You take it uphill and I'll take it down!"

"My friend, Pete, has been practicing the violin for six years."
"Great. I bet he's mighty good at it by now."
"No, he ain't. It took him five years to learn that you don't blow a violin."

Marie was twelve years old and was now taking singing lessons. After her usual one-hour-practice at home, her brother, Stan, asked: "Why don't you sing just Christmas carols?"

"Dullsville!" Marie replied. "Why should I?"
"Because then you'd only have to sing once a year."

First student: "What do you have to know to play a cymbal in the orchestra?"
Second student: "Not a darned thing. You just have to know when."

Tommy Funk had dropped out of school and his buddy asked: "Why?"
"I got discouraged, that's all. I flunked every subject except geography."
"Every subject except geography? How do you explain that?"
"I didn't take geography!"

Little brother: "What's gossip?"
Big sister: "Ear pollution."
Little brother: "Well, then, what's dandruff?"
Big sister: "Hair pollution."

Two high schoolers were walking home from school. "What should we do tonight?" one asked.
"Let's flip a coin," replied the other. "If it comes up heads, we'll go to the movies. If it comes up tails, we'll play pool. If it stands on edge, we'll study."

Knock-knock.
Who's there?
Hatch.
Hatch who?
God bless you.

Sam and Jimmy were struggling with a huge table in a doorway. They pushed and pulled and upped it and downed it until both were exhausted. Between gasps for air, Sam managed to say, "We better give up...'cause we'll never get this table into the house."

"Into the house?" screamed Jimmy. "I thought we were moving it out of the house!"

———————— 🙎🙍 ————————

Sister: "I've made the chicken soup."
Brother: "Thank heaven for that. I thought we had to eat it!"

———————— 🙎🙍 ————————

Two eighth graders were discussing their friend, Amos. "That guy, Amos," one said to the other, "he's the most conceited guy I know. Do you know that on his last birthday, he sent a letter of congratulations to his Mom!"

———————— 🙎🙍 ————————

Little four-year-old Susie was alone in her room when her brother knocked on the door and asked to come in.

"No! You can't come in. Mommy always says that little boys shouldn't see little girls in their nightgowns." The brother didn't know how to respond to that, so he just stood there thinking about it. Suddenly Susie's voice announced a solution: "You can come in now. I took it off!"

———————— 🙎🙍 ————————

Knock-knock.
Who's there?
Cereal.
Cereal who?
Cereal pleasure to meet you.

———————— 🙎🙍 ————————

Little girl: "My baby brother is only one year old but he's been walking, now, for six months."
Little boy: "My goodness...isn't he awful tired?"

"*I THINK HE MEANS TO RUN AWAY FOR GOOD THIS TIME.*"

Joey: "Have you heard? I have a new baby sister."
Billy: "What's her name?"
Joey: "Who knows. She won't tell me."

Two boys were examining the bathroom scale. "How do you make this thing work?" one lad asked.

"I don't know," his buddy replied. "All I know is that when you stand on the thing, it makes you cuss a blue streak!"

Bobby: "Say, Tommy, have you ever had measles, scarlet fever or mumps?"

Tommy: "Nope. All I've ever had was cornflakes and Granola."

Little boy to pal, as they leave a movie: "I like television a lot better. It ain't so far to the bathroom."

There's a lady who is determined that when her twelve-year-old son Alfred grows up, he will be not only a Fred Astaire, but a Ronald Reagan as well. So, she marches him to dancing school every Wednesday afternoon and, furthermore, watches to see that he not only pushes little girls around the room, more or less in time with the music, but talks to them at the same time. Alfred is not what you'd call fond of the entire procedure.

Last Wednesday, Alfred was doing what he fondly believed to be a waltz with a brand-new dancing partner when his mother called: "Engage her in conversation!" He took a deep breath and gallantly informed his partner: "You sure do sweat less than any fat girl I've ever danced with!"

Alfred won't have to go back to that dancing school for a long time.

―――――― 🧍🧍 ――――――

What is the coldest place in a theater?
Z Row!

―――――― 🧍🧍 ――――――

Why is a guidebook like handcuffs?
Cause it's for tourists. (2 wrists)

―――――― 🧍🧍 ――――――

Why is a lazy dog like a hill?
Cause it's a slow pup. (slope up)

―――――― 🧍🧍 ――――――

Two boys wanted to ask a favor of their mom. "You ask her," demanded Eric, age 10.

"No, you ask her," said Peter, age 9, "you've known her much longer."

―――――― 🧍🧍 ――――――

Ella: "Sally, can you tell me how to spell banana?"
Sally: "Maybe. Trouble is…I don't know when to stop!"

―――――― 🧍🧍 ――――――

Did you hear about the farmer who ran short of proper feed and had to feed his hens sawdust? Well, they laid ten eggs. Nine of the baby chicks had wooden legs and the tenth was a woodpecker!

Carl: "What's the noisiest game in the world?"
Florin: "Tennis. You can't play it without raising a racket."

———————— 🧑‍🤝‍🧑 ————————

Sam: "My dog's got no nose."
Joe: "How awful! How does he smell?
Sam: "Terrible."

———————— 🧑‍🤝‍🧑 ————————

Polly: "Does your grandmother read the Bible?"
Elaine: "Sure does. Day and night."
Polly: "But why does she read it so much?"
Elaine: "I guess she's cramming for her finals."

———————— 🧑‍🤝‍🧑 ————————

First-grader: "Hey, Pop, "I learned to say 'Yes, sir' and 'No, sir' in school today."
Father: "Did you really?"
First-grader: "Yep!"

———————— 🧑‍🤝‍🧑 ————————

Small boy turning to his friend as a pretty girl walks by: "Wow! Ain't she terrific? If I ever stop hating girls, she'll be the one I'll stop hating first!"

———————— 🧑‍🤝‍🧑 ————————

Little boy to his buddy: "Mom told me today that storks don't really bring babies. Wow! You'd never believe what she told me!"

———————— 🧑‍🤝‍🧑 ————————

Kids' Proverbs

We are not to run in class even when teacher don't see us because even if teacher don't see us, Jesus can and He might tell the principal.

Though I am now a child, I will one day be a man or woman.

I plan to get married one day. Longer than one day, really. It is just that this is how it is usually said.

According to some people's beliefs, there is something that is halfway between Heaven and Hell. It's called pubertory.

I have resolved this year not to fight my sister unless she fights me first or makes me mad or I feel like it.

High up in the sky, the air is very thin. It is only close to the ground that we find the fat kind.

"What's the difference between a nut and a bolt?"

"A bolt is a thing like a stick of hard metal such as iron with a square bunch on one end and a lot of scratching around the other end. A nut is similar to the bolt only just the opposite, being a hole in a little chunk of iron, sawed off short, with wrinkles around the inside of the hole."

Demothenes was a great talker who practiced with a mouth full of pebbles. It really works and you can try it with bubblegum.

It is not true, the story of Ben Franklin flying his kite in an electric storm. Only a nut would try it.

If General Grant's formula for success could be summed up in one sentence, it would be this: "Always start everything you finish."

Joseph didn't wear bathrobes like other men in the Bible. He liked sports coats and had one of many colors.

Marconi invented the noodle and stuff like that.

Macadam was the first Scotchman.

St. Christopher always looks after travelers unless they go too fast.

———————— 🧑‍🤝‍🧑 ————————

Here are some answers to questions on the history of America:
"Where did our pioneers come from?"
"I am not sure but I know it is not the stork."

———————— 🧑‍🤝‍🧑 ————————

Knock-knock.
Who's there?
Pencil.
Pencil who?
Pencil fall down if you don't wear a belt!

———————— 🧑‍🤝‍🧑 ————————

Sam: "I know a kid who's got four legs."
Sally: "Yeah? What's his name?"
Sam: "Billy."

———————— 🧑‍🤝‍🧑 ————————

Knock-knock.
Who's there?
Debbie.
Debbie who?
Debbie stung me.

———————— 🧑‍🤝‍🧑 ————————

Mary: "Is that a real diamond ring you're wearing, Edith?"
Edith: "Well, if it isn't, I've been cheated out of fifty cents."

———————— 🧑‍🤝‍🧑 ————————

"My mother tried to buy a round-trip ticket to Chicago today and the agent said he couldn't sell her one!"
"What excuse did he give for that?"
He said, "All our tickets are square!"

Tommy: "What are the names of your twin pups, Jim?"
Jim: "Trashy and Smashy."
Tommy: "Which one is Trashy?"
Jim: "The one standing next to Smashy."

Jeremy: "My Dad says the price of everything is going up, up, up. Food, clothes...everything. He says he'd like to see something go down!"
Jim: "Would you like to show him my report card?"

Knock-knock.
Who's there?
Oswald.
Oswald who?
Oswald my bubble gum.

Elmer: "Get outa that seat, Joe! That's my seat."
Pete: "Nuts to you. Just prove it's your seat."
Elmer: "OK. I left my cake and ice cream on MY seat!"

A boy walked into a pharmacy and asked the pharmacist to give him something to cure the hiccups. The pharmacist merely leaned over and slapped the kid on the back.
"Why did you do that to me?" asked the boy.
"Well, you don't have the hiccups now, do you!"
"No, but my Mom out in the car still does!" the kid replied.

Knock-knock.
Who's there?
Olga.
Olga who?
Olga home if you don't quit cussin'.

Two lads were hiking through the Minnesota woods when they came upon a huge bear. One boy sat down, took a pair of track shoes out his knapsack and started to put them on.

"You're wasting your time," said the other boy. "You can't outrun that bear even with your track shoes on."

The other lad replied: "I don't have to outrun the bear, I just have to outrun you."

Two boys had just met and were introducing themselves. "I'm Al Reid," one boy said. "I'm Pete Elephanzagriatok," said the other.

"Wow! What a name. If I were you, I'd change it."

"I've asked for a change at court," the boy replied.

"Very wise. What name did you ask for?"

"Instead of Pete, I asked for Charles!"

Two kids were hiking through the Maine woods and were surrounded by huge granite cliffs. "I wonder where all this stone came from?" one boy asked.

"I know," said the other lad. "It came down when the glaciers came through here."

"Well, the rock is here but where are the glaciers?" asked the other.

"Well, er, uh, ahem. Well, I suppose the glaciers went back for more rock," was the reply.

Jerry: "I've eaten beef all my life and now I'm as strong as a bull."

Paul: "That's queer. I've eaten fish all my life and yet I can't swim a stroke."

Jonesy: "While we're camping, can I cook breakfast in my pajamas?"

Reedy: "Yes, you can, but...a pot or pan would be better."

Jimmy: "It rained the whole darned time me and my family were on vacation."

Morrie: "Well, it looks like you got a nice tan, anyway."

Jimmy: "That's not a tan...it's rust!"

Johnny: "How do you get fur from a tiger?"
Eddie: "You run as fast as you can in the opposite direction."

———————— 🧒 ————————

Knock-knock.
Who's there?
Midas.
Midas who.
Midas well open the door 'cause I ain't goin' home.

———————— 🧒 ————————

Dick: "I'm sure worried about our buddy, George."
Cal: "Why? What's he done?"
Dick: "Well, we walked into the post office the other day and there on the wall was posted a sign reading: MAN WANTED. Well, George went to the information window and applied for the job!"

———————— 🧒 ————————

Jeremy: "What's the difference between a thief and a church steeple?"
Finney: "One steals from the people and the other peals from the steeple!"

———————— 🧒 ————————

"Eddie, my teacher this year is Miss Edgar. And they say she rules the fourth grade with an iron fist. Boy!"
"I can sure believe that! You ought to hear her play the piano at our singing class!"

———————— 🧒 ————————

Peter: "We got one tough teacher this year. She told us to say 'Yes, sir' and 'No, sir'."
Elmer: "That's not so unusual."
Pete: "Well, it sure is when your teacher's name is Ms. Ilmaners!"

———————— 🧒 ————————

Bart: "Had a great time last summer. I learned how to ride a horse. I also learned how to eat standing up!"

81

"I tell you...the mosquitoes were so big at the resort we stayed in last summer that they had their own landing strip and came with their own landing gear. And those derned mosquitoes were such pests! They bit me to pieces. Why, I had to have a neighbor boy come over to help me scratch!"

"I wanta ask you something, George...when mosquitoes go on vacation, do they complain about all the people?"

"You shoulda been with me this summer at camp. We had a lot of tough times with skunks. How do they smell? They smell like our gym class! But I never changed clothes once this summer at camp and, y'know what? Toward the end of the season, the skunks ran away from me."

Mary: "Get away from me, Jamie. You remind me of the ocean."
Jamie: "Why is that? Because I'm so handsome?"
Mary: "No! Because you make me sick!"

Saul: "Hey, Jeremy! I got a new sister and she looks just like me."
Jeremy: "Don't let that worry you, Saul, so long as she's healthy."

Eddie: "This here's my dog, Rover. He's gentle as heck. He'll eat off your hand."
Sam: "That's what I'm afraid of. I need 'em both!"

Selma: "Our dog is just like one of the family."
Pearl: "Yeah? Which one?"

One of the unusual qualities about my family is that my cousin also happens to be the son of my father's sister.

Besides my mother and father, I have a fellow-sister and three *bothers.*

———————— 👫 ————————

The Halloween party I went to last year wasn't so much. I screamed only twice.

———————— 👫 ————————

The six-year-old boy and girl were wading in the ocean, near shore, but the water was a bit rough. So they walked back onto the dry sand and removed their clothes. As they walked back into the ocean to wade, once again, the boy glanced at the girl, stopped in shock and said, "Wow! I didn't know there was that much difference between Catholics and Protestants!"

———————— 👫 ————————

Dear God: It's OK that you made different religions but don't you get mixed-up sometimes? Arnold.

———————— 👫 ————————

"My Dad really made a deep impression on me last week."
"Yeah? Sit down and tell me about it."
"I can't. That's where he impressed me."

———————— 👫 ————————

Polly: "Is your big sister spoiled?"
Elaine: "No, not at all. It's just that awful perfume she wears."

———————— 👫 ————————

Eddie: "Hey, Charlie, you scratched me. Don't you ever file your nails?"
Charlie: "Nope. I just pitch 'em in the wastebasket."

———————— 👫 ————————

Stan: "I asked my dad if he was growing taller and he seemed surprised at my question."
"Why do you ask that?" he said.
So I said: "Because your head is pushing up through your hair."

83

Elmer: "Hey, George, did you hear about the tire that had a nervous breakdown?"

George: "Nope. Tell me about it."

Elmer: "It just couldn't take any more pressure!"

———————— 🧑‍🤝‍🧑 ————————

Stan: "Did you hear about the dog who went with his master to the flea market?"

Bob: "Nope. I sure didn't. Tell me about it."

Stan: "Not much to tell. That dog stole the show."

———————— 🧑‍🤝‍🧑 ————————

Polly: "Did you hear about the girl who swallowed some dimes and nickels?"

Elaine: "No, I sure didn't. Tell me about her."

Polly: "Well, she just wanted to see some change in herself."

———————— 🧑‍🤝‍🧑 ————————

Dick: "Hey, Jamie, did you hear about the big fire at the soap factory?"

Jamie: "No, tell me, did anyone get burned?"

Dick: "Everybody got off safe. They slid down the lather!"

———————— 🧑‍🤝‍🧑 ————————

Alan: "Did you hear about the absent-minded professor who looked into the mirror for over an hour?"

Morrie: "No, I haven't heard. Tell me about him."

Alan: "He was trying to remember where he'd seen that face before."

———————— 🧑‍🤝‍🧑 ————————

Marshall: "Do you know what this guy said when he wanted to stop the boat?"

Bob: "No, tell me."

Marshall: "He yelled, 'whoa, whoa, whoa the boat.'"

———————— 🧑‍🤝‍🧑 ————————

Jonas: "Did you hear about the stupid farmer who ran a steamroller over his field of potatoes?"

Adam: "Nope. Not a word."

Jonas: "Well, the dope thought he'd get a crop of mashed potatoes."

84

"BRUSHING YOUR TEETH ISN'T SO BAD IF YOU USE PEANUT BUTTER!"

Pete: "If you had a hundred-pound worm in your garden, how would you get rid of it?"

Emil: "Hm-m-m, well, let's see. Oh yeah. Here's how. Bring in a two-hundred-pound robin!"

———————————————————

Elmer: "Why did the skeleton refuse to cross the road?"

Al: "Simply because he didn't have the guts to do it."

———————————————————

Adam: "What did the judge say when a skunk walked into the courtroom?"

Jonas: "He said: 'Odor in the courtroom!'"

———————————————————

An eighth grade class was visiting the local FBI office and they were looking at a wall full of photographs. The FBI agent leading the group said: "These represent the most-wanted criminals in our area. We hope these photographs will help us catch them."

A boy in the group spoke up: "How come you didn't keep them when you took the photographs?"

Sassy Schooldays

Little bits of nerve,
Little grains of sand,
Make the biggest blockhead
Pass a hard exam.

Ashes to ashes,
Dust to dust,
Oil those brains
Before they rust.

Red, white and blue,
I don't speak to you.

Flypaper, flypaper,
Gooey, gooey, gooey,
Flypaper, flypaper,
Hope it sticks on Louie.

Cross my heart and hope to die,
Eat a banana and holler Hi!

Now you are graduating,
Isn't that fine!
You've been in the eighth grade
Since 1989.

Pins and needles,
Needles and pins,
Sass me again
And I'll kick your shins.

Teacher, Teacher,
I declare,
I see Mary's underwear.

Hickory leaves and calico trees,
All schoolteachers are hard to please.

The more we study, the more we know,
The more we know, the more we forget.
The more we forget, the less we know.
The less we know, the less we forget.
The less we forget, the more we know.
Why study?

On a hill there is a mill,
From the mill, there is a walk,
Under the walk, there is a key.
Can you spell this name for me?
(Milwaukee)

A knife and a fork,
A bottle and a cork.
That's the way to spell
New York

Chicken in the car
And the car won't go,
That's the way to spell
Chicago.

P with a little o,
S with a t,

O double f,
And i-c-e.
(Post Office)

———————— 🧒🧒 ————————

A cin and a natty,
A skinny and a fatty,
That's the way to spell Cincinnati.

———————— 🧒🧒 ————————

Bill had a billboard and also a board bill,
But the board bill bored Bill so that he
Sold the billboard to pay the board bill.

———————— 🧒🧒 ————————

If dumbness were an occupation,
You would be a great sensation.

———————— 🧒🧒 ————————

Pete: "Had a bad time last night. I fell over twenty feet!"
Bob: "You seem OK. How come you didn't get hurt?"
Pete: "I was only trying to get to my seat at the movies."

———————— 🧒🧒 ————————

"My mother really talked to the airplane pilot when we got on the plane."
"Really? What'd she talk about."
"Oh, she just told him not to go faster than sound 'cause she and I wanted to talk a lot."

———————— 🧒🧒 ————————

Latin's a dead language,
Dead, dead, dead as can be!
It knocked off all the Romans,
And now, it's killing me.

"Here it is . . . S-E-X."

CHAPTER III

Parents Love to Talk to Other Parents

"My daughter's sex education class didn't worry me," the concerned father said, "until they scheduled a field trip."

Every father and mother knows that when they consider the telephone, why, teenagers just can't seem to get the hang of it.

Young Chris was diligently practicing away on the piano when there came a determined banging on the door. It was the cop from the corner, looking very formidable indeed. "Gotta investigate a call from the lady who lives next door," he said to Chris's father. "She swore two fellers named Chopin and Debussy was being murdered in here."

Bob Hope saw nothing suprising in the fact that babies start bawling the moment they are born. "In the first place," points out Hope, "they're hungry. And in the second place, by the time they're ten minutes old, they owe the Department of Internal Revenue $2,500."

Opening gambit of a very sad statement: "No sooner had we sold Junior's buggy than..."

A young mother-to-be visited her gynecologist for a routine check-up, and was told that she would be blessed with twins. So the Doc decided the husband should know at once. He had the nurse drag hubby out of the front seat of his car parked below.

"What's the big idea?" hubby protested. "I'm liable to get a ticket for being double-parked outside."

"Well, Sir," the nurse said, "your wife's in the same situation inside."

A thoughtful pediatrician reminded a comparatively new father, "Don't spank your child on an empty stomach. Be sure to eat something first."

Then he noticed that the baby had white hair. "This kid worrying about something?" Doc asked.

"It's not the kid at all," the father replied. "It's my wife. She's near-sighted and keeps powdering the wrong end."

There's great truth in an observation made by Mrs. Edward Yonkers of Decatur, IL, after she and her husband returned with their four small children from a visit with family and friends in Peoria over a Christmas holiday.

"We made everybody we visited happy twice," she said. "Once when we arrived and a second time when we left!"

Never cry if the kid spilled the milk...it could have been whiskey!

The following words of wisdom are from *When It's Laughter You're After* by Stewart Harral:

Juvenile delinquency, it is said, is the result of parents trying to train children without starting at the bottom.

Any task around the house is fascinating to a child until he's old enough to do it.

When you observe children of six years throwing a tantrum, you wonder who will manage them when they are forty.

Today's children start to school with one big advantage. They know two letters of the alphabet—TV.

There are no problem children—only children who have problems.

The three things that children wear out faster than shoes are, Mom, Pop and Teacher.

An allowance is something you pay your children to live with you.

Child psychology: how children manage their parents.

Nowadays it seems that the kids run about everything in the house...but the lawn mower and the vacuum cleaner.

If you want to prevent your children from hearing what you say, pretend you're talking to them.

The richest inheritance parents can give their children is a few minutes of their time each day.

Children are like canoes, they are more easily controlled if paddled from the rear.

Most parents can remember when their children were in the "no-it-all" stage.

Those hardest to convince that they are at the retirement age are kids at bedtime.

If you want to know whether a parent has been a success or failure, wait till you find out what happens to the grandchildren.

A friend observed that before marriage he had four theories about children and now that he has four children, he has no theories.

Most parents have difficulty selecting a name for their new baby—some have wealthy relatives!

The way some kids act makes you wonder if their parents embarked on the sea of matrimony without a paddle.

If you think it's easy to take candy away from a baby—try it sometime!

Some kids grow by leaps and bounds—especially those in the apartment overhead.

When you do manage to get a suitable pet for your kid, you learn that the city has an ordinance against alligators!

When a child takes "No" for an answer, he's probably thinking of still another way to ask the question.

Most children are descended from a long, long line their mothers listened to.

When It's Laughter You're After by Stewart Harral
© by the University of Oklahoma Press, Publishing
Division of the University. Fourth printing 1969.

"I'm sure that our little Benny gets all his intelligence from me!" said the proud Papa.

"Very likely," his wife said, "because I still have mine."

Seeing a man stagger as he walked was old hat to 5-year-old Suzanne. She said, "He walks just like my baby sister."

Kids give you an ongoing medical condition: They're either a lump in the throat or a pain in the (ahem) neck.

On West Monroe Street, there lives a New Yorker who has been brooding about his adored sixteen-year-old daughter, Susie, whose interest in life is confined to one subject: clothes. Arithmetic, history, sports and literature, she disdains. All she does is read Vogue, Harper's Bazaar, Women's Wear and all the fashion columns in the daily newspapers.

One evening, she returned home from her 1997 modeling school and casually reported that the class had been lectured on the facts of life by an expert on sex.

"At last," thought the father, "Susie has acquired a new interest." He asked her: "Aren't there questions about things you heard today that you want to ask?"

"Just one," replied the daughter. "What can a girl wear for a thing like that?"

The son of a prominent Bostonian came home for his first vacation from college at the age of eighteen with grades so good the entire family was proud. His six-year-old brother, a bit upset because of the adulation poured upon the older brother, decided he wanted to get into the act himself, and interrupted loudly, "I got an 'A' in arithmetic today."

His father replied, "I didn't know they taught arithmetic in kindergarten. What's one and one?"

The five-year-old thought that one over, then replied, "We haven't gotten that far yet."

Which state is a father? Pa.

A mother was just about frantic with trouble from her four hard-to-handle kids. A friend asked if she'd have children if she had it to do over again.

"Yes, I guess I would," she replied, "but they'd sure as heck be different than the ones I've got now."

A man with a small boy entered a barbershop and asked for a haircut. When the barber had finished with him, the man said, "I'm going down the street for a beer. Please cut my kid's hair."

The barber cut the boy's hair, then waited for the man to return. Finally, he turned to the kid and asked, "Where the dickens did your father go?"

"Oh," said the boy, "he ain't my father. He's the guy who stopped me in the street and asked if I'd like a free haircut."

The family barber looked at our 10-year-old boy's greasy, slick hair and then asked, "Do you want it cut or just the oil changed?"

" IT SAYS HERE THAT A GOOD EDUCATION IS LIKE MONEY IN THE BANK -- WHATEVER THAT IS!"

A mother, shopping in a department store, aided by three clerks and several bystanders, was futilely trying to quiet her noisy, destructive little son. Then she noticed a distinguished psychiatrist was watching them.

"Could you do anything with this child?" she asked.

The learned man grasped the lad by an arm, led him aside and whispered a few words to him with immediate and amazing results.

"What on earth did you say to him?" the mother gasped.

"I just said, 'If you don't straighten up, I'll spank your pants off!'"

A father read a list of six questions that his small son would need to answer in school that day.

"Did you miss any of the six?" asked the father.

"Yes," replied the boy. "I missed the first three and the last two."

Some students drink at the fountain of knowledge—others just gargle.

John J. Plomp says that you know children are growing up when they start asking questions that have answers.

Why should bowling alleys be quiet?
So that you can hear a pin drop!

There was a time when parents had a lot of kids. Now kids have a lot of parents.

The kid was making everybody miserable on the airplane—running up and down the aisle, waking people, spilling the food. Suddenly, things quieted. "What happened?" one passenger asked.

"I took care of it," replied the hostess.

"How?"

"I told him to go outside and play!"

"We must lower the voting age to fourteen," said one teen's father. "That's when they know everything."

During a telephone conversation with my six-year-old grandson, Bert, he said, "Grandpa, I'm sick and tired of our Sunday School studying about Pharoah and the lights."

"Lights, Bert? What kind of lights?" I asked.

Just then his father took the phone: "He means Israelites, Grandpa."

"Don't be fooled," said the ad in the morning paper, "that airport money, if authorized, will put an unjust tax burden on your children and grandchildren."

"Holy smokes," said my pinch-penny friend. "I was going to vote against this thing, but if my children and grandchildren are going to pay for it, I believe I'll be able to afford it."

The family is a court of justice that never shuts down for night or day.

Malcolm DeChazal

Everybody knows how to raise children except the people who have them.

P.J. O'Rourke, *The Bachelor Home Companion.*
1987

Daughters are best. They don't migrate.

Alan Bennett, *Talking Heads.*   1988

Biff, the Talking Dog

By Carl Goerch

I'd practically forgotten all about it until I saw a skit on television the other night that reminded me of it. It also brought back memories of one of the most enjoyable afternoons I ever have spent in all my life.

One of my buddies many years ago was Bricky Connor, whose father was a gardener on one of the large estates at Tarrytown, N.Y. Bricky was a lad of great ingenuity and clever ideas. He was always thinking up something new and, in a good many instances, his ideas got himself and others into plenty of trouble.

He and I were together on this particular afternoon. Playing around the yard was Biff, a medium-sized dog of unknown parentage. Bricky had had him ever since he was a little bit of a thing.

The two of us—Bricky and I—were tossing a baseball around. One of my throws got past him and he had to run over toward the fence to retrieve it. While doing so, he happened to notice a long rubber hose which his father had left there to dry.

Bricky took a second look at the hose, glanced at Biff and then, with a wide grin, announced: "We'll make Biff talk."

"How?" I wanted to know.

"Come on," he said, "and I'll show you."

He outlined his plan as we went to the shed where Mr. Connor kept quite a number of gardening tools. Each of us got a shovel. We dug a long, shallow trench from behind the shed to a point near the sidewalk in front of the house. Into this trench, we placed the rubber hose and then covered it up. One end of the hose was behind the shed; the other was up front, near the sidewalk. Next, we grabbed Biff and tied him to a wooden peg, just a foot or two away from the sidewalk. After that, Bricky went into the house and came out with a funnel, which we inserted in the end of the hose behind the shed. It made an excellent mouthpiece.

And that completed the preliminary arrangements. In our place of concealment behind the shed we waited for our first victim while Biff sat calmly near the other end of the hose, perfectly satisfied and contented.

I wish I could remember the names of the individuals who came along but I'm not exactly sure about all of them. As I recall, however, the first one was a middle-aged man by the name of Mr. Tom Powers. Bricky pressed his face against the funnel and, just as Mr. Powers was opposite Biff, shouted out:

"Hello, Mr. Powers!"

Mr. Powers looked around, saw nobody and started to move on.

"How're you feeling, Mr. Powers?"

He came to an abrupt stop. The end of the hose was right close to Biff but we had concealed it by putting some tall grass around it. Mr. Powers couldn't see it. He regarded Biff suspiciously and for the first time realized that the voice couldn't possibly have come from anyone else except the dog.

You should have seen him. He backed away from tail-wagging Biff and then swung around and walked off as rapidly as he could, casting occasional glances over his shoulder at the dog.

Equally interesting was Mrs. Ethel Combs's reaction. She had been to the grocery store and had three or four bundles in her arms. She observed Biff and said: "Hi, Biff!" Then, just as she got past him, Biff spoke up and said: "How about a bone, Mrs. Combs?"

Well, Sir, the lady jumped as though somebody had hit her in the rear with a barrel-stave. She dropped two of her bundles and, while stooping to pick them up, gazed at Biff in complete consternation. Then she moved away as rapidly as she could, paying no attention when Biff hollered after her: "Goody-bye, Mrs. Combs!"

For the next hour or two, we had more fun than you could shake a stick at. Old and young alike regarded Biff in amazement. They weren't sure, of course, whether it was the dog that was doing the talking but, at the same time, they couldn't see any other source whence the voice could be coming. The expressions on their faces were wonderful to watch.

The climax came when Frank Shields hove in sight. Or perhaps it would be better to classify it as an anti-climax. Mr. Shields at that time was about thirty years old. He was an affable fellow but he had one weakness—he loved to drink. On frequent occasions, he drank too much for his own good, and this happened to be one of them. He had spent most of the day in Al Cureau's saloon and was just able to navigate as he wended his way homeward.

We waited until he came within range. Bricky placed the funnel up against his face once more and hollered: "Hello, Frank!"

Mr. Shields stopped. He looked around, saw nobody and started off again.

"It's me—Biff—talking to you," said the voice.

Mr. Shields turned slowly around once more. His bleary eyes focused on the dog. "Oh," he said, "it's you. How are you, Biff?"

"I'm all right, Frank. What time is it?"

With considerable effort, he pulled out his watch, gazed at it intently and then announced: "It's half-past five."

"Thank you, Frank," said Biff.

"You're welcome," said Mr. Shields, and he staggered on his way without giving any sign that anything of an unusual nature had taken place.

As I recall, we never did give the stunt away and for some time after-wards, there were quite a number of people in the neighborhood who regarded Biff suspiciously every time they saw him.

Just for the Fun of It by Carl Goerch
Edwards & Broughton Co., Raleigh, NC   1954
Reprinted with permission of the heirs of Carl Goerch.

———————— 🎎 ————————

What flower is a fierce animal?
Dandelion.

———————— 🎎 ————————

One of the most important things to remember about infant care is:
Never change diapers in mid-stream.

Don Marquis

———————— 🎎 ————————

Isn't it amazing—the contrasts in life. For example, consider the fellow that married your daughter. He was way beneath her in all phases of life; way, way below her. But their kid, my grandchild, is just the smartest, pret-tiest, nicest, most intelligent kid ever born.

———————— 🎎 ————————

When you've seen a nude infant doing a backward somersault, you know why clothing exists.

"OOPS...THE STUFF FROM LAST WEEK!"

Here's humor from 'way down south' in North Carolina, *Tar Heel Laughter,* edited by Richard Walser, University of North Carolina Press. 1974

A boy once took it in his head
That he would exercise his sled.
He took that sled into the road
And, lord a massa, how he slod.
And as he slid he laughing cried,
"What fun upon my sled to slide."
And as he laughed, before he knewed,
He from that sliding sled was slude.
Upon the slab where he was laid,
They carved this line: "This boy was slade."

> *Tar Heel Laughter,* by Richard Walser, Editor
> University of North Carolina Press,
> Chapel Hill, NC.   1974

Tragic Incident

Probably the most tragic incident involving truth and children occurred when some Asheville friends called the home of a couple they play bridge with.

"Let me speak to your mommy," the lady asked the little boy who answered.

"She's in the bathtub," he said.

"Let me speak to your daddy."

"He's in the bathtub with mommy," the little fellow explained.

> A.C. Snow, Raleigh Times.   Dec. 1971

She's getting married next month and she's awfully busy collecting things for her torso.

Mother got the butcher knife out and prepared to carve the jack-o-lantern from the fat pumpkin.

"Mama!" wailed her two-year-old son Drew. "You gonna kill it?"

One Santa Claus grabbed up a guitar and conked the other Santa Claus over the head with it, and that was when the fight started.

Too Many Santa Clauses

The setting for this tale is in a country school not far from the town of Lenoir in Watauga County.

A couple of weeks before Christmas, teachers and other members of the Parent-Teachers Association decided to put on a rip-snortin' Christmas program. The children got tremendously interested and one of the first things the kids wanted to know was whether Santa Claus would be there. They were told that every effort would be made to bring the old gentleman to the schoolhouse.

Arrangements were made with Mr. Jim Walker to dress up and take the part of St. Nicholas. Mr. Walker said he would get his wife to make him an appropriate suit and they could depend upon his being present.

Another group, not knowing about all this, called on Mr. Tom Hadley and made him the same proposition, and Mr. Hadley said he'd be glad to cooperate.

The celebration took place on the night of December 21. When the program started at eight o'clock, the school auditorium was packed and jammed with children and grown-ups. Several carols were sung, the preacher made an appropriate Christmas talk and then—and then—in walked Santa Claus—in other words, Mr. Walker. The children applauded joyously.

Santa had come all the way from the North Pole to pay them a visit and they were delighted.

And now, momentarily, we turn to Mr. Hadley.

It was close to Christmas. Mr. Hadley felt that the advent of the Yuletide season justified him in taking a drink. So, he drank a toast to himself, followed by one to Santa Claus, Mrs. Santa Claus and the nine reindeer, including Rudolph.

Then he started for the schoolhouse. He entered the back door of the auditorium and walked out on the platform. The children gasped in amazement. They hadn't been sure whether one Santa Claus would show up and here—all of a sudden—were two of them.

They yelled, stamped their feet and clapped their hands.

Mr. Hadley bowed in appreciation of such a wonderful reception. Then he happened to look over toward the side of the stage and saw Mr. Walker.

Ha-ha! An interloper. An imposter.

He walked somewhat unsteadily over toward Mr. Walker and asked, "What are you doing here?"

Said Mr. Walker, "I'm Santa Claus!"

"You're not...I'm Santa Claus, and besides—you're drunk."

Mr. Hadley looked around him. Members of the school orchestra had left their instruments on the stage. A guitar was within easy reach. He grabbed it, held it firmly in his right hand, took a long swing, and crowned Mr. Walker with it.

Mr. Walker staggered back from the blow. The children went wild. Mr. Walker reached on a table, picked up a book and slung it at Mr. Hadley. He socked him squarely in the face with it.

Then the two of them went at it with their fists, and the children really went wild. "Hit 'im, Santa Claus! Sock him in the jaw! Hit 'im in the belly." The entire auditorium by this time was in an uproar. Four or five men sprang forward and succeeded in separating them. They were ushered unceremoniously out of the building and were told to stay out.

Then the school principal said that in view of unforeseen circumstances, he, himself, would enact the part of Santa Claus. The kids didn't give a rap about the rest of the program. They had seen enough to last them a lifetime, and to this day they haven't quit talking about the dandy fight that Santa Claus and his brother put on for them.

Mr. Walker and Mr. Hadley still don't speak to each other.

It's a truism that men believe in heredity, at least until their sons make asses of themselves.

The Ransom of Red Chief

O. Henry

It looked like a good thing: but wait till I tell you. We were down South, in Alabama—Bill Driscott and myself—when this kidnapping idea struck us. It was, as Bill afterward expressed it, "during a moment of temporary mental apparition"; but we didn't find that out till later.

There was a town down there, as flat as a flannel-cake, and called Summit, of course. It contained inhabitants of as undeleterious and self-satisfied a class of peasantry as ever clustered around a Maypole.

Bill and me had a joint capital of about six hundred dollars, and we needed just two thousand dollars more to pull off a fraudulent town-lot scheme in Western Illinois with. We talked it over on the front steps of the hotel. Philogrogenitiveness, says we, is strong in semi-rural communities; therefore, and for other reasons, a kidnapping project ought to do better there than in the radius of newspapers that send reporters out in plain clothes to stir up talk about such things. We knew that Summit couldn't get after us with anything stronger than constables and, maybe, some lackadaisical bloodhounds and a diatribe or two in the *Weekly Farmer's Budget.* So, it looked good.

We selected for our victim the only child of a prominent citizen named Ebenezer Dorset. The father was respectable and tight, a mortgage fancier and a stern, upright collection-plate passer and forecloser. The kid was a boy of ten, with bas-relief freckles, and hair the color of the cover of the magazine you buy at the newsstand when you want to catch a train. Bill and me figured that Ebenezer would melt down for a ransom of two thousand dollars to a cent. But wait till I tell you.

About two miles from Summit was a little mountain, covered with a dense cedar brake. On the rear elevation of this mountain was a cave. There we stored provisions.

One evening after sundown, we drove in a buggy past old Dorset's house. The kid was in the street, throwing rocks at a kitten on the opposite fence.

"Hey, little boy!" says Bill, "would you like to have a bag of candy and a nice ride?"

The boy catches Bill neatly in the eye with a piece of brick.

"That will cost the old man an extra five hundred dollars," says Bill, climbing over the wheel.

That boy put up a fight like a welter-weight cinnamon bear; but, at last, we got him down in the bottom of the buggy and drove away. We took him up to the cave, and I hitched the horse in the cedar brake. After dark, I drove the buggy to the little village, three miles away, where we had hired it, and walked back to the mountain.

Bill was pasting court-plaster over the scratches and bruises on his features. There was a fire burning behind the big rock at the entrance of the cave, and the boy was watching a pot of boiling coffee, with two buzzard tail-feathers stuck in his red hair. He points a stick at me when I come up and says:

"Ha! cursed paleface, do you dare to enter the camp of Red Chief, the terror of the plains?"

"He's all right now," says Bill, rolling up his trousers and examining some bruises on his shins. "We're playing Indian. We're making Buffalo Bill's show look like magic-lantern views of Palestine in the town hall. I'm Old Hank, the Trapper, Red Chief's captive, and I'm to be scalped at daybreak. By Geronimo! that kid can kick hard."

Yes, sir, that boy seemed to be having the time of his life. The fun of camping out in a cave had made him forget that he was a captive himself. He immediately christened me Snake-eye, the Spy, and announced that, when his braves returned from the warpath, I was to be broiled at the stake at the rising of the sun.

Then we had supper; and he filled his mouth full of bacon and bread and gravy, and began to talk. He made a during-dinner speech something like this:

"I like this fine. I never camped out before; but I had a pet 'possum once, and I was nine last birthday. I hate to go to school. Rats ate up sixteen of Jimmy Talbot's aunt's speckled hen's eggs. Are there any real Indians in these woods? I want some more gravy. Does the trees moving make the wind blow? We had five puppies. What makes your nose so red, Hank? My father has lots of money. Are the stars hot? I whipped Ed Walker twice, Saturday. I don't like girls. You dassant catch toads unless with a string. Do oxen make any noise? Why are oranges round? Have you got beds to sleep on in this cave? Amos Murray has got six toes. A parrot can talk, but a monkey or fish can't. How many does it take to make twelve?"

Every few minutes he would remember that he was a pesky redskin, and pick up his stick rifle and tiptoe to the mouth of the cave to rubber for the scouts of the hated paleface. Now and then, he would let out a warwhoop that made Old Hank the Trapper shiver. That boy had Bill terrorized from the start.

"Red Chief," says I to the kid, "would you like to go home?"

"Aw, what for?" says he. "I don't have any fun at home. I hate to go to school. I like to camp out. You won't take me back home again, Snake-eye, will you?"

"Not right away," says I. "We'll stay here in the cave awhile."

"All right!" says he. "That'll be fine. I never had such fun in all my life."

We went to bed about eleven o'clock. We spread down some wide blankets and quilts and put Red Chief between us. We weren't afraid he'd run away. He kept us awake for three hours, jumping up and reaching for his rifle and screeching: "Hist! pard," in mine and Bill's ears, as the fancied crackle of a twig or the rustle of a leaf revealed to his young imagination the stealthy approach of the outlaw band. At last, I fell into a troubled sleep, and dreamed that I had been kidnapped and chained to a tree by a ferocious pirate with red hair.

Just at daybreak, I was awakened by a series of awful screams from Bill. They weren't yells, or howls, or shouts, or whoops, or yawps, such as you'd expect from a manly set of vocal organs—they were simply indecent, terrifying, humiliating screams, such as women emit when they see ghosts or caterpillars. It's an awful thing to hear a strong, desperate, fat man scream incontinently in a cave at daybreak.

I jumped up to see what the matter was. Red Chief was sitting on Bill's chest, with one hand twined in Bill's hair. In the other, he had the sharp case-knife we used for slicing bacon; and he was industriously and realistically trying to take Bill's scalp, according to the sentence that had been pronounced upon him the evening before.

I got the knife away from the kid and made him lie down again. But from that moment, Bill's spirit was broken. He laid down on his side of the bed, but he never closed an eye again in sleep as long as that boy was with us. I dozed off for a while, but along toward sun-up, I remembered that Red Chief had said I was to be burned at the stake at the rising of the sun. I wasn't nervous or afraid; but I sat up and lit my pipe and leaned against a rock.

"What you getting up so soon for, Sam?" asked Bill.

"Me?" says I. "Oh, I got a kind of pain in my shoulder. I thought sitting up would rest it."

"You're a liar!" says Bill. "You're afraid. You was to be burned at sunrise, and you was afraid he'd do it. And he would, too, if he could find a match. Ain't it awful, Sam? Do you think anybody will pay out money to get a little imp like that back home?"

"Sure," said I. "A rowdy kid like that is just the kind that parents dote on. Now, you and the Chief get up and cook breakfast, while I go up on the top of this mountain and reconnoitre."

I went up on the peak of the little mountain and ran my eye over the contiguous vicinity. Over towards Summit, I expected to see the sturdy yeomanry of the village armed with scythes and pitchforks beating the countryside for the dastardly kidnappers. But what I saw was a peaceful landscape dotted with one man plowing with a dun mule. Nobody was dragging the creek; no couriers dashed hither and yon, bringing tidings of no news to the distracted parents. There was a sylvan attitude of somnolent sleepiness pervading that section of the external outward surface of Alabama that lay exposed to my view. "Perhaps," says I to myself, "it has not yet been discovered that the wolves have borne away the tender lambkin from the fold. Heaven help the wolves!" says I, and I went down the mountain to breakfast.

When I got to the cave, I found Bill backed up against the side of it, breathing hard, and the boy threatening to smash him with a rock half as big as a coconut.

"He put a red-hot boiled potato down my back," explained Bill, "and then mashed it with his foot; and I boxed his ears. Have you got a gun about you, Sam?"

I took the rock away from the boy and kind of patched up the argument. "I'll fix you," says the kid to Bill. "No man ever yet struck the Red Chief but he got paid for it. You better beware!"

After breakfast, the kid takes a piece of leather with strings wrapped around it out of his pocket and goes outside the cave unwinding it.

"What's he up to now?" says Bill, anxiously. "You don't think he'll run away, do you, Sam?"

"No fear of it," says I. "He don't seem to be much of a home body. But we've got to fix up some plan about the ransom. There don't seem to be much excitement around Summit on account of his disappearance; but maybe they haven't realized yet that he's gone. His folks may think he's spending the night with Aunt Jane or one of the neighbors. Anyhow, he'll be missed today. Tonight we must get a message to his father demanding the two thousand dollars for his return."

Just then we heard a kind of warwhoop, such as David might have emitted when he knocked out the champion Goliath. It was a sling that Red Chief had pulled out of his pocket, and he was whirling it around his head.

I dodged and heard a heavy thud and a kind of a sigh from Bill, like a horse gives out when you take his saddle off. A rock the size of an egg had caught Bill just behind his left ear. He loosened himself all over and fell in the fire across the frying pan of hot water for washing the dishes. I dragged him out and poured cold water on his head for half an hour.

By and by, Bill sits up and feels behind his ear and says: "Sam, do you know who my favorite Biblical character is?"

"Take it easy," says I. "You'll come to your senses presently."

"King Herod," says he. "You won't go away and leave me here alone, will you, Sam?"

I went out and caught that boy and shook him until his freckles rattled.

"If you don't behave," says I, "I'll take you straight home. Now, are you going to be good, or not?"

"I was only funning," says he, sullenly. "I didn't mean to hurt Old Hank. But what did he hit me for? I'll behave, Snake-eye, if you won't send me home, and if you'll let me play the Black Scout today."

"I don't know the game," says I. "That's for you and Mr. Bill to decide. He's your playmate for the day. I'm going away for a while, on business. Now, you come in and make friends with him and say you are sorry for hurting him, or home you go, at once."

I made him and Bill shake hands, and then I took Bill aside and told him I was going to Poplar Grove, a little village three miles from the cave, and find out what I could about how the kidnapping had been regarded in Summit. Also, I thought it best to send a peremptory letter to old man Dorset that day, demanding the ransom and dictating how it should be paid.

"You know, Sam" says Bill, "I've stood by you without batting an eye in earthquakes, fire and flood—in poker games, dynamite outrages, police raids, train robberies, and cyclones. I never lost my nerve yet till we kidnapped that two-legged skyrocket of a kid. He's got me going. You won't leave me long with him, will you, Sam?"

"I'll be back some time this afternoon," says I. "You must keep the boy amused and quiet till I return. And now we'll write the letter to old Dorset."

Bill and I got paper and pencil and worked on the letter while Red Chief, with a blanket wrapped around him, strutted up and down, guarding the mouth of the cave. Bill begged me tearfully to make the ransom fifteen hundred dollars instead of two thousand. "I ain't attempting," says he, "to decry the celebrated moral aspect of parental affection, but we're dealing with humans, and it ain't human for anybody to give up two thousand dollars for that forty-pound chunk of freckled wildcat. I'm willing to take a chance at fifteen hundred dollars. You can charge the difference up to me."

So, to relieve Bill, I acceded, and we collaborated a letter that ran this way:

Ebenezer Dorset, Esq.:

We have your boy concealed in a place far from Summit. It is useless for you or the most skilful detectives to attempt to find him. Absolutely, the only terms on which you can have him restored to you are these: We demand fifteen hundred dollars in large bills for his return; the money to be left at midnight tonight at the same spot and in the same box as your reply—as hereinafter described. If you agree to these terms, send your answer in writing by a soli-

*tary messenger tonight at half-past eight o'clock. After crossing
Owl Creek on the road to Poplar Grove, there are three large trees
about a hundred yards apart, close to the fence of the wheat field
on the right-hand side. At the bottom of the fence-post, opposite
the third tree, will be found a small pasteboard box.*

*The messenger will place the answer in this box and return
immediately to Summit.*

*If you attempt any treachery or fail to comply with our demand
as stated, you will never see your boy again.*

*If you pay the money as demanded, he will be returned to you
safe and well within three hours. These terms are final, and if you
do not accede to them, no further communication will be attempted.*

Two Desperate Men

I addressed this letter to Dorset, and put it in my pocket. As I was
about to start, the kid comes up to me and says:

"Aw, Snake-eye, you said I could play the Black Scout while you was
gone."

"Play it, of course," says I. "Mr. Bill will play with you. What kind of a
game is it?"

"I'm the Black Scout," says Red Chief, "And I have to ride to the
stockade to warn the settlers that the Indians are coming. I'm tired of playing Indian myself. I want to be the Black Scout."

"All right," says I, "It sounds harmless to me. I guess Mr. Bill will help
you foil the pesky savages."

"What am I to do?" asks Bill, looking at the kid suspiciously.

"You are the hoss," says Black Scout. "Get down on your hands and
knees. How can I ride to the stockade without a hoss?"

"You'd better keep him interested," said I, "till we get the scheme
going. Loosen up."

Bill gets down on his all fours, and a look comes in his eye like a rabbit's when you catch it in a trap.

"How far is it to the stockade, kid?" he asks, in a husky manner of
voice.

"Ninety miles," says the Black Scout. "And you have to hump yourself
to get there on time. Whoa, now!"

The Black Scout jumps on Bill's back and digs his heels in his side.

"For Heaven's sake," says Bill, "hurry back, Sam, as soon as you can.
I wish we hadn't made the ransom more than a thousand. Say, you quit
kicking me or I'll get up and warm you good."

I walked over to Poplar Grove and sat around the post-office and store,
talking with the chaw-bacons that came in to trade. One whiskerando says
that he hears Summit is all upset on account of Elder Dorset's boy having

been lost or stolen. That was all I wanted to know. I bought some smoking tobacco, referred casually to the price of black-eyed peas, posted my letter surreptitiously, and came away. The postmaster said the mail-carrier would come by in an hour to take the mail to Summit.

When I got back to the cave, Bill and the boy were not to be found. I explored the vicinity of the cave, and risked a yodel or two, but there was no response.

So I lighted my pipe and sat down on a mossy bank to await developments.

In about half an hour, I heard the bushes rustle, and Bill wabbled out into the little glade in front of the cave. Behind him was the kid, stepping softly like a scout, with a broad grin on his face. Bill stopped, took off his hat and wiped his face with a red handkerchief. The kid stopped about eight feet behind him.

"Sam." says Bill, "I suppose you'll think I'm a renegade, but I couldn't help it. I'm a grown person with masculine proclivities and habits of self-defense, but there is a time when all systems of egotism and predominance fail. The boy is gone. I sent him home. All is off. There was martyrs in old times," goes on Bill, "that suffered death rather than give up the particular graft they enjoyed. None of 'em were ever subjugated to such supernatural tortures as I have been. I tried to be faithful to our articles of depredation; but there came a limit."

"What's the trouble, Bill?" I ask him.

"I was rode," says Bill, "The ninety miles to the stockade, not barring an inch. Then, when the settlers was rescued, I was given oats. Sand ain't a palatable substitute. And then, for an hour, I had to try to explain to him why there was nothin' in holes, how a road can run both ways, and what makes the grass green. I tell you, Sam, a human can only stand so much. I takes him by the neck of his clothes and drags him down the mountain. On the way, he kicks my legs black and blue from the knees down; and I've got to have two or three bites on my thumb and hand cauterized.

"But he's gone"—continues Bill—"gone home. I showed him the road to Summit and kicked him about eight feet nearer that at one kick. I'm sorry we lose the ransom; but it was either that or Bill Driscott to the madhouse."

Bill is puffing and blowing, but there is a look of ineffable peace and growing content on his rose-pink features.

"Bill," says I, "there isn't any heart disease in your family, is there?"

"No," says Bill, "nothing chronic except malaria and accidents. Why?"

"Then you might turn around," says I, "and have a look behind you."

Bill turns and sees the boy and loses his complexion and sits down plump on the ground and begins to pluck aimlessly at grass and little sticks. For an hour, I was afraid of his mind. And then I told him that my scheme was to put the whole job through immediately and that we would get the ransom and be off with it by midnight if old Dorset fell in with our proposition. So Bill braced up enough to give the kid a weak sort of a smile and a promise to play the Russian in a Japanese war with him as soon as he felt a little better.

I had a scheme for collecting that ransom without danger of being caught by counterplots that ought to commend itself to professional kid-nappers. The tree under which the answer was to be left—and the money later on—was close to the road fence with big, bare fields on all sides. If a gang of constables should be watching for any one to come for the note, they could see him a long way off, crossing the fields or in the road. But no, sirree! At half-past eight, I was up in that tree as well hidden as a tree toad, waiting for the messenger to arrive.

Exactly on time, a half-grown boy rides up the road on a bicycle, locates the pasteboard bow at the foot of the fence-post, slips a folded piece of paper into it and pedals away again back towards Summit.

I waited an hour and then concluded the thing was square. I slide down the tree, got the note, slipped along the fence till I struck the woods, and was back at the cave in another half an hour. I opened the note, got near the lantern, and read it to Bill. It was written with a pen in a crabbed hand, and the sum and substance of it was this:

Two Desperate Men.

Gentlemen: I received your letter today by post, in regard to the ransom you ask for the return of my son. I think you are a little high in your demands, and I hereby make you a counter-proposition, which I am inclined to believe you will accept. You bring Johnny home and pay me two hundred and fifty dollars in cash, and I agree to take him off your hands. You had better come at night for the neighbors believe he is lost, and I couldn't be responsible for what they would do to anybody they saw bringing him back. Very respectfully,

Ebenezer Dorset

"Great pirates of Penzance," says I; "of all the impudent—"

But I glanced at Bill, and hesitated. He had the most appealing look in his eyes I ever saw on the face of a dumb or a talking brute.

"Sam," says he, "what's two hundred and fifty dollars, after all? We've got the money. One more night of this kid will send me to a bed in Bedlam. Besides being a thorough gentleman, I think Mr. Dorset is a spendthrift for making us such a liberal offer. You ain't going to let the chance go, are you?"

"To tell you the truth, Bill," says I, "this little he ewe lamb has some-what got on my nerves, too. We'll take him home, pay the ransom, and make our getaway."

We took him home that night. We got him to go by telling him that his father had bought a silver-mounted rifle and a pair of moccasins for him and we were to hunt bears the next day.

It was just twelve o'clock when we knocked at Ebenezer's front door. Just at the moment when I should have been abstracting the fifteen hundred dollars from the box under the tree, according to the original proposition, Bill was counting out two hundred and fifty dollars into Dorset's hand.

When the kid found out we were going to leave him at home, he started up a howl like a calliope and fastened himself as tight as a leech to Bill's leg. His father peeled him away gradually, like a porous plaster.

"How long can you hold him?" asks Bill.

"I'm not as strong as I used to be," says old Dorset, "but I think I can promise you ten minutes."

"Enough," says Bill. "In ten minutes, I shall cross the Central, Southern and Middle Western States, and be legging it trippingly for the Canadian border.

And, dark as it was and as fat as Bill was, and as good a runner as I am, he was a good mile and a half out of Summit before I could catch up with him.

"WOULD YOU STOP THAT INFERNAL GIGGLING?!"

When kids ask tough questions, put a spin on the saying: Invention is the necessity of mothers.

A woman whose son was at summer camp got a letter from the director. "Robert is one of the most promising youngsters we have ever had here," he rhapsodized. "He is a great athlete, has a world of vitality and enthusiasm and his sportsmanship and leadership leave nothing to be desired. If every boy here was such a great example of American youth as Robert, we would feel we had succeeded far beyond our fondest hopes."

The mother wrote back: "I am glad to hear that Robert is doing so well. I have a son there, too—named George. How is he doing?"

By the time parents quit worrying about how the children will turn out, it's time to worry about when they'll come in.

When you go on vacation with a car full of children, pets, toys and suitcases, how can they call it "getting away from it all?"

By the age of 14, the average boy has outgrown 30 pairs of shoes, 26 shirts, 14 pairs of pants and 2 parents.

They say that a home with a five-year-old is a place where you not only wash the bathroom in its entirety, but the soap, too!

"Every one of our neighbors complains about our Jimmy," said his Mom. "And I don't blame them because he is a little devil."

"I'll take care of him," said his father. "I'll buy him a bicycle."

"That won't help," his mother replied. "It won't change his bad behavior."

"No, it won't," replied his father. "But it'll certainly spread it over a much wider territory."

The quickest and easiest way for a parent to get a child's attention is to just sit down, look comfortable and close the eyes.

Two parents in Edwardsville, Illinois are worried about their kids' eyesight. The girl can't find anything to wear in her closet full of clothes and the boy can't find a single thing to eat in the refrigerator!

"CHAUNCEY WAS THE FIRST PERSON ON THE BLOCK TO BUY A TELEVISION, BUT YESTERDAY HE WAS THE FIRST TO THROW HIS OUT."

Isn't it simply amazing how a little soap and water can turn a complete stranger into your own child?

I never met a kid I liked.

W. C. Fields

The boy was seventeen and the girl sixteen, but the parents opposed their marriage. Still, when the minister asked the groom to repeat after him, "With all my worldly goods, I thee endow," mother whispered in father's ear: "There goes his baseball glove!"

It is a recognized fact that the only things kids wear out faster than shoes are their parents.

Eventually, every kid gets what is coming to him. Yes sir! He grows up and then he, too, becomes a parent!

Mosquitoes and small children have much in common. The moment they stop making noise and buzzing, you can be sure they are into something!

Why do we keep bemoaning the younger generation! After all, there's nothing wrong with them that the older generation didn't outgrow.

Two fathers were discussing their kids. One said, "My three boys sure stick together…like the Three Musketeers. When one gets into trouble, the others will never tell on him."

"That's fine," said the other father. "But how do you ever know the guilty one so that you can punish him?"

"No trouble at all! I just send them all to bed without their supper. Then, the next morning, I spank the dickens out of the one with the black eye."

There's not a man in America who at one time or another hasn't had a secret desire to boot a child in the ass.

W. C. Fields

"MAY I HAVE A WORD WITH YOU, MR. HOOPER?"

Two businessmen were having lunch and talking not only business but about their families. "I got six boys," one said.

"You're lucky," the other man replied. "I sure wish I had six kids."

The other asked: "Don't you have any children?"

"You bet," he said. "I got ten!"

I love children...parboiled!

W. C. Fields

Dad stood watching his son mow the lawn. Mother asked: "How on earth did you get him to do that?"

"Simple," said dad. "I just told him that I lost the car keys somewhere in the grass."

Today, any father who aspires to have his kid follow in his footsteps had better be sure he makes deep, deep tracks!

———————— 🧑‍🤝‍🧑 ————————

"The nerve of that supermarket!" mumbled Mrs. Jones angrily as she picked up the telephone and prepared to call them.

When they answered the phone, she identified herself and demanded to know why he short-weighed little boys.

"I sent Howard to your store," she said, "To get two pounds of grapes. He has just arrived home and the grapes weighed only a pound and a half."

"Our scales are inspected regularly," the manager assured her. "But...have you weighed Howard yet?"

———————— 🧑‍🤝‍🧑 ————————

Childhood: That time of life when you make funny faces in the mirror. Middle age: That time of life when the mirror gets even.

———————— 🧑‍🤝‍🧑 ————————

Parents are people who have pictures in their wallets where they used to have money.

———————— 🧑‍🤝‍🧑 ————————

God has impeccable good sense and that's why he has children but...no grandchildren!

———————— 🧑‍🤝‍🧑 ————————

Can you recognize the father of six who said, "I'm mighty proud to say that I've worked 28 years...have calculated with care, reduced all possible expenses, all so that I could give my kids what I never had." And that, friends, is a portrait of a father up to his armpits in debt!

———————— 🧑‍🤝‍🧑 ————————

Every adult should have a least one child to teach. That's the way adults learn!

———————— 🧑‍🤝‍🧑 ————————

I've learned how much fun grandchildren can be. They are wonderful. Why, if I'd known that early enough, I'd have had them first!

"It seems that I've spent a lifetime saying, 'Sit up straight,' 'Use your napkin!' 'Close your mouth when you chew!' 'Don't speak when your mouth is full!' Just when I finally got my husband using good manners, the kids came along."

Wilma: "I'm going to try something new with the dog and kids this summer."
Elma: "What's that?"
Wilma: "I'm sending the dog to camp and the kids to obedience school."

Those things that are most worth knowing you learn after you know it all.

There are three ways to get something done:
1. Do it yourself.
2. Hire someone to do it.
3. Forbid your kids to do it.

Husband to wife as they start out to dinner, leaving the sitter home with their young sons: "I tell you that when they begin asking for a blonde instead of a brunette, they're old enough to stay home alone!"

A businessman came home one evening totally exhausted. He said to his optimistic wife, "I've had a bad day at the office, so I'll welcome tonight the good news you always have for me."
"It's better than ever tonight, Sweetheart," she said. "You know we have five children—and the great news is that four of them didn't break an arm today."

What do you suppose today's youngest generation will tell their kids that they did without?

"From the day your baby is born," counseled a famous scholar, "you must teach him to do without things. Children today love luxury too much. They have execrable manners, flaunt authority, have no respect for their elders. They no longer rise when their parents or teachers enter the room. What kind of awful creatures will they be when they grow up?"

The genius who wrote these words, incidentally, was Socrates, who died in 399 BC.

———————— 🧒🧒 ————————

Christmas is that time of year when good old Santa Claus leaves at your home all the goodies that it'll take your Dad a full year to fill up again.

———————— 🧒🧒 ————————

Mother, pay attention! Be truly careful because you may just be the only Bible your youngster ever reads!

———————— 🧒🧒 ————————

Did you ever wonder what books the younger generation reads today? A recent poll discovered that there are two items: Mom's cookbook and Dad's checkbook.

" NO WONDER YOU CAN'T GET THE NEWS. YOU'RE WATCHING THE MICROWAVE OVEN. "

An American truism: Insanity is hereditary...you get it from your kids.

Doc Jones was a good man, so when Mrs. Elmer Jorgensen was about to have her *twelfth* child, he drove out to her home to deliver the baby. Everything went fine. But just as he was about to leave, the doctor said, "Elmer, just as I was coming up the driveway, a duck cut across my path. I almost hit it."

"That wasn't a duck, Doc," Elmer replied, "it was a stork with its legs worn down!"

Johnny Levy locked himself in the bathroom and his mother could not get him to come out. In desperation, she called the fire department. She told them the problem. The big, bearded fireman asked the gender of the child. "A little boy," she said. The fireman then walked up the stairs, stood before the bathroom door and bellowed, "Come out, little girl!"

Upset and angry that he'd been called a girl, the kid unlocked the door and walked out to stick his tongue out at the fireman.

"It works just about every time I try it!" the fireman explained.

A country woman had just delivered her eighth baby and was complaining to her neighbor who had come to pay a visit. "I sure am tired of having babies."

"Then why don't you just stop," said her neighbor.

"I'll tell you why. It's the only way I know of to keep the youngest from being spoiled!"

You've heard the phrase, "Mama's little helper?" "Well, Margie Pearson changed that a bit. She calls her kid, 'Mama's little yelper'!"

Is there a minimum number of six-year-olds needed to create a birthday party?

Yes, there is! Seven! Two to blow out the candles, three to cover the rug with cake-droppings and two to break the television set.

No family should go on an auto trip unless the car has more windows than the family has kids.

———————— 🕺 ————————

Familiarity brings contempt—and children.
                              Mark Twain

———————— 🕺 ————————

If a child shows himself incorrigible, he should be decently and quietly beheaded at the age of twelve.
                              Don Marquis

———————— 🕺 ————————

One of the hardest jobs for a parent is making a child realize that "no" is a complete sentence.

———————— 🕺 ————————

America's early philanthropist and richest citizen, John D. Rockefeller, was raised in a strong and disciplined family. One time, his mother was giving him a severe whipping for an offense that he ceaselessly and loudly denied. When she was finished, she said, "Once I got started, John, it seemed unwise to stop. However, if proven that you did not do this mischief, I'll credit your account for next time."

———————— 🕺 ————————

Imagination: Something that sits up with Mom and Dad the first time their teenager stays out late.

———————— 🕺 ————————

Isn't it a blessing that small kids are washable!

———————— 🕺 ————————

The secret to raising a child judiciously is in knowing when to give it a hand—and where.

The child who is always a jump ahead of his class is, without a doubt, the only one who can read the clock.

The nicest compliment a child can pay his parents is to be a good example for them.

Training a child to follow a narrow, straight path is easy for parents...All they have to do is merely lead the way.

A child with big ideas is one who is going to try to up his allowance.

When a child marches off to school frowning, you can be sure his mother didn't believe him when he said he had the day off.

A sick boy, truly sick, is one who comes down with something on a Saturday morning.

————————— 🤸 —————————

A considerate, wise child is one who asks the guests only such questions as they can answer.

————————— 🤸 —————————

A smart kid knows how to throw a tantrum—and when!

————————— 🤸 —————————

Discipline is a big help in training a child, but only love will make him come running into your arms when you come home from work empty-handed.

————————— 🤸 —————————

Children represent God's way of telling you the party is over.

————————— 🤸 —————————

It's best not to try to make your kids in your own image. Lord knows, one of you is enough.

————————— 🤸 —————————

Children seem to be natural mimics. They certainly act like their parents no matter what one does to teach them good manners.

————————— 🤸 —————————

Our kids would be much better behaved if they knew they'd have to chop wood or churn butter to keep the TV going.

————————— 🤸 —————————

Kids certainly are a great comfort in our old age and...and, not only that, they get us there quicker.

————————— 🤸 —————————

An axiom: Sometimes, bending a kid over can straighten him out.

Of children as of procreation—the pleasure momentary, the posture ridiculous, the expense damnable.

Evelyn Waugh

Children should neither be seen nor heard from—again.

W.C. Fields

There are three terrible ages of childhood—1 to 10, 10 to 20, 20 to 30.

Cleveland Amory

The best way to keep the children at home is to make the home atmosphere pleasant—and let the air out of the tires.

Dorothy Parker

Making the Baby Mind

We know of a lady in Raleigh who has a two-year-old son. He gets quite contrary and she has to spank him frequently in order to make him behave.

One day a doctor told her that she oughtn't to spank the youngster when he begins to cut up because it might be that his contrariness was due to indisposition of one kind or another.

The lady now heeds his advice. She provided herself with a thermometer. When the baby starts howling and screaming, she rushes to the bathroom, gets the thermometer and thrusts it into the child's mouth.

If one or two degrees of fever is indicated, she cuddles up the youngster and nurses him tenderly. But if his temperature is normal, she drops the thermometer and proceeds to whale hell out of him.

Just For the Fun of It, by Carl Goerch
Edwards & Broughton Co., Raleigh, NC   1954

Having a baby takes a lot out of a woman.

A world-famous pickpocket fell in love with another famous pickpocket and they were married. Soon, the woman was pregnant and all the underworld waited to see what kind of baby these two crooks, both notorious pickpockets, would produce. Well! When the baby arrived, the doctor could not pry the baby's hand open! After repeated efforts, he gave up and left the room. As soon as he was gone the baby opened his hand and what do you think...In it was the doctor's wrist watch!

One of the most exciting experiences you can have is to be at a party and have your baby-sitter telephone you to ask where you keep the fire extinguisher!

A mystery of science that desperately needs to be solved is why a kid can't walk around a mud puddle.

One of the great puzzles in married life is just that how a father only 5'6" tall can convince his son, now 6'2"tall, that all that junk food is bad for him!

A situation of "mixed emotions" occurs when your boy gets an 'A' in sex education.

Nature makes boys and girls lovely to look at so they can be tolerated until they acquire some sense.

William Lyons Phelps, 1865-1943

Adam and Eve had advantages but the principal one was...they escaped teething.

Mark Twain

The denunciation of the young is a necessary part of the hygiene of older people and greatly assists in the circulation of the blood.

Logan Pearsall Smith

Youth is such a wonderful thing. What a crime to waste it on children.

George Bernard Shaw

The time not to become a father is eighteen years before a war.

E.B. White

Child Psychology

I have just finished reading a magazine story by a psychiatrist with a lot of letters behind his name. He was writing about children and how we should raise them.

I'm always a little suspicious of folks who have pat formulas for anything, especially about raising children. They always overlook one simple fact—all children are different; therefore, what will work with one child won't work with another.

This article said that any form of harsh punishment should be avoided, and it went on to list five or six acceptable kinds of punishment. But it overlooked the most obvious means known to mankind to discourage bad behavior in children. It overlooked the method that has been working for countless generations.

It's a simple matter. You look the child in the eye and, with all the sincerity you can muster, say, "Darling, if you ever do that again, Soap Salley will get you." The child then will say, "Who is Soap Salley?" And in a calm, rational voice, you explain that Soap Salley is an ugly old hag of a woman who makes soap out of bad children.

If that doesn't work, you might want to go to what we call phase two, where you discuss in some detail the Boogie Man.

History probably will prove that Soap Salley and Boogie Man will work in the majority of cases, but if that should fail, you may try the ultimate: Call a contractor and ask him to give you an estimate on building a good, old-fashioned shed out behind your house.

The Cornbread Chronicles   1983
Reprinted with permission of Ludlow Porch

SCHWADRon

If Abraham's son had been a teenager, it wouldn't have been a sacrifice.

Scott Spendlove

When my kids become wild and unruly, I use a nice, safe playpen. When they're finished, I climb out.

Erma Bombeck

There's nothing wrong with teenagers that reasoning with them won't aggravate.

Anonymous

Father: "I know Johnny is a difficult boy. But we used to live on the south side of Chicago where if a kid has all his teeth, he's considered a sissy.

Little Willie

When Willie was a little boy,
Not more than five or six,
Right constantly he did annoy
His mother with his tricks.

Yet not a picayune cared I
For what he did or said,
Unless, as happened frequently,
The rascal wet the bed.

Closely he cuddled up to me
And put his hand in mine,
Till all at once I seemed to be
Afloat in seas of brine.
Sabean orders clogged the air,
And filled my soul with dread,
Yet I could only grin and bear
When Willie wet the bed.

'Tis many times that rascal has
Soaked all the bed-clothes through,
Whereat I'd feebly light the gas
And wonder what to do.
Yet there he lay, so peaceful-like,
God bless his curly head!
I quite forgave the little tyke
For wetting of the bed.

Ah, me! Those happy days have flown,
My boy's a father too,
And little Willies of his own
Do what he used to do.

And I, ah! All that's left for me
Are dreams of pleasure fled;
My life's not what it used to be
When Willie wet the bed!

Eugene Field   1850-1895

Before I got married, I had six theories about bringing up children.
Now I have six children...and no theories.

Lord Rochester

"Where's our son Joey?" father asked of his mother. "I'm not sure," she replied. "I think he's gone ice skating. If it's as thick as he thinks it is, he's skating, all right. But if it's as thick as I think it is, he's probably swimming."

A baby, according to Peeksville pediatrician Max Vogel, is an alimentary canal with a loud voice at one end and no responsibility at the other.

When Mix Went to School

"School days, school days, dear old Golden Rule days—that's the song I've heer'd 'em sing," says Rawhide Rawlins, "an' it may be all right now, but there was nothin' dear about school days when I got my learnin'. As near as I can remember them he-schoolmarms we had was made of the same material as a bronco-buster. Anyway, the one I went to in Missouri had every kid whip-broke. He'd call a name an' pick up a hickory, an' the owner of the name would come tremblin' to the desk.

"Charlie Mix—maybe some of you knowed him—that used to run the stage station at Stanford, tells me about his school days, an' it sure sounds natural. As near as I can remember, he's foaled back in the hills in New York state. There's a bunch of long, ganglin' kids in this neck of the woods that's mostly the offspring of old-time lumber jacks that's drifted down in that country, an' nobody has to tell you that this breed will fight a buzz-saw an' give it three turns the start.

"These old grangers bring in all kinds of teachers for this school, but none of 'em can stay the week out. The last one the kids trim is pretty game an' is over average as a rough-an'-tumble fighter, but his age is agin him. He's tall an' heavy in the shoulders like a work bull, an' he wears long moss on his chin which he's sure proud of, but it turns out it don't help him none to win a battle. Two or three of these Reubens would be easy for him, but when they start doublin' up on him about ten strong, one or two hangin' in his whiskers, another couple ham-stringin' him and the rest swingin' on him with slates, it makes him dizzy. Eye-gougin' an' bitin' ain't barred either, an' this wisdom-bringer has got the same chance of winnin' as a grasshopper that hops into an anthill. He comes to the school in a spring buggy with a high-strung span of roadsters, but he leaves in a light spring wagon, layin' on a goosehair bedtick, with several old ladies bathin' his wounds. The team is a quiet pair of plow animals, an' the driver is told to move along slow an' avoid all bumps.

"It looks like a life vacation to the boys, but the old folks think different. They don't 'low to have their lovin' offspring grow up into no ignorant heathen. So one night these old maws an' paws pull a kind of medicine smoke, an' two of the oldest braves is detailed to go to the big camp, work the herd an' cut out a corral boss for these kids. They go down to New York City, an' after perusin' aroun' they locate a prize-fighter that's out of work. They question him, an' findin' he can read an' write an' knows the multiplication table, they hire him.

"Next morning, Mix tells me, teacher shows up an' the boys are all there itchin' to tear into him. But Mix says there's somethin' about this teacher's looks that makes him superstitious. Of course, he don't say nothin'—not wantin' to show yaller—but somehow he's got a hunch that somethin's goin' to happen.

"This gent's head is smaller than's usual in humans. There don't seem to be much space above his eyes, an' his smile, which is meant to be pleasant, is scary. There's a low place where his nose ought to be, an' he could look through a keyhole with both eyes at once. His neck's enough larger than his head so that he could back out of his shirt without unbuttoning his collar. From here down, he's built all ways for scrappin', an' when he's standin' at rest his front feet hang about even with his knees. All this Mix takes in at a glance.

"When the school room quiets down, the new teacher pulls a nice little talk. 'Boys,' says he, 'I ain't huntin' for trouble, but it's been whispered around that this bunch is fighty, an' I'm here to tell you as a gentleman that if there's any battle pulled, you boys is goin' to take second money.'

"The last word ain't left his mouth till one of the big kids blats at him.

"'Come here,' says he, kind of pleasant, to the kid that did it. The kid starts, but the whole bunch is with him.

"The teacher don't move nor turn a hair, but he kind of shuffles his feet like he's rubbin' the rosin. The first kid that reaches him, he side steps an' puts him to sleep with a left hook. The next one he shoots up under a desk with an upper-cut, and the kid lays there snorin'. They begin goin' down so fast Mix can't count 'em , but the last he remembers he sees the big dipper an' the north star, an' a comet cuts a hole through the moon. When he comes to, it looks like the battle of Bull Run, an' teacher is bending' over, pourin' water on him from a bucket. He can hear what few girl scholars there is outside crying.

"When he gets through bringin' his scholars back to life, teacher tells the boys to get their song books an' line up.

"'Now,' says he, 'turn to page 40 an' we will sing that beautiful little song:

"Every Monday mornin' we are glad to go to school,
For we love our lovin' teacher an' obey his kindly rule.

"'He makes us sing that every mornin',' says Mix, 'an' we was sure broke gentle.'"

> From *Trails Plowed Under* by Charles M. Russell.
> Copyright 1927 by Doubleday, a division of Bantam
> Doubleday Dell Publishing Group, Inc. Used by
> permission of Doubleday, a division of Bantam
> Doubleday Dell Publishing Group, Inc.

Speak roughly to your little boy,
And beat him when he sneezes;
He only does it to annoy,
Because he knows it teases.
> Lewis Carroll 1832-1898
> *Alice's Adventures in Wonderland.*   1865

Children from the age of five to ten should watch more television. Television depicts adults as rotten SOB's, given to fistfights, gunplay, and other mayhem. Kids who believe this about grownups aren't likely to argue about bedtime.

P.J. O'Rourke, *The Bachelor Home Companion*   1987

––––––––––– 🧑🧑 –––––––––––

If a man's character is to be abused, say what you will, there's nobody like a relation to do the business.

William Makepeace Thackeray   1811-1863
Vanity Fair.   1947

––––––––––– 🧑🧑 –––––––––––

Cockroaches have been given a bad rap. They don't bite, smell, or get into your booze. Would that all houseguests were as well behaved.

P. J. O'Rourke   1947-
The Bachelor Home Companion (1987)

"OF COURSE I KNOW WHAT HE WANTS WHEN HE CRIES. HE WANTS YOU."

There is this horrible idea, beginning with Jean-Jacques Rousseau and still going strong in college classrooms, that natural man is naturally good...Anybody who's ever met a toddler knows this is nonsense.

P. J. O'Rourke   1947-
Parliament of Whores

————— 🧑‍🤝‍🧑 —————

Some husbands are the living gospel, absolute and unmitigated proof that a woman can, really can...take a joke!

————— 🧑‍🤝‍🧑 —————

Humor is something that tickles the brain and laughter is invented to scratch it.

————— 🧑‍🤝‍🧑 —————

Anybody can stay young if they work hard, have a positive mental attitude and lie about their age!

————— 🧑‍🤝‍🧑 —————

A good laugh is like manure — doesn't do any good unless you spread it around.

————— 🧑‍🤝‍🧑 —————

Whoever named it necking was a poor judge of anatomy.

Groucho Marx

————— 🧑‍🤝‍🧑 —————

A good wife will give up just about anything for the husband...except to forego efforts to improve him.

————— 🧑‍🤝‍🧑 —————

The absolute, most difficult times in a marriage always follow the wedding ceremony.

Every man is a darned fool at least ten minutes of every day. The smart feller never exceeds that limit.

The optimistic husband gets out of bed, goes to the window and says: "Good morning, Lord." But the sourpuss says: "Good lord, it's morning!"

A passerby stopped to yell at a kid: "I'm going to tell your Mom that you've been throwing rocks at cars!"
Another passerby: "I'd suggest that you tell that to his father."
First passerby: "Thanks, but y'see, I am his father."

Sayings by Famous People about the Joy(?) of Parenthood

They tell me there is no more toilet paper in the house. How can I be expected to act a romantic part and remember to order TOILET PAPER!
Margot Peters Mrs. Pat   1984
Mrs. Patrick Campbell   1865-1940

Housewife. You know...sleep-in-maids.
Come Blow Your Horn   1961
Neil Simon   1927-

A trick that everyone abhors
In little girls is slamming doors.

Rebecca   1907
Hilaire Belloc, 1870-1953

After a good dinner, one can forgive anybody, even one's own relations.
A Woman of No Importance.   1893
Oscar Wilde, 1854-1900

Fathers should be neither seen nor heard. That is the only proper basis for family life.
An Ideal Husband.   1895
Oscar Wilde, 1854-1900

Mom and Pop were just a couple of kids when they got married. He was eighteen, she was sixteen and I was three.

> *Lady Sings the Blues.*   1958
> Billie Holliday, 1915-59

If you must go flopping yourself down, flop in favor of your husband and child, and not in opposition to 'em.

> *A Tale of Two Cities.*   1859
> Charles Dickens 1812-1870

Parents should conduct their arguments in quiet, respectful tones, but in a foreign language. You'd be surprised what an inducement that is to the education of children.

> Judith Martin 1938-
> *Washington Post* 1979-1982
> Advice from Miss Manners column

All bachelors love dogs, and we would love children just as much if they could be taught to retrieve.

> *The Bachelor Home Companion.*   1987
> P.J. O'Rourke 1947-

Conran's Law of Housework—it expands to fill the time available plus half an hour.

> *Superwoman 2*   1977
> Shirley Conran 1932-

" JUST PROTECTION FROM THOSE SILLY CURLERS !"

Hatred of domestic work is a natural and admirable result of civilization.

———————— 🧒🧒 ————————

The great advantage of a hotel is that it's a refuge from home life.

———————— 🧒🧒 ————————

The laughter of children is like a light in the window to show the heart is home.

———————— 🧒🧒 ————————

The father was pacing the hospital floor and hoping it was a girl.
"Why a girl? Don't you want a son?" the nurse asked.
"No, no son. I wouldn't want anybody to go through what I have gone through the last three hours."

———————— 🧒🧒 ————————

The hardest time to put a baby to sleep is when he's sixteen years old.

———————— 🧒🧒 ————————

There may be some doubt as to who are the best people to have charge of children, but there can be no doubt that parents are the worst.
                                                                George Bernard Shaw

———————— 🧒🧒 ————————

An old friend stopped off to visit the Nixons. And that lady just talked and talked and talked. Finally, she left and the little girl took her mother's hand and said, "I'm glad she's gone. My! Wasn't she boring!"
"But, dear, she was only here such a little while...less than an hour."
"Maybe so, Mom," the little girl replied. "But that lady stays longer in an hour than most of your friends do in a week!"

———————— 🧒🧒 ————————

Little Paul said to his father: "Daddy, I'm going to the backyard now. I'm gonna play baseball with God."
"Really! Tell me, Son, how do you play baseball with God?"
"Oh, I just throw the ball up in the air and God throws it back to me."

Most parents have observed that kids are pretty much alike—quite similar in most disrespects!

———————— 🧍🧍 ————————

There is one tried-and-true way to keep youth from slipping away and that is...to hide the car keys!

———————— 🧍🧍 ————————

Kids start school today with a considerable advantage in that the alphabet is not entirely unknown...they know two letters...TV.

———————— 🧍🧍 ————————

If, in discussions with your wife or others, you don't want the kids to know what you are saying, the one sure way to keep them ignorant of your talk is to act like you are talking to them!

———————— 🧍🧍 ————————

Of all humans, the most difficult to convince are children at bedtime.

———————— 🧍🧍 ————————

Isn't it amazing...the contrasts in life! For example, consider the fellow that married your daughter. He was way beneath her in all phases of life-way, way below her. But their kid, my grandchild, is just the smartest, prettiest, nicest, most intelligent kid ever born.

———————— 🧍🧍 ————————

Grandma Thomas gave Christmas presents to her many grandchildren every year. Unfortunately, the kids never bothered to thank her, in spite of the orders to do so from their parents. But one year things switched! It seems that Grandma sent each of the grandchildren a check and the next day each child came to her home to thank her. A friend to whom she was telling this story asked: "So they came to thank you this year. How do you explain that?"

"This year, I didn't sign the checks!" Grandma replied.

———————— 🧍🧍 ————————

The time not to become a father is eighteen years before a war.

E. B. White

Mothers are fonder than fathers of their children because they are more certain they are their own.

Aristotle

———————— 🧑‍🧒 ————————

Telling lies is a fault in a boy, an art in a lover, an accomplishment in a bachelor and second nature in a married woman.

Helen Rowland

———————— 🧑‍🧒 ————————

In America, there are two classes of travel—first-class and with children.

Robert Benchley   1898-1945

———————— 🧑‍🧒 ————————

My mother was only sixty years old when she developed chest pains. The doctor suggested she walk at least a mile a day to strengthen her heart and she's been doing that every day for fifteen years. Now that she is seventy five years old, we haven't a clue as to where she is.

———————— 🧑‍🧒 ————————

Isn't it just wonderful the way kids brighten a home? They just never turn off the lights.

———————— 🧑‍🧒 ————————

Bring up a child in the way he should go and be sure to go that way yourself!

———————— 🧑‍🧒 ————————

For the first twenty years of a man's life, his father asks where he is going. For the next twenty years, his wife asks the same thing. And when he's dead, the mourners ask the same thing!

———————— 🧑‍🧒 ————————

Isn't it strange that when your kids are young, they think of you as their dreamboat? Then they get older and you become...their supply ship!

A family with eleven kids came home from a vacation trip. A friend asked the father: "Where did you stop?"

The father replied: "At darned near every service station!"

Someone defined a family as: "A group of people, each of whom likes a different breakfast cereal."

It was their first baby and Matt Turner simply didn't know how to diaper the kid. His wife took over saying: "It's really very simple, Dear. Just consider the layout as a baseball diamond. Bring second base to home plate and lay the baby down between first and third. Then, when you're ready, bring first, third and home together and pin them. But be sure to dust home plate with talcum powder. Got that?"

Mrs. Turner, you must agree, was one sensible woman!

A friend of mine the other day said: "My kids are at the most perfect age...too old to cry at night and too young to borrow the car."

To my embarrassment, I was born in bed with a lady.

Wilson Mizner

I love children, especially when they cry, for then someone takes them away.

Nancy Mitford

A kid is the kind of person who doesn't understand why anyone would want to give away a perfectly good puppy.

A nice, middle-aged man cuts our grass every summer. One day we got to talking and I asked him: "George, how come you never married? Women don't bite."

George replied: "Maybe not. But they can sure as hell gnaw!"

When it becomes time for parents to quit worrying why their kids don't turn out the lights, it's time to begin worrying why they do!

Mrs. Jacobs returned one afternoon from a day of shopping to find pinned on the door, a note saying: "Darling, you will find your Mother's Day present upstairs on your bed."
She rushed upstairs, smiling in anticipation, and there on the bed was...her husband!

If you are doing a survey on retirement and you want to know the most difficult age for retirement, consider children at bedtime.

Everyone marvels in absolute awe of a lion tamer housed in a cage with lions...that is, everyone but a school bus driver.

God's way of making that final separation with children somewhat easier was to bring that period of adolescence!

The babysitter was beside herself trying to handle the three Mason kids. The parents were very late coming home. When they finally arrived, the babysitter said, "Don't bother to apologize for being late...I wouldn't be anxious to get home early, either!"

Even worse that a coffee-cup spill
Is a bunch of kids suddenly still!

Children have a penchant for accurate repetition of their parents sayings...especially if the parents are sorry they said them.

Don't take up a man's time talking about the smartness of your children; he wants to talk to you about the smartness of his children.

Edgar Watson Howe, 1853-1957

By the time the youngest children have learned to keep the place tidy, the oldest grandchildren are on hand to tear it to pieces again.

Christopher Morley, 1890-

When Woodrow Wilson was president of the United States, he recalled the time when his father took him to visit their neighbor. When the man saw the Wilson family's horse and buggy he wondered aloud: "Reverend Wilson, how comes it that you're so thin but your horse is mighty fat and well-rounded?"

Reverend Wilson began a mild answer but he was interrupted by his son Woodrow, who said, "The reason is that my father feeds the horse but the congregation feeds my father."

Double Bubble

Have you ever stopped to think of the good things that pass out of your life when you are grown? Some things we outgrow, and some things we get too sophisticated to do. For example, when was the last time you had a piece of Double Bubble gum? Do you remember the taste of Double Bubble? Vastly superior to chateaubriand, if I do say so myself.

And when was the last time you had a good piggyback ride? Do you remember how much fun it was when you could ride piggyback on somebody?

And how about walking barefooted in the mud? I don't remember why I did it, but I do remember it was great fun.

And do you remember how much fun it was to put on your bathing suit and have somebody squirt you with the garden hose? Boy, that first squirt was cold as ice, but once you got soaked, it was great fun.

When was the last time you read a good Captain Marvel comic book, or skipped rocks across the lake, or rode a bicycle with no hands?

When was the last time you showed off in front of a girl, or got a brand-new pocket knife for your birthday? When was the last time you played with a frog, swung on a rope, or went to a wiener roast? When was the last time you went to a prom party, or went skinny dipping?

When was the last time you read *Treasure Island,* or saw a Durango Kid movie?

You know what I think? I think being a grown-up isn't all it's cracked up to be.

The Cornbelt Chronicle   1983
Reprinted with permission of Ludlow Porch

———————— 🏃🏃 ————————

You truly are bored when you discover that you can't wait for the kids to come home from school.

———————— 🏃🏃 ————————

People who say they sleep like a baby usually don't have one.

Leo J. Burke

———————— 🏃🏃 ————————

Dad and Mom had gone to a professional prizefight. At about the fifth round when both fighters were showing bloody faces and bruises, Mom turned to Pop and said, "Dear, do you think we ought to call home and see how that new sitter is getting along with the kids?"

———————— 🏃🏃 ————————

This is the story of a young mother whose first-born was delivered at sea. The ship's doctor put her in the seven-berth cabin reserved for the sick, and as the passage was unusually smooth she was alone in the berth. She sent a radio message to her husband:

'EVERYTHING FINE. WE HAVE A BIG CABIN ALL TO OURSELVES. SEVEN BIRTHS. MOTHER.'

The astonished husband wired back his congratulations, saying:

'WHEN YOU GET SEVEN; YOU DON'T CALL THEM BIRTHS, YOU CALL THEM LITTERS.'

———————— 🏃🏃 ————————

Mom: "Do you think we should take junior with us to the zoo?"
Pop: "Absolutely not. If they want him, let them come and get him."

———————— 🏃🏃 ————————

When I was born, I was so surprised that I didn't talk for a year and a half.

Gracie Allen

If you want to stay young, associate with young people. But to get old real fast...try keeping up with them!

———————— 🧑‍🧒 ————————

Chicago is truly a baseball town—among other things! So, I rushed my wife, who was expecting our second baby, to the hospital. But, as it happened, nature decided to make us wait and the doctor sent me home to get some sleep. I did as he ordered, too distracted to bother about any other matters, even if it was the first day of the World Series!

That afternoon, the phone rang and it was the doctor to tell me that all had gone well and that I was father to a boy.

"When did it arrive?" I asked.

"In the middle of the fifth inning!" he replied.

———————— 🧑‍🧒 ————————

Money isn't everything...but it sure does keep the children in touch.

———————— 🧑‍🧒 ————————

Why is a little boy like a piece of untreated flannel?

They both shrink from washing.

———————— 🧑‍🧒 ————————

Question: What do you call a tourniquet worn on the left hand that stops circulation?

Answer: A wedding ring.

———————— 🧑‍🧒 ————————

Two boys had just about upset everyone in church with their whispered (scarcely!) arguments. A parishioner leaned over and whispered to their father: "Sibling rivalry, eh?"

"Nope," father replied..."Sible War!"

———————— 🧑‍🧒 ————————

One of the most important things to remember about infant care is: Never change diapers in mid-stream.

Don Marquis

If you want complete privacy so that the kids don't hear what you are saying, then just pretend that you're talking to them.

Parents are dead wrong when they think that their children have an inborn fear of water. It is NOT water they fear, but only the soap introduced with it.

"How's your son doing?" a friend asked.
"Just great...in a manner of speaking. He's got a B.A., M.A., Ph.D., but no J.O.B."

A symbol of the times is the family who prays their youngest son will get married before the oldest boy gets divorced and moves back with them.

A pedestrian is a man with two cars, a wife and a teenager.

Someone described a father as "A banker provided by nature!"

That guy is so derned henpecked that his wife makes him wash and iron his own...his very own aprons!

There are so many divorces nowadays that a recently formed chain of jewelry stores has offered rental engagement rings.

Boys will be boys and so will a lot of middle-aged men.
Frank M. (Kim) Hubbard

A boy, of all beasts, is the most difficult to manage.

Plato

———————— 🧒🧒 ————————

A bachelor never quite gets over the idea that he is a thing of beauty and a boy forever.

Helen Rowland

———————— 🧒🧒 ————————

Train your child in the way you now know you should have gone yourself.

Howard Spurgeon, 1834-1892

———————— 🧒🧒 ————————

A Sunday School is a prison in which children do penance for the evil conscience of their parents.

H. L. Mencken

"They were really no trouble at all."

Parents were invented to make children happy by giving them something to ignore.

———————— 🧍🧍 ————————

The fundamental defect of fathers is that they want their children to be a credit to them.

Bertrand Russell

———————— 🧍🧍 ————————

What maintains one vice would bring up two children.

Benjamin Franklin, 1706-1790

———————— 🧍🧍 ————————

If children grew up according to early indications, we should have nothing but geniuses.

Johann Wolfgang von Goethe, 1749-1832

———————— 🧍🧍 ————————

One of the best things in the world is to be a boy, it requires no experience, but needs some practice to be a good one.

Chas. D. Warner, 1829-1900

———————— 🧍🧍 ————————

A couple with four or five kids is a lot happier than a couple with four or five million dollars. Y'know why? Because they don't need to keep pushing and straining and pulling for more.

———————— 🧍🧍 ————————

Every baby born into the world is a finer one than the last.

Charles Dickens, 1812-1870

———————— 🧍🧍 ————————

Setting a good example for your children takes all the fun out of middle age.

William Feather

The first half of our lives is ruined by our parents and the second half by our children.

———————— 🧑‍🤝‍🧑 ————————

My parents have been visiting me for a few days. I just dropped them off at the airport. They leave tomorrow.

Margaret Smith

———————— 🧑‍🤝‍🧑 ————————

Children begin by loving their parents; as they grow older they judge them; sometimes they forgive them.

Oscar Wilde, 1856-1900

———————— 🧑‍🤝‍🧑 ————————

Everytime a boy shows his hands, someone suggests that he wash them!

Edgar Watson Howe, 1853-1937

———————— 🧑‍🤝‍🧑 ————————

There is nothing so aggravating as a fresh boy who is too old to ignore and too young to kick.

Elbert Hubbard, 1856-1915

———————— 🧑‍🤝‍🧑 ————————

The parent who could see his boy as he really is would shake his head and say, "Willie is no good; I'll sell him."

Stephen Leacock, 1869-1944

———————— 🧑‍🤝‍🧑 ————————

A boy is, of all wild beasts, the most difficult to manage.

———————— 🧑‍🤝‍🧑 ————————

It used to be a good hotel but that proves nothing—I used to be a good boy.

Mark Twain, 1835-1910

When I Was Christened

When I was christened
they held me up
and poured some water
out of a cup.

The trouble was
it fell on me,
and I and water
don't agree.

A lot of christeners
stood and listened:
I let them know
that I was christened.

David McCord   1897

————— 🧍🧍 —————

Proud mother, holding infant for neighbor to see: "He's eating solids now—keys, newspapers, pencils."

————— 🧍🧍 —————

Squaw (missing child as she walks into wigwam): "I could have sworn I was wearing him when I came in."

————— 🧍🧍 —————

Did you hear about the Louisville mother who speaks of her nursery as the Inner Spanctum?

————— 🧍🧍 —————

A mother's life is not a happy one. She is torn between the fear that some designing female will carry off her son and that no designing male will do the same for her daughter.

L'Enfant Glacé

When Baby's cries grew hard to bear
I popped him in the Frigidaire.
I never would have done so if
I'd known that he'd be frozen stiff.
My wife said: "George, I'm so unhappé
Our darling's now completely *frappé!*"

Harry Graham, 1874-1936

———————— 🧑‍🤝‍🧑 ————————

A lot of mothers in the last generation had their daughters vaccinated in places they wrongly thought would never show.

———————— 🧑‍🤝‍🧑 ————————

What a mother should save for a rainy day is patience.

———————— 🧑‍🤝‍🧑 ————————

Many a mother's life is disorganized around her children.

———————— 🧑‍🤝‍🧑 ————————

Mother: A woman who takes twenty years to make a man of her boy so that another woman can make a fool of him in twenty minutes.

———————— 🧑‍🤝‍🧑 ————————

Mother's definition of leisure: The spare time a woman has in which she can do some other kind of work.

———————— 🧑‍🤝‍🧑 ————————

When children ask embarrassing questions, invention is the necessity of mother.

———————— 🧑‍🤝‍🧑 ————————

A woman got into a taxi and the driver immediately shot into traffic, cutting in and out, changing lanes quickly and making hair-raising turns.

"Be careful, please," the woman admonished the cabby. "I have ten children at home!"

"You have ten children," the cabby exclaimed, "and you're telling ME to be careful!"

A pat on the back develops character if given enough, often enough and low enough.

Many kids, when they begin to sow wild oats, discover that their parents are busy praying for a crop failure.

CHAPTER IV

Parents to Kids

It was a lovely day in the park and father was pushing a baby carriage in which the baby was just screaming like crazy. The father kept murmuring, "Take it easy, Eddie. Just relax and stay calm. Steady, Eddie, steady. Everything is gonna be just fine."

A lady passed by and heard the man speak to his baby. She stopped and said, "You certainly do know how to talk to an upset child, Sir." Then she leaned over and spoke to the child. "What seems to be wrong, Eddie?"

The father said, "You got it wrong, Ma'am. He's Jimmy. I'm Eddie."

Two brave explorers met in the depth of an African jungle. One said, "I'm here because I love the primitive and wish to commune with it so I can broaden my outlook. But what about you?"

"To tell you the truth, Sir, I came here because my daughter has begun taking piano lessons!"

A lady who lived in a Chicago suburb had a son who loved to swim. But one day the boy fell in their swimming pool! The mother fished him out, took him in the house, undressed him and told him to stay in his room while she dried and ironed his clothes.

Sometime later, she heard a lot of noise in the basement, walked to the basement door and called down, "Are you down there wetting your pants again?"

A man's voice replied: "No, Ma'am, I'm not! I'm just reading the meter!"

A farmer in Maryland grabbed his ten-year-old son and asked: "Did you cut down that cherry tree?"

"Yes, Daddy, I did," the boy replied, sobbing. "I cannot tell a lie."

The father grabbed the lad, put him across his knee and whaled the tar out of him. "But, Daddy," the boy cried, "George Washington's father didn't do that to him when he cut down that cherry tree when he was a boy."

"That's true," the boy's father replied. "But George Washington's father wasn't sitting in the tree when he cut it down!"

A famous newspaper columnist once told about his son whom he had never had to lay his hands on...except in self-defense!

"Mommy," cried little Tommy exultantly, "I just found a lost baseball."
"How do you know it was lost?" his mother asked.
"Because the kid across the street is still looking for it."

Their old friend, Mrs. Edward Spivak, was visiting them in their home. She asked the little girl: "Margie, tell me what you plan to do when you are grown-up and a big girl like your Mommy?"
"Well," replied Margie, "I think I'll reduce."

Sally Jean came home from camp with a silver cup awarded for packing her trunk more neatly than any other girl.
"That's remarkable," said her mother. "Why, Sally Jean, here at home you never clean up the mess you constantly leave. How did you do it at camp?"
"Simple, Mom." replied Sally Jean. "I just never unpacked."

My son would call me, "Daddy" when he was a youngster in grade school. Then, when he was in high school, he called me "Pop". Now that he's in college he calls me collect!

Father: "Yes, you're a regular little pig! Wouldn't give your brother any of that candy!
Do you know what a little pig is?"
Kid: "Er—er—sure—er—pig—is—er—hog's little boy."

Joker Number One
Cadmus Press, Galesburg, IL 1910

151

When Billy was three years old, his grandmother came to visit the family. She hadn't visited them for several months and thought that the youngster might not remember her. So she went to his room to see him standing in his bed. She said, "Hello, darling. Do you know who I am?"

The boy stood for a moment, then said, "Don't you know who *you* are?"

The farm family was expecting twins and was delighted but puzzled. They couldn't think of a proper set of names for the twins. So they asked their four-year-old son what names he'd like. He thought for a bit, then said, "Alice!"

"But there will be twins, Dear," Mom responded. "We need two names. Alice is fine, but what about a second?"

"Alice Chalmers," the boy responded.

A salesman knocks on the door and a little boy opens it. "Can I speak with your daddy or Mommy?" the salesman asked.

"They aren't home," the lad responded.

"Well, is there anyone else here I could speak to?"

The little boy nods and leaves to get the person. Pretty soon, he's back and says: "Sorry, Mister, but I can't lift her out of bed!"

The five-year-old loved his daddy and hated to see him leave every day to go to work. He asked: "Mom, why does Daddy have to leave us and go to work every day?"

Mother replied, "So he can earn money to bring home so that we can pay our bills and put food on the table."

"Are you saying that if he doesn't go to work every day, we'll have to eat off the floor?"

A little boy entered the department store and walked to the lingerie department. He told the clerk: "It's my Mom's birthday and I want to get her a nice slip for a present. Trouble is...I don't know the size."

"Can you guess?" asked the clerk.

"Well, I dunno," the boy hesitated. "She's just perfect is all I know."

"That'll do it," said the clerk and wrapped up a size thirty-four.

A few days later, the boy's mother came back to the store to exchange the slip for a size fifty!

All of which proves that "perfect" is in the eyes of the beholder.

"Johnny Jones," yelled his Mom. "How is it that I find your hand stuck in the cookie jar?"

"Well, Mom!" said Johnny, "I guess it's because you wear those derned rubber-soled shoes."

"Eddie Condon," the father shouted at his ten-year-old son. "Do you know what they do to boys that tell lies?"

"Sure do, Pop. They get to ride on trains for half fare."

Aunt Jane was visiting the Fogartys and sitting in their living room. "So tell me, Bobby," she asked the ten-year-old. "How do you like going to school?"

Bobby replied, "The going is just fine. So's coming back. But it's the in-between that I don't like."

Some years back, the Louisville radio station WAKY (pronounced "Wacky") offered a prize to persons who answered their telephones by saying "Hello, WAKY." All over town, a phone call, especially those answered by a child, would start with the "Hello, WAKY" greeting.

"I've had to tell our children to quit answering the calls that way," said the wife of a Louisville doctor. "It's driving away my husband's patients."

You see, her husband is a psychiatrist.

From *Joe Creason's Kentucky*
Reprinted with permission of William S. Creason

The proud mother stood beside the piano and announced to her guests, assembled for a party, "My little Julie has agreed to arrange a little piece for you."

"That's just great," exclaimed one of the guests. "We could use a little peace."

OLD MC DONALD'S ANSWERING MACHINE

"But, Daddy," exclaimed little George, "all governments in this country—county, state, federal—all of them use the 'one man, one vote,' principal. It just makes sense that here, in our house, I have something to say about what I can and can't do."

"That makes sense, son," said his father. "But don't forget, in our democratic society, the president, state governors, city mayors, county boards, also have the power to veto any and all legislation or proposal presented to them. And this head of state still votes nay."

Last Cajun Straw

I got a frien' w'at got a li'l boy chirren not quite savan, an' up to de time he not quite savan he don' said a word. An' his ma-ma an' pa-pa dey worry, hoo manh, you KNOW. So dey took dat li'l boy chirren to de doc—taire an' he look him over an' say, "He hokay physical. Mebbe up dair (an' he hit his head), but you better brought him home an' see w'at happen."

Den one day at breakfas' dat li'l fallow say, "Ma-ma, dis toas' is burn like de devil, I ga—ron´-tee." Well, his ma-ma do a handsprung r'at now, an' his pa-pa los' his spoke plumb, he so sopprise. Den his ma-ma say, "Son, how come you don' say nothin' an' den you say somet'ing after all dese year?"

An' dat li'l boy chirren say, "Up to now, averyt'ing been hokay!"

From Justin Wilson's Cajun Humor
by Justin Wilson and Howard Jacobs.
Copyright © by Justin Wilson and Howard Jacobs

The mother was furious. "Paul!" she yelled. "Why are you making such awful faces at your bulldog?"

"Well, Ma, he started it!"

Mom was taking her son, Jamie, with her to the supermarket and the kid did nothing but ask questions...from the moment they started walking to just before they got to the store. He asked about birds, trees, people, cars, earth, sky...on and on with his questions. Finally, Mom lost patience and growled: "Jamie, if you don't shut up...quit asking questions...I'm going to paddle your bottom right here in the street!"

"Maybe so, Mama, but just where would you sit?"

Intemperance

Jack and Jill went up the hill—
Not for a drink of water—
And that is why they both fell down—
They drank what they hadn't orter.

Child: "Mother, can I climb the tree in the backyard?"

Mother: "Yes. But if you fall and break your legs, don't come running to me."

Mom had just put her two boys to bed and slumped into the living room for a much-needed rest. But then there came screaming and yelling from the kid's bedroom!

She rushed back into the bedroom and yelled. "All right! That's enough! And who started all this?"

"It was Paul!" said the older boy. "He started this whole thing by hitting me back!"

Little Albert's dad took him to his first football game. The lad was deeply impressed, as you might suspect, when you learn that at bedtime, the boy said his prayers: "God bless Mama! God bless Papa! Rah! Rah! Rah!"

There's a mighty true old saying that, "If you give a kid an inch, he just might become a ruler!"

"Mama?" asked the coed. "What do you say to a feller when he whispers sweet nothings in your ear?"

"You simply answer him by saying 'sweet nothing doing' in his ear."

An inhibited little girl in Indiana was the six-year-old daughter of a prominent physician.

Her mother was entertaining some important people when the little girl trudged down the stairs, her pajamas open at the rump and quite wet. "What's the matter?" asked her mother.

"Someone left the lid up," she answered, "and I damn near drowned."

"Well, Bobby, what did you learn in school today?" father asked his son.

"Today the teacher taught us writing."

"So...tell me what you wrote."

"I don't know, Daddy. Teacher hasn't taught us reading yet."

An eight-year-old ran to his father and asked, "Daddy, where are the Himalayas?"

His father responded: "How should I know! Go ask your Mommy. She puts everything away around here!"

Pop advised his son, Joe: "Cheerful people resist disease more forcefully than glum ones do. And that, Joey, is why the surly bird catches the germ."

"How comes it, Bobby," Pop said to his twelve-year-old, "that you've never enough time to do it right...but always enough time to do it over!"

A father is a man who expects his boy to be every bit as good a man as he meant to be.

The only advice I get about raising children is to be consistent. But how can I be consistent? They never do the same thing twice.

To the five-year-old boy with an injured arm who came into the office of Dr. V.A. Jackson, a Lexington doctor then practicing in Clinton, a picture was a picture.

The doctor looked at the bad wing while the kid grimaced in pain.

"Well, now," the doctor said, "we'll just have to take a picture of that arm."

"Doctor," asked the kid, holding back the tears, "do I have to smile?"

From *Joe Creason's Kentucky*
Reprinted with permission of William S. Creason

When I was sixteen, I thought I was in love and it made me sick. Sicker than a dog. My pap tuck me to the doctor, and come to find out it wasn't love. It was worms.

A child's tears are the most efficient water power in the world.

Every child should have an occasional pat on the back as long as it is applied low enough and hard enough.

Bishop Fulton J. Sheen

To my daughter Lenore, without whose never-failing sympathy and encouragement, this book would have been finished in half the time.

To the Heart of a Goof.   1926
P. G. Wodehouse

I was readying my little girl for the day when she asked me, "Mama, where are we going today?" I told her, "Nowhere." She turned to me and said, "But I want to go Yes where!"

Little Emily came home from a full day spent with her father. "Tell me, Sweetheart," her mother said, "did you have a lot of fun with your Daddy?"

"I sure did. It was lotsa fun. And best of all came when we were ready to come home. Daddy stopped to get us a drink at this place he knew. I had a Sprite and Daddy had a glass of water with an olive in it."

ONCE UPON A TIME THERE WERE THREE LITTLE PIGS,
SO I ATE THEM. END OF STORY. NOW GO TO SLEEP.

Nine-year-old Elmer was told he could go fishing only if he took his little sister along. He agreed, but, at the end of the day, he came in the house, saying, "I'll never take her fishing again. I didn't catch a thing."

Mom said, "I don't think she'll be noisy next time. You should explain to her that the fish won't bite when there's noise like talking. Then she'll be quiet."

"She wasn't noisy, Mom," the boy said. "It's just that she ate all the bait!"

The teacher of the Sunday School class had an emergency operation and the minister, the superintendent and head of the Sunday School committee called on Mrs. Jones to see if she would substitute until the regular teacher was well enough to return to the job. They all waited at the door until Mrs. Jones' daughter went upstairs to get her mother.

Once upstairs, Mrs. Jones told her daughter to go right back downstairs and tell the company to wait in the living room for just a few minutes. "You tell them I'm just loaded down with work."

The little girl ran back downstairs to the door, invited the guests in and waited while they seated themselves. Then she said, "Mama will be down in a little while. But right now, she's just loaded!"

"Charles!" exclaimed his mother, "You must not...simply must not pull the cat's tail!"

"But, Mama," the boy insisted, "I'm not pulling Tabby's tail. I'm just holdin' on to it. It's the cat that's doin' all the pullin'."

What is it that runs over the field, comes home at night, and sticks its tongue out from under the bed?

A wagon.

The best revenge is to live long enough to be a problem to your kids.

Adults are obsolete children.

                                Dr. Seuss

The little guy was crushed. His dog had just been killed by a car and the boy couldn't stop crying. At last his mother said, "Jimmy, don't let Rover's death get you down. Your dog is in heaven now and with God."

Jimmy did stop sobbing for a moment, then said, "Oh, Mom...what would God want with a dead dog!"

My father gave me these hints on speechmaking: Be sincere...be brief...be seated.

James Roosevelt

I have heard a well-built woman compared in her motion to a ship under sail, yet I would advise no wise man to be her owner if her freight be nothing but what she carries between wind and water.

Francis Osborn advising his son not to marry a beautiful but poor girl

I can't imagine what my kids will tell their kids they had to do without.

A salesman at the door asked the little boy: "Sonny, is your Mother home?"

"Nope. She ain't."

"Young feller," the salesman said, frowning, "watch your...grammar!"

"Oh, her. She's out in the kitchen gettin' dinner ready."

Two kids, one three and the other four, were playing together when one of them sneezed. "Mommy! Mommy!" cried one the other. "Helen just got 'bless you' all over me!"

In the 1920s when the boy started sowing wild oats, his father started the thrashing machine.

"Hey, Mom," Sally asked, "do men go to heaven, too?"

"Of course, they do," responded her mother. "Why do you ask?"

"Well, I just never see any pictures of angels with whiskers."

"I can assure you that some men, good men, do go to heaven. But, you see, it's a very close shave."

There isn't a single thing wrong with the younger generation that the older generation didn't outgrow.

His daddy told Bobby that quite soon he'd have a new member in the family. A baby was due. "And would you rather have a baby sister or a baby brother?" Mama asked.

"If it don't make no difference to you, I'd just as soon have a new puppy!" the lad replied.

Don't be afraid of four-letter words to be used with your kids, such as duty, earn, love, give, work and care.

All was going quietly and peacefully that evening in the living room when suddenly there was a loud crash. Little Eddie had knocked a vase off the table!

"Eddie Jenkins!" his mother exploded. "What on earth am I going to do with you. Nothing but naughty things! And every time you do things like you just did, I get another...gray...hair!"

Little Eddie glanced at the totally silver-thatched hair of his grandmother and said, "Wow, Mom! You must have been one naughty girl when you were a kid!"

Presidential Secretary Bill Moyers once recalled a telegram sent by his father: "Always tell the truth. If you can't always tell the truth, don't lie."

My little boy, Jonah, wouldn't be quiet while he was in bed and we were all waiting for him to go to sleep. "Mama, Mama," he called for this and that and I was about to go nuts! Finally, I said, "Jonah, if you call me one more time, I'm coming in and spank you!"

There was a short space of quiet, then the boy whispered, "Mrs. Adams...could I have a drink?"

――――――― 🧒👧 ―――――――

Table Manners of Children

Young children who have to wait till older people have eaten all there is in the house, should not open the dining-room door during the meal and ask the host if he is going to eat all day. It makes the company feel ill at ease, and lays up wrath in the parents' heart.

Children should not appear displeased with the regular courses at dinner, and then fill up on pie. Eat the less expensive food first, and then organize a picnic in the preserves afterward.

Do not close out the last of your soup by taking the plate in your mouth and pouring the liquid down your childish neck. You might spill it on your bosom, and it enlarges and distorts the mouth unnecessarily.

When asked what part of the fowl you prefer, do not say you will take the part that goes over the fence last. This remark is very humorous, but the rising generation ought to originate some new table jokes that will be worthy of the age in which we live.

Children should early learn the use of the fork, and how to handle it. This knowledge can be acquired by allowing them to pry up the carpet tacks with this instrument, and other little exercises, such as the parent mind may suggest.

The child should be taught at once not to wave his bread around over the table, while in conversation, or to fill his mouth full of potatoes, and then converse in a rich tone of voice with some one out in the yard. He might get his dinner down his trachea and cause his parents great anxiety.

In picking up a plate or saucer filled with soup or with moist food, the child should be taught not to parboil his thumb in the contents of the dish, and to avoid swallowing soup bones or other indigestible debris.

Toothpicks are generally the last course, and children should not be permitted to pick their teeth and kick the table through the other exercises. While grace is being said at table, children should know that it is a breach of good breeding to smouge fruit cake just because their parents' heads are bowed down, and their attention for the moment turned in another direction. Children ought not to be permitted to find fault with the dinner, or fool with the cat while they are eating. Boys should, before going to the table, empty all the frogs and grasshoppers out of their pockets, or those insects might crawl out during the festivities, and jump into the gravy.

If a fly wades into your jelly up to his gambrels, do not mash him with your spoon before all the guests, as death is at all times depressing to those who are at dinner, and retards digestion. Take the fly out carefully, with what naturally adheres to his person, and wipe him on the table cloth.

It will demonstrate your perfect command of yourself, and afford much amusement for the company. Do not stand up in your chair and try to spear a roll with your fork. It is not good manners to do so, and you might slip and bust your crust, by so doing. Say "thank you," and "much obliged," and "beg pardon," wherever you can work in these remarks, as it throws people off their guard, and gives you an opportunity to get in your work on the pastry and other bric-a-brac near you at the time.

Bill Nye's Redbook by Bill Nye
Wiley Book Co., New York   1891

"DON'T SLAM . . .

. . . the door."

THE SATURDAY EVENING

Dialogue between Father and Daughter

Father: "Then, what do you say to the poem of Mizpah?"
Daughter: "An out-and-out masterpiece—that's what it is, Pa!"

Robert Browning, 1812-1889

Good and Bad Children

Children, you are very little,
And your bones are very brittle;
If you would grow great and stately,
You must try to walk sedately.

You must still be bright and quiet,
And content with simple diet;
And remain, through all bewild'ring,
Innocent and honest children.

Happy hearts and happy faces,
Happy play in grassy places—
That was how, in ancient ages,
Children grew to kings and sages.

But the unkind and the unruly,
And the sort who eat unduly,
They must never hope for glory—
Theirs is quite a different story!

Cruel children, crying babies,
All grow up as geese and gabies,
Hated, as their age increases,
By their nephews and their nieces.

Robert Louis Stevenson, 1850-1894

A Parental Ode to My Son,
Aged Three Years and Five Months

Thou happy, happy elf!
(But stop,—first let me kiss away that tear)—
Thou tiny image of myself!
(My love, he's poking peas into his hear!)
Thou merry, laughing sprite!

With spirits feather-light,
Untouch'd by sorrow and unsoil'd by sin—
(Good heavens! The child is swallowing a pin!)
  Thou little tricksy Puck!
With antic toys so funnily bestuck,
Light as the singing bird that wings the air—
(The door! the door! he'll tumble down the stair!)
  Thou darling of thy sire!
(Why, Jane, he'll set his pinafore a-fire!)
  Thou imp of mirth and joy!
In love's dear chain so strong and bright a link,
Thou idol of thy parents—(Drat the boy!
  There goes my ink!)

  Thou cherub—but of earth;
Fit playfellow for Fays, by moonlight pale,
  In harmless sport and mirth,
(That dog will bite him if he pulls its tail!)
  Thou human humming-bee, extracting honey
From ev'ry blossom in the world that blows,
  Singing in Youth's Elysium ever sunny—
(Another tumble!—that's his precious nose!)

  Thy father's pride and hope!
(He'll break the mirror with that skipping-rope!)
With pure heart newly stamp'd from Nature's mint—
(Where *did* he learn that squint?)
  Thou young domestic dove!
(He'll have that jug off, with another shove!)
  Dear nursling of the hymeneal nest!
  (Are those torn clothes his best!)
  Little epitome of man!
(He'll climb upon the table, that's his plan!)
Touch'd with the beauteous tints of dawning life—
  (He's got a knife!)

  Thou enviable being!
No storms, no clouds, in the blue sky foreseeing,
  Play on, play on,
  My elfin John!
Toss the light ball—bestride the stick—
(I knew so many cakes would make him sick!)
With fancies buoyant as the thistledown,
Prompting the face grotesque, and antic brisk,
  With many a lamb-like frisk—
(He's got the scissors, snipping at your gown!)

165

Thou pretty opening rose!
(Go to your mother, child, and wipe your nose!)
Balmy, and breathing music like the South,
(He really brings my heart into my mouth!)
Fresh as the morn, and brilliant as its star,—
(I wish that window had an iron bar!)
Bold as the hawk, yet gentle as the dove—
(I'll tell you what, my love,
I cannot write, unless he's sent above!)

Thomas Hood, 1899-1945

———————— 🮱 ————————

I call you bad, my little child,
Upon the title page,
Because a manner rude and wild
Is common at your age.

A Bad Child's Book of Beasts   1896
Hilaire Belloc, 1870-1953

———————— 🮱 ————————

At her first school concert, the young singing student noticed that an elderly man was sobbing quietly.

Quite moved by this, she walked up to the man and said. "I loved singing "The Eyes of Texas" and I feel terribly good that my singing moved you so much. Are you a Texan?"

"No, young lady, I'm a musician!"

———————— 🮱 ————————

Childhood is that time in life when it's fun to make faces in the mirror. Middle-age is the time the mirror gets even.

———————— 🮱 ————————

Bus driver: "That boy is over twelve, ma'am and you must pay full fare!"

Mother: "How can he be over twelve when I've been married only ten years!"

Bus driver: "Looky here, Ma'am. I collect bus fares...not confessions."

Adam and Eve in the garden dwelt,
Life was jolly and jivy;
But what, do you figure, they would have felt
If the leaves had been poison ivy?

Mary Sisery went to a department store to pay an installment on her baby buggy. She gave over the money to the clerk and said, "That's the final installment, I think."

"That's right," said the clerk, after taking her money and giving her a receipt. And how's the baby doing?"

"Just great. She got married last week!"

Grandma Peters was mailing the ancient family Bible to her grandson in New York. The postal clerk asked, "Does this package contain anything breakable?"

"You bet. It has the Ten Commandments."

Mrs. Peterson went to the doctor: "I'm terribly worried about my boy Jimmy. He thinks he's a chicken."

The doctor asked, "And how long has this been going on?"

"Almost a year," Mrs. Peterson replied.

"Well for goodness sakes! Why didn't you bring him to see me sooner?"

"Because we needed the eggs!"

Money can't bring happiness,
Nor can it make us glad.
But we'll always take a chance, for sure,
At being rich and sad.

Edgar Sampson was a man not known for good manners. One time in a restaurant, he tucked his napkin under his collar. The head waiter was aghast but didn't want to insult a paying guest, so he said to a young employee new at the business of waitering, "Go over to that clod and tell him to take the napkin out of his collar and put it on his lap. But do it so as not to insult him."

The new waiter approached the clod and said, "Would you like a shave and haircut as well?"

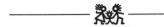

It was at Sunday School that the teacher asked her class, "Who knocked down the wall of Jericho? Stanley?"

"It wasn't me!"

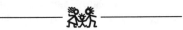

Hillbilly Sally got a letter one day, read it, then burst out crying.

"What's the matter, Sally?" her friend Annabelle asked.

"It's my very special nephew. He has three feet."

"Oh no, Sally! That's not possible."

"Well, the letter tells it all. It says he's grown another foot!"

Infant: A disturber of the peace. A household object that gets you down in the daytime and up at night!

Johnny Rogers rushed home from school and excitedly told his parents that he'd been awarded a prime part in a play at school. "I play a man who's been married twenty years," Johnny told them.

"Good boy, Johnny," said his dad. "You keep it up and one of these days they'll give you a speaking part."

A country woman heard her son using nasty, bad language and she said to him: "Where on earth did you learn those awful words?"

"From Shakespeare...at school."

"Well, I don't want you to ever play with him again!"

Father: "Did Elmer bring you home last night?"

Daughter: "He sure did. It was late, though. Did the noise disturb you?"

Father: "It wasn't the noise...it was the silence."

Her only child was having an awful day. If it wasn't one thing, it was another and finally the little boy knocked over a lamp and broke it into little pieces. "That does it," shrieked the mother. "You're going to be an only child—or worse—your sister is going to be one!"

The students were impatiently lined up at the entrance of the football stadium waiting for it to open so they could buy tickets to see the high school football team play. When a man came up to the head of the line and attempted to move in, the kids were really upset and cursed him, then shoved him back. Three times the man attempted to get to the head of the line and each time, the students refused to allow it.

Finally the man shouted, "If you guys don't stop throwing me out of the line, nobody's going to see the game today. I've got the key to open the door!"

Hendrickson

"Looking for snake food—why?"

169

The little girl asked her mother, "Do all fairy tales start with 'Once upon a time'?"

Her mother replied: "Not always. Sometimes they begin with 'I'll be working late at the office tonight, Dear'."

"Does Papa tell you stories like that?"

"He used to."

"What made him change?"

"Well, one day he said to me that he'd be working late and I asked, 'Can I depend on that?'"

Son: "Daddy, how old do I have to be to do as I please?"

Daddy: "I really don't know, Son. Nobody has ever yet lived that long!"

Son: "Dad, what's the name of your birthstone?"

Dad: "It's not a birthstone, son, it's a grindstone."

Son: "How would you define *luck,* Dad?"

Dad: "Luck? Well, let's see. I guess I'd say it meant that another fellow succeeded at something at which I had failed."

Ralph: "Dad, what does *bigamy* mean? Does it mean a man has one wife too many?"

Dad: "Not always, Son. A man can have one wife too many and still not be a bigamist."

My grandson and I were watching a mother bird feed her baby. Soon the mother bird flew away, probably for more food. Then another bird landed in the nest, next to the baby. My grandson said: "Hey, Granpa! That must be the babysitter!"

CHAPTER V

Kids in Church

Mrs. Beeker had taught Sunday School for thirty years and told this story at an area meeting of Sunday School teachers. She told of a class of six-year-olds who were dabbling in water colors. Each was asked to tell what subject they were painting and Joey White said, "I'm painting a picture of God."

"Well, isn't that nice," Mrs. Beeker said. "But nobody has ever seen God or knows what He looks like."

"Maybe not before this," Joey White replied. "But when I'm done they will."

A Sunday School teacher was telling the children about heaven and how we must act to get there. "So tell me, Stanley, what must we do before we can expect to be forgiven our sins?"

"Well...well...well," Stanley muttered, "first we got to...to sin!"

The five-year-old had just returned from church where she had witnessed the baptism of four people. Her uncle asked her to tell him about it.

"First off...the preacher preached a whole lot and then he changed his suit and went down the steps into a big tub of water. And do you know what? After that he really, truly washed off four people!"

In Sunday School, the teacher asked, "Now children, can anyone tell me what may be found in Mark, but not in Luke or John?"

"I can," said Clark Townsend.

"Then please do," said the teacher.

"The letter 'a'," said Clark.

Little Tommy was constantly in trouble for the mischief he was forever doing. "How do you expect ever to get into heaven, Tommy, doing all the bad things you do?"

"That's easy," Tommy replied. "I'll run in and then run out, run in and then run out and I'll keep it up until they say, 'Either stay in or stay out,' and then I'll stay in."

We took our little boy to church one Sunday for the first time. We watched as ten men went to the pulpit to begin communion and then the preacher said a prayer. Elmer, our three-year-old, asked who the man in the robe was and who the other men were. Father told him that the robed man was a preacher and that he was talking to God.

Elmer watched things for a bit, then said, "Which one is God?"

The Sunday School teacher was discussing the Book of Exodus with her third grade class. "Can anyone tell me who led the children of Israel out of Egypt?" she asked.

Nobody hazarded a reply so she pointed and nodded to one little guy in the back, "Dickie, can you tell us who led them out of Egypt?"

"It wasn't me," Dickie replied. "We just moved here from Indiana."

The minister was invited to dinner at a parishioner's home. It was a home where the women's liberation movement was often discussed. So, before they began to eat, the minister said grace. Finished with the prayer, he said, "Amen!" It was then that the family's four-year-old shook her head and said, frowning, "A Woman!"

Where was Solomon's temple?
On the side of his head.

"You raise your children like you'd throw a ball," said the minister. "While they're in your hands, give them the best start you can for they must go the rest of the way themselves."

A little boy was peeling an apple with a knife and cut his finger. And did he cuss! Wow! But a preacher was passing by, heard every profane word of the lad and began to remonstrate: "That's terrible language, young man. Your profanity sends chills up and down my spine!"

"Haha," the little guy replied. "You should have heard my daddy when he hit his toe with our sledge hammer. You'd have froze to death!"

A Sunday School teacher asked little Eddie a critical question: "Where is God?"

Eddie remained silent so the teacher repeated the question a bit more stridently this time. "Come, come, Eddie...where is He?"

But Eddie ran screaming from the classroom, out the school door and ran on home to his father. "Daddy, Daddy," he screamed. "The teacher said God was missing and she's blaming me for it!"

Asked about prayers at home, Marshall replied: "We don't say prayers at home while at dinner. We just sit down and eat, that is...unless our relatives come over."

Tom was about to get dressed for school when he heard his mother call to him, "Tommy, put on a clean pair of socks. Do you hear me?"

"Yep! Sure do."

"And I want you to do that every day. Do you hear me?"

"Yep. Sure do," he replied.

A week later, he called down to his Mother, "Hey, Mom, I can't get my shoes on!"

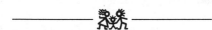

On their way to church, the family drove past a cemetery. Their four-year-old asked, "What are all those blocks of stone doing out there?"

The six-year-old answered, "They put those over all the dead people to keep them in the ground."

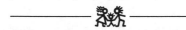

Who is the best doctor mentioned in the Bible?
Job, because he had the most patience (patients).

The Small Boy Who Scandalized the Congregation

In accordance with the custom of that period, there were no free pews, except for the extremely poor. The owner of each of these sittings, after carefully packing his family away in the limited space available for that purpose, closed the door of his pew.

As before stated, it was a very warm day and little "Jabe," who for some family reason or other was at present living with his three maiden aunts, came to church attired only in his gingham shirt and cotton trousers. Jabe was not old enough to appreciate the solemnity of the occasion and it was beyond his understanding how people could be so foolish as to be willing to sit perfectly still for two mortal hours in church. Therefore, when he found that his attendance at church was inevitable that morning, he looked about to provide himself with diversion for the long period of hateful inactivity. The maiden aunts were very devout. They gave their entire attention to the parson. Except to occasionally lay a restraining hand on the "wiggling" urchin who was stationed between them, they seemed to have forgotten him.

In the pew immediately behind little Jabe and his aunts, there were several young girls. Even at this time, it was often necessary to frown upon the effervescent spirits of girls in their teens. It can therefore be readily understood how horrified and scandalized were the "pillars" of the church, when in the midst of the service, one of these young ladies squealed hysterically. The minister ceased his discourse and one of the deacons hastily demanded an explanation, which even in that austere congregation seemed to be not only satisfying but amusing. Little Jabe on his way to church, loitering behind his faithful aunts, had spied a small snake on the roadside, pounced upon it and tucked it inside his little gingham shirt. When the pastor had got well along in "fifthly," Jabe had taken the snake by the tail and allowed his head to emerge from his shirt front with the above named disastrous consequences to the dignity of the morning service.

New England Joke Lore, by Arthur G. Crandall
F. A. Davis Co., Philadelphia, PA   1922

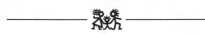

The pastor was ranting and shouting about sin and the need to counter it with God's grace.

A little boy, hearing the pastor rave on and on, whispered to his father, "Daddy, you always tell me that the Pastor is close to God. Well, how come, if he's so close, he has to shout like that?"

"ABOUT THE NEW BARBIE DOLL, MOM...
I'VE DECIDED TO GO OVER YOUR HEAD."

In Sunday School, the first graders had been singing songs of the teacher's choice. After several had been sung, the teacher asked, "Is there a special song that any of you would like us to sing?"

One little guy said, "Yeah! How about 'Deep in the Heart of Texas'."

The family had just finished saying grace before their dinner and was prepared to begin the meal when little Tony asked: "Daddy? Does God have a last name?"

The little girl walked to the teacher's desk and asked: "They say that Adam and Eve were the first two people on earth. Is that right?"

"That's what the Bible has to say about it," replied the teacher.

"And they had only two boys, right?" the child asked.

"Again, that's what the Bible tells us," was the reply.

"Well, then, please tell me this...if boys can't have babies, where did the rest of us come from?"

Mrs. Evers took her five-year-old with her to the post office to mail a letter to her friend who had just lost her mother. The boy was eager to put the letter in the slot designated for this particular package. Since there were several slots, the lad couldn't make up his mind which one to use. With the letter posed in hand, ready to mail, the lad asked: "Mom, is this the slot that goes to heaven?"

———————— 🧒🧒 ————————

Why was Adam's first day long?
Because there was no Eve.

———————— 🧒🧒 ————————

It was at Sunday School that the preacher asked, "Class, if each of you had two apples...a big one and a little one...which one would you give to your brother?"
"I got a question," one boy asked.
"Yes? What is it?" the teacher replied.
"Am I supposed to give it to my big brother or my little brother?"

———————— 🧒🧒 ————————

The Sunday School class was discussing the Ten Commandments, and were at the one beginning "Honor thy father and thy mother" when the teacher stopped to ask, "Now tell me, children, are there any commandments that tell us how to treat brothers and sisters?"
One little fellow replied: "How about...'Thou shalt not kill?'"

———————— 🧒🧒 ————————

The little girl was in bed, ready to go to sleep. Suddenly, she sat up saying: "I almost forgot! I'm going to say my prayers. Anybody want anything?"

———————— 🧒🧒 ————————

It was little Jamie's first time in church and, as he sat quietly, the choir, all dressed in white robes, filed out and faced the congregation.
"Daddy?" the little boy asked, "are all those people going to get a haircut?"

———————— 🧒🧒 ————————

Preacher: "Do you offer a prayer before meals?"
Little boy: "Heck no! My Ma is a good cook!"

176

What three words (which read the same backwards and forwards) might Adam have used to introduce himself to Eve?
"Madam, I'm Adam."

Little Adolph was in church with his father and it was the lad's first visit there. The boy fell asleep but finally awakened to ask: "Daddy, has he finished yet?"
His daddy replied: "Yep, he's finished...but he ain't stopped!"

The fact that boys are allowed to exist at all is evidence of a remarkable Christian forbearance among men.

Ambrose Bierce

The GI had just returned from Vietnam and stood with his intended at the altar, waiting for the minister to bless and conclude his marriage.
When the marriage vows were completed and the groom was kissing the bride, a little boy was heard to ask his father, "Daddy, is he spreading the pollen on her now?"

My two daughters were given parts in a Christmas play to be presented at their grade school. The two girls were arguing about which one had the most important part and my oldest, Sally, was arrogantly superior.
"There's no doubt about it...I've got the biggest, best part in the play."
"Which part do you have?" father asked.
"I play the virgin. And anybody'll tell you it's much harder being a virgin than an angel."

All of the class at Sunday School had to draw names for a Valentine's Day party for which each boy was asked to bring a sack of candy to share with one of the girls in the class.
"Dadblame it!" moaned Tommy. "I wanted Mary's name but someone else got it."
"Don't let it bother you," the teacher soothed. "There are lots of nice, pretty girls in class."

"I know that," Tommy replied. "But Mary is the only girl in class who's not allowed to eat candy."

The children in Sunday School class really had a high old time with the Lord's Prayer.

One child began it with, "Howard be thy name."

Another child had this interpretation: "Lead me not into Penn Station."

Still another child interpreted it this way, "Our Father, who are in heaven, how'd you know my name."

"Did you heard the story of the church bell?"

"Nope. It ain't been tolled yet."

"Tell me something about what you learned in Sunday School today," the father asked his son.

"Well, they told us all about the story in Exodus…how the Hebrews got chased to the Red Sea, and how they all got into huge boats docked there so's to get them over to the other side. But when the Egyptian soldiers tried to follow them, the sea just rolled up and covered every last one of 'em. The Egyptians were all drowned and the Jews, all of them, were saved.

"Come on, now!" laughed his father. "Did the teacher really tell you that stuff?"

"No, not really. But if I told you what she did tell us, you'd never in a million years believe me."

The little guy came running into the house after Sunday School. He was sucking on a huge lollipop. "And where, young man, did you get that lollipop?" his mother asked.

"I bought it with that quarter you gave me for Sunday School," the boy replied.

"But that quarter I gave you was for Sunday School," mother replied.

"I know that, Mom," the boy said, "but the minister met me at the door and he let me in free."

"Class, what is the meaning of 'repentance'?"

"I know, teacher," one little girl said. The teacher nodded to her.

"Well, it means that you're sorry enough about what you did to quit doing it."

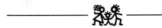

The Sunday School class was discussing the presence of Jesus with all people at all times. "Can anyone give me an example of Jesus' presence with all of us?"

A little boy raised his hand. "Jesus is the one who opens the door for me when we go to the supermarket and then closes it after us after we're done shopping."

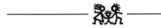

The Sunday School class was about to finish the session but there were still a few minutes of time left. The teacher asked the class to write down the name of their favorite hymn.

All but Mary did just that, but Mary sat with downcast eyes and wrote nothing.

"Can't you think of one hymn that pleases you?" asked the teacher.

So little Mary wrote something on her paper and passed it to the teacher. "What's this, Mary? Tommy Fredericks?"

"That's him," Mary said, blushing.

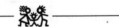

When the little five-year-old returned from Sunday School, her mother asked her to tell what she'd learned in Sunday School.

"Well, Mama, we learned the song about the bad dog that had fleas."

Not having heard of any such song, Mother asked the little girl to sing a bit of it. So she started singing: "Fleas, naughty dog..."

"Oh, now I understand," mother interrupted. You mean 'Feliz Navidad'."

One Sunday, my husband and I went to a special church service but did not take our daughter because she would have been bored. We took her to a nearby nursery.

After services, I picked her up and, on the way home, asked if she'd made any new friends.

She said, "New friends, Mommy? No, I sure didn't make 'em. They were there when I got there."

179

It was the weekly Sunday School class and the teacher asked, "How many of you children want to go to heaven?"

All raised their hands except Georgie. "And just why don't you want to go to heaven, Georgie?" the teacher asked.

"I do want to go," Georgie replied, "but not with this bunch!"

———————— 🧒🧒 ————————

Little Paul was in church for the first time. He asked his mother, "What are we supposed to do now?"

"Say our prayers," Mother replied.

"Really? And with all our clothes on?"

———————— 🧒🧒 ————————

Little Al had asked, in his prayers, for a little brother to keep him company, but to no avail. He became discouraged, finally, and said to his mother: "I'm not gonna ask Him for one anymore."

But not long afterward, little Al was led into his mother's room and there he saw her with twin boys who had arrived that night.

"Gosh," he remarked after standing silently for a time. "It sure is a good thing I quit praying when I did!"

"THIS IS ONE CHURCH PLAY I'LL HAVE TO SEE. THE CASTING IS PERFECT!"

Kids are the most honest of all. Consider this statement by a little boy who, at the conclusion of church services, when the preacher asked: "Does anyone have anything to say?", replied: "I'm sleepy and I just want to go home!"

Did you hear about the boy who grew tall so fast that even his shadow couldn't keep up with him? Not only that but he had to stand on a chair to comb his hair!

The ten-year-old son of an Army Persian Gulf veteran listened avidly at the Sunday School teacher's description of nailing Jesus to the cross.

When the teacher finished there was a pause, then the boy asked: "Just where in hell were the Marines?"

The teacher said: "People who tell lies don't go to heaven!"

Student: "Gosh-all-get-out, it must be lonely as heck up there with only George Washington and God."

When asked if she said her prayers every night, little Emily said, "Well, not every night...but I do say 'em when I need something."

"Of all the parables in the Bible, which one do you like best?" the teacher asked a boy in her Sunday School class.

"I like the one about the guy who loafs and fishes."

Their son, Peter, came home from Sunday School and asked: "Daddy, we've had nothing in Sunday School for several weeks but stuff about the children of Israel crossing the Red Sea and how they built the Temple and how they marched forty years in the desert. Golly, didn't grown-ups do *anything at all?*"

Little Johnny's folks asked him to write what he had learned in Sunday School last Sunday. Here's what he put down: "I learned about a little boy named Andy. He was pretty active, too. Andy walks with me, Andy talks with me, Andy tells me I belong to him."

"Tell me, Adelaide, why do you believe in God?"
"I guess it's because...because...well...it just runs in our family."

"Can anyone in this class tell me why it is wrong to cut off a cat's tail?"
Edith raised her little hand: "I think I know. It's because the Bible tells us, 'What God has joined together, let no man put asunder.'"

The teacher asked his fifth grade Sunday School class to write the Ten Commandments. One boy put this down for the fifth: "Humor thy father and thy mother."

Miss Murphy, teacher of a third grade Sunday School class, was teaching the 23rd Psalm. The class recited it in chorus but there was an odd sound to the recitation that gave Miss Murphy pause. So, one by one, she had the students recite until finally she came to one kid who ended the prayer with "Surely good Miss Murphy shall follow me all the days of my life."

A boy came home from Sunday School and, at lunch, asked his Dad if Noah had a wife with him on the ark.
"Of course, he had a wife," the father replied. "Have you never heard of Joan of Ark?"

Teacher: "What do you think a land flowing with milk and honey would be like?"
Student: "Re-e-e-al sticky!"

The preacher was describing Judgment Day to his Sunday congregation: "And there's gonna be floods, lightning, thunder, fire, landslides and earthquakes!" roared the Preacher.

Seated in the fifth row beside his mother was a little boy. He tugged on her sleeve and when she turned to him, he asked: "Mommy, will I get out of school then?"

The theologian Harry Emerson Fosdick offered this lovely example of a little girl's prayer: "O God, make the bad people good and the good people nice."

Sunday School teacher: "Can anyone tell me the story of Adam and Eve?"

A little girl raised her hand and the teacher nodded to her. "Well, God first created Adam," the little girl began, "then God looked at Adam, shook his head and said, 'I can do better than that'. And He created Eve."

The Sunday School class had finished the story of Adam and Eve and the teacher wanted to know just how much of the story had been absorbed by the class. So she asked Maryann to repeat the story.

"Well, y'see...God made Adam first but Adam got kinda lonesome all by himself out there and so God waited till Adam was asleep, then took all his brains out and made Eve. And that was that."

Little Eddie came home from Sunday School and he was very excited. "I got a part in the Sunday School Christmas play," he exulted.

"And what part did you get?" his mother asked.

"I get to play the part of one of the three wise guys."

Sunday School teacher: "Class, if you were to give advice to our missionaries to the cannibals of Africa, what advice would you give them?"

Student: "To study how to teach them to be vegetarians."

The Sunday School teacher was talking to her first grade class about heaven. She described it long and lovingly and when finished, she asked: "And now, class, do any of you want to go to heaven?"

The entire class raised their hands, all except little Casper. The teacher noticed this and asked: "Why didn't you raise your hand like all the others, Casper?"

"Well, y'see, my mom gave me strict orders to come straight home after Sunday School today!"

The Sunday School class was studying the Bible story of Lot and his wife escaping the sinful city of Sodom. The teacher had just finished the part of Lot's wife turning into a pillar of salt when she disobeyed orders by looking back at sinful Sodom.

One little fellow raised his hand and said. "That's not so terrible or unusual. Why, my Mom was driving her car, looked back and turned into a light pole!"

The teacher was telling her Sunday School class the story of Sodom and Gomorrah and was making a tremendous impression with her story. "Lot was warned to take his wife and flee out of the city that was going to be destroyed. They were not to look back, but Lot's wife did look back and was turned into a pillar of salt.

"And now, children, are there any questions?"

One boy raised his hand. "Yes, I do have a question. Whatever happened to the flea?"

"Rabbi, I've got real trouble with my son Amos. He's ready for his Bar Mitzvah, but all he talks about is baseball."

"You shouldn't worry, Mr. Levy. Your Amos is only doing what Jews have done for centuries. There are several references to baseball in the Bible."

"What! You're kidding. Give me some examples."

"Here they are," said the Rabbi. "Eve stole first. Then Adam stole second. Then there was Gideon who rattled the pitcher and Goliath was struck out by David. You'll recall the prodigal son made a home run. So, you see, your son is right on target. With so many big troubles in the world, you should worry about them...not your son."

The devil couldn't do everything so he made children.

"Children," said the Sunday School teacher, "Now that we've finished the story of Jonah and the whale, is there one of you who could tell us the meaning of the story?"

A little boy raised his hand. "I can teacher," he said. "The Jonah story teaches us that you can't keep a good man down."

At Sunday School, the teacher asked, "Who knocked down the walls at Jericho?" Little Johnny said, "It wasn't me!" The teacher was stunned. The next day, she ran across Johnny's mother in the supermarket and said to her: "I'm really worried about your son, Johnny, because in class I asked, "Who knocked down the walls of Jericho?" and he replied: "I didn't do it." The mother said, "If my boy said he didn't knock that wall down, you can be sure he didn't do it!"

Again, the teacher was stunned. The very next day, she went to see the boy's father at work. "I'm worried about your son," she told the father. "At school when I asked him who knocked down the walls of Jericho, he said it wasn't him. Then I told your wife what he said and she told me, 'If my boy said he didn't tear that wall down, he didn't do it!'"

The father said, "Look...we don't want no trouble. Just tell me how much it'll cost to repair that wall!"

Little Judy was in the church pew beside her mother attending a wedding. After awhile, she tugged on her mother's sleeve and asked: "Mommy, did the lady in the white dress change her mind?"

"Why do you ask, child?"

"Well, she went up the aisle with one man but came back down it with another!"

The teacher passed the plate around her class for the weekly contribution. But Ruthie put not one cent in the plate!

"Do you know where little girls go who don't put their contribution in the collection plate?" the teacher asked, frowning.

"I sure do," responded Ruthie. "I go to the movies!"

"When we go to heaven, do we take our earthly personality with us?"

"Daddy, I got to tell you...since you changed us to this super-modern, progressive church, things have really changed. Why, instead of telling us to bring Christmas presents to each other in our Sunday School class, the teacher told us to bring gift certificates."

————————— 🧒🧒 —————————

Teacher: "So God sent you a baby brother yesterday, Sally?"
Sally: "He sure did. And He's gonna clothe the baby, too."
Teacher: "What? How do you mean that?"
Sally: "Well, I heard my daddy say just this morning, 'God only knows where that baby's clothes are gonna come from!'"

————————— 🧒🧒 —————————

Teacher: "Stanley, what would you like to do in Sunday School today?"
Stanley: "Graduate!"

————————— 🧒🧒 —————————

Mother: "Did you do well in Sunday School today, Albert?"
Albert: "Yep! Real good. The teacher didn't call on me."

The little boy came home from Sunday School and, to the consternation of his parents, began to pull nickels, dimes and quarters out of his pockets! "Jimmy! Where did you get all that money?" his father demanded.

"At Sunday School," Jimmy replied. "Dad, you wouldn't believe all the bowls of change they were passing around and everybody just helped themselves!"

The Sunday School teacher had just finished reading her class the Book of Genesis. "Are there any questions?" she asked the class.

"I got one," a little boy said. "My daddy says that we didn't come from Adam, that we came from apes. How about that?"

"Young man, we do not discuss private family matters in this Sunday School!"

For the last five weeks, the Sunday School teacher had been reading to her class the Book of Genesis. A little boy in the front row was her most avid listener. But one Sunday morning, the little guy didn't want to go to Sunday School and his mother asked him why.

"It just isn't fun anymore," the boy replied. "Not since Moses died."

Teacher: "What kind of illumination did Noah have on the ark?"
Pupil: "Flood lights!"

"What do you get if all the ornaments fall off the trees, along with most of the pine needles and Santa Claus leaves muddy footprints on the floor?"

"A Merry Christ...mess."

The Sunday School teacher was talking about God. "Class, when you got up, washed, dressed, had breakfast and so on, did any of you find God?"

"I didn't see Him, but I know He was in our bathroom at home."

"Come now...how come you are so sure of that?"

"Because I heard my Dad say: 'Jeezus Keerist, when are you going to get done in there?'"

Teacher: "Why did Noah take two kinds of every animal into the ark?"
Student: "Because he didn't dig all that stuff about the stork!"

Mom: "You'll like Sunday School, Sally. You'll be with at least a hundred souls just like you."
Sally: "Is that so? I wonder how many heels'll be there!"

Their Sunday School superintendent was surprised to find a large sign above the drinking fountain that read: "OLD FACEFUL!"

There is not a lot of difference among kids of Sunday School age. Really, they are all alike in most disrespects!

"And what," the teacher asked, "do we learn from the story of Jonah and the whale?"
"We learned," replied Emil, "that people can make whales sick!"

"Tell me, Class, do any of you know what religion Abraham's father practiced?"
"I do, Teacher," one little boy said, raising his hand.
"Then tell the class, please," teacher responded.
"I think it was...I think they called it...Idle Worship."

"Class, you should never use 'A' before a plural. For example, don't say 'a horses' or 'a birds'."
One little boy held up his hand. "But teacher, our minister always says 'A-men!'"

Little Nathan was a constant problem at grade school and the principal called a conference with his parents. There, they decided that it would be best to put Nathan in a parochial school. And this they did.

Amazingly, the boy did wonderfully well and was no problem for his new school. His father and mother were enormously pleased and asked him just why he did so much better and was so well-mannered at parochial school.

"Well, Pop and Mom, I tell you...on that first day, when I walked into my new school, I saw the figure of that guy nailed hand and foot to the cross and I said to myself: 'Wow! They really mean business here at this school!'"

A man and his eight-year-old son went to church one Sunday morning. At the conclusion of the services, the man turned to his son and said, "That was the worst sermon I ever heard. Too long and without meaning! And the choir was atrocious."

The little boy looked up at his dad and replied: "What did you expect, Daddy...for a dime!"

The Sunday School class was asked for the meaning of *faith*. Little Eddie held up his hand and the teacher nodded to him.

"Faith means...means that you believe in things you know ain't so."

"Your Dad's a minister...is that right?"

"Yep. Sure is and he's the best, gentlest, smoothest sermon-giver in town."

"What do you mean?"

"Well, when Mom and I go to hear him on Sunday morning, everybody goes to sleep 'cept Mom and me."

It was Jonathan's first Sunday morning in church and he stood before a plaque, wondering what it was. The minister walked by and Jonathan asked: "Sir...Mr. Pastor...what are these brown things on the wall?"

"Those are bronze plaques honoring members of this church who died in service," said the minister.

"In the service? Which one would that be? The nine o'clock or the ten o'clock?"

Sunday School teacher to pupil, Edward: "Why, Edward, in our daily prayers, do we ask for our 'daily bread' instead of asking for a week's supply?"

Edward replied, "So we get it fresh every day?"

A priest joined his new congregation in the peanut-growing section of Georgia. He was in the confessional booth, one day, when three boys entered for absolution. He asked how they had sinned. Two of the three boys responded, saying: "We been throwin' peanuts in the river, Father, and we're ashamed."

"But I don't see a sin in throwing mere peanuts in the river and you are granted absolution." Then he turned to the third boy and asked. "And you, young fellow, what is your sin?"

"I'm Peanuts," was the reply.

The little son said to his father, "Daddy, I'm building a church with my building blocks and we have to be awfully quiet now."

The father smiled, pleased that his son had taken to heart his words on proper behavior in church. "And why do we have to be quiet?" he asked.

"Daddy, you know why! Because the people are asleep!"

Jackie: "What's the difference between a thief and a church bell?"

Mackie: "One peals from the people...the other peels from the steeple."

A mother and her son went to a new church one Sunday, one they'd never before visited. On the way home, the Mother asked her son how he liked the service.

"Gee, Mom," the lad replied, "the music sure was swell, but I thought the commercial was just...too...long!"

The sermon was on family life—and the erosion of it—in our contemporary society. But the sermon went on and on until, at last, the minister ended the sermon by saying: "What more can I say?"

From the back of the church a muted voice sounded: "Try 'Amen'."

Five-year-old Patrick was kneeling beside his bed, saying his prayers. "Dear Lord above," he began, "we had one heckuva good time at church today. I sure wish You'd been there with us."

"I REFUSE TO SAY GRACE FOR A SPINACH CASSEROLE."

A minister was explaining the facts of life to his Sunday School class. The kids listened, absolutely entranced. Finally, one boy raised his hand and asked: "Sir, does God know all about this?"

The Sunday School teacher, Ellen Watkins, was trying to make the boy behave. "I'm very fearful, John, that I'll never see you in heaven. Isn't that terrible?"

"Gosh, yes! What have you been doing to bring that on you, Miss Watkins?"

"You got this a bit wrong, Eddie," the Sunday School teacher said to little Eddie. "The part where you say, 'Beware of Satan' is just fine, but then you added, or *evil* have his way."

The Sunday School teacher wrote home to Jimmy's mother. "Your little boy is too interested in the girls to learn anything at Sunday School. I'm doing my best to teach him otherwise."

The lad's mother wrote back: "Dear Teacher...Please let me know what methods you use to teach Jimmy about leaving the girls alone. For years, I've been trying to change his daddy, who has the same problem!"

Sunday School teacher: "Willie, can you tell me what becomes of boys who swear...after they've grown up?"

Willie: "Yep! They learn to play golf."

Sunday School teacher: "Can anyone tell me of a commandment with only four words in it?"

Tommy: "I can, teacher."

Teacher: "Please tell us what it is."

Tommy: "Keep Off the Grass!"

Sunday School teacher: "Can anyone tell me what happens to a man who thinks only of his body but never his soul?"

Student: "Well, he'll sure as heck get mighty fat!"

Sunday School teacher: "Can anyone tell me about Goliath?"

Albert: "I can. He's the one who David rocked to sleep."

Clergyman, after finishing his story: "Now, children, are there any questions?"

Peter: "Yes Sir. Could you tell us how you get into your collar?"

Teacher: "When Lot's wife looked back, what happened to her?"
Scholarly type: "She turned into sodium chloride, that's what!"

The little guy had been absent from Sunday School for three weeks and teacher said, "I'm glad you could come today. We missed you."
The little fellow replied: "I almost didn't make it today. I started to go to the ballgame but daddy wouldn't let me."
"I'm real glad he didn't let you go. I hope he told you why. Did he?"
"Yep! Sure did. He only had one ticket and he wanted to go."

Preacher: "Remember, class, it is better to give than to receive. Do you agree?"
Student: "You bet! I sure do. My Dad uses that motto in his business everyday."
Preacher: "That's good to hear. What is your father's business?"
Student: "He's a professional prize fighter."

Mom: "And what did you learn in Sunday School today, Ruthy?"
Ruthy: "We studied the Ten Commandments. Seems like they're always broke!"

A scorner and atheist wrote: "GOD IS NOWHERE" on the church door. Luckily, a little girl changed it to read: 'GOD IS NOW HERE."

In the beginning class at Sunday School, the kids were having trouble identifying the various saints. They simply could not identify St. Matthew or St. Nicholas and the teacher was upset. She asked about this saint and that saint but with little or no response from the children. Finally, she asked: "Can anyone tell me anything at all about St. Peter?"
"I can, Teacher," said a little girl.
"Good," said the teacher, beaming. "Please tell us what you know."
"Well, first, wasn't he a wabbit?"

It was the first class at Bible School that four-year-old Bobbie had attended. The lesson involved the time Jesus fed thousands with only five loaves and two fish. "How do you suppose that Jesus was able to feed so many people with so little food?" the teacher asked.

"'Bout the only thing He *could* do was take 'em to McDonalds!"

Spitballing Father While He Was Preaching

That Darned Minister's Son

by Haydn S. Pearson

There is one episode in my life that sets me apart. So far as I can discover, I am the only minister's son who ever threw spitballs at his father while the latter was preaching a sermon.

I don't want to be misunderstood. Ordinarily, I do not object at all to going to church. It is a pleasant, quiet, relaxing environment. A person can sit and plan his program for the coming week; he can review his accomplishments of the past. Or he can just sit.

It was a hot, sultry July Sunday in 1911, when I was ten years old. The Hancock Congregational Church is a big, beautiful church. It sits beside the village common, looking down the valley toward Peterborough and Mount Monadnock. Behind it is a semicircular row of the best-preserved horse sheds in New England.

The first floor of the building is the Town Hall. Upstairs is the large auditorium that will hold an audience of four hundred people. Back in 1910, the average Sunday crowd was probably fifty or sixty. They sat in the rear pews of the church. I remember I once asked Father if it did not bother him to have the people sit so far back. He said, "No, that's human nature, and it gives me a chance to exercise my voice."

But the elder's family did not sit in a back pew. We sat in the fourth pew from the front, left-hand side of the middle aisle. Mildred and Edith used to argue the issue vehemently. Why should they have to sit way up front where all the women and girls in the rear could study the parson's family—especially their hats and coats? It has long been a New England tradition that the minister's family should sit well up front. And that is where we sat, for Father was a believer in tradition. Mother sat on the inside, Nona next to her, then Mildred, and Edith beside me.

It did not bother me, so far as I can recall, to sit up front. Clothes were, and still are, according to comments, a minor concern with me.

This particular Sunday morning, I could not seem to get comfortable with my thoughts. There were no fishing trips to plan; mail-order time was weeks away. I did not care to review mentally "The Unbelievable Adventures of a Lone Trapper in the Artic Circle."

Father's preaching was not holding my attention. Not that Father was not a good preacher. He was powerful and dynamic. He often told good stories in his sermons and used illustrations from nature and farming that everyone liked because they understood what he was talking about. He exhorted the faithful to be more so and regularly gave the devil about all it deserved.

It was muggy, close, and uncomfortable in the church. I glanced over at Mother and saw that she was nodding off. She had been on the go since six o'clock, feeding her tribe, washing the milk pails, getting the four children, a man, and herself ready for church. The spirit of the Evil One entered me and I reached forward for a hymnbook. It did not disturb Mother. She was actually snoozing. I tore out a leaf of the Responsive Readings in the rear of the book. I tore the leaf in half, crumpled it slowly and carefully in my hand. Then I put it in my mouth and worked it into a solid round missile.

Father organized his sermons well, by firstlys, secondlys, and thirdlys. And when he came to the grand climax of a division of his sermon, he had the habit of rising on his toes and throwing his muscular arms wide, as if to include the whole world.

By and by, I had the spitball made to suit me. It was firm and round; it was large enough to handle efficiently. I took another look at Mother and shoved Edith over a bit. Then when Father was hitting on all fours, raised on his toes and arms wide-flung, I let go with a quick, snappy sidearm throw.

I am a bit ashamed to admit it, but I missed Father by at least four feet.

I have been told that even if New Hampshire men are not very smart, they are persistent. I made a second spitball and bided my time while Father got steamed up to the climax of the next point. This time I aimed more carefully. The spitball whizzed by Father's ear, and just for the merest fraction of a second, I thought he paused. Probably he thought it was an unusually large fly.

I was improving. I took special pains with the third one. I made it a little larger; I chewed it a little longer. I pushed Edith over a little farther. Then I waited. I was patient. I have been called a patient man—as well as other adjectives. I knew Father had several points to cover and there was plenty of time. I waited while he checked off two or three climaxes. Then he came to another. Mother was still snoozing. Mildred and Nona were making horrible faces, trying to stop me. Edith, as usual, was co-operative.

Came the crucial moment. Father towered above us, his voice deep with emotion, his arms outspread. I let drive quick and hard.

The spitball went straight and true. Persistence and patience always pay off. The ball caught Father right in the middle of his chin.

It was one of those epochal moments in life. Silence was as thick as a double feather bed over that church.

A look of utter astonishment was in Father's eyes. His arms dropped slowly, very, very slowly to his sides. Slowly he bowed his head and looked down at the platform by his feet. Slowly he raised his head, and for some strange reason he looked straight at me.

Psychologists, those men and women who can use seven-syllable words without faltering, tell us that, in moments of great crisis, picayunish trivialities, etch unforgettable gullies in our cerebral convolutions. It is thir-ty-seven years since that July day, and two minor points are still as clear as first November ice in my mind.

Eight or ten pews behind us, Eddie Kent sat with his father and moth-er. When Eddie grew excited he had a high, shrill, falsetto giggle. When that spitball conked Father on the chin, Eddie's giggle just sort of climbed upward toward the rafters. Then it was sliced off abruptly as his mother's elbow jabbed into his ribs. At the very instant the giggle was left dangling high in the air, a young cockerel out behind Charlie Sheldon's barn let go with one of those croaking, raucous, quavering, long-drawn-out, juvenile cockerdoodledoos.

Silence again muffled the church. Father's eyes bored into mine, and I suppose the ravages of a criminal career were deeply lined in my face.

After one of those moments that seems an eternity, Father said, "Excuse me," in a low, firm voice.

With portentous, unhurried dignity, he walked across the pulpit plat-form. He methodically descended the four steps. I could tell from the set of his shoulders that he was in complete command of the situation. He started up the aisle. As he went by the pew, he crooked a forefinger in my direction.

I got up and followed Father that long last mile. I remember the horri-ble clatter we made as we went over the big hot-air register. We went out into the entry. There Father sat down, took me across his knees, and per-formed a task that more parents today should perform on their offspring.

Then he opened the door to the auditorium, closed it carefully but emphatically, took me by the shoulder, marched me down the aisle, sat me down in the pew with a thud, climbed into the pulpit and finished his ser-mon as if nothing had happened.

That Darned Minister's Son, by Haydn S. Pearson
Doubleday & Company, Garden City, NY   1950

Reprinted with permission of The
Saturday Evening Post Society.

Dear God,
Thank you for
the baby brother
but what I prayed
for was a puppy

Joyce

Dear God,

I didn't think orange went with purple until I saw the sunset you made on Tve. That was <u>Cool</u>.

EUGENE

Dear God,

Is reverend Coe a friend of yours, or do you just know him through business?

Donny

Dear God,
Is it true my father
Won't get in Heaven
if he uses his Bowling
Words in the house?
Anita

Dear God,

How come you did all those
miracles in the old days and
don't do any now?

Seymour

Dear God,
Instead of letting people die
and haveing to make new ones
why don't you just
Keep the ones you got now?

Jane

CHAPTER VI

Kids to Parents

It was the maid's day out and her employer, a prominent publisher, volunteered to take the heat off his wife and tackle the huge task of putting their five-year-old to bed. The exhausted wife lay down on the chaise lounge and picked up the evening papers. An hour later, the five-year-old stole into the room and whispered, "Daddy's asleep at last!"

Back in the 1930s, a little boy watched a milkman deliver bottles of milk from his horse-drawn milk wagon. When the boy noticed the milkman come out of the house and start to climb in his wagon, the lad said, "Mister, that horse'll never get you back to your shop."

"Any why not?" responded the milkman.

"Because he's just lost all his gasoline," the boy explained.

A five-year-old boy was watching his mother change the baby's diapers. But the mother didn't sprinkle the baby's bottom with talcum powder but put him directly into his diaper. The five-year-old remarked: "Mom...oh, Mom...you forgot to salt him!"

The tax assessor was going through the house and asked the owner's little girl: "Does your daddy have a den?"

"Oh no," she replied, "He growls all over our house."

Eight-year-old Cynthia was sent off to Boston for a visit with her old-maid aunt. Her last-minute instructions were "Remember, Aunt Clara is a bit on the prissy side. If you have to go to the bathroom, be sure to say, 'I'd like to powder my nose.'" Cynthia made such a hit with Aunt Clara that when the time came for her to leave, she was told, "I really loved having you here, Cynthia. On your next visit, you must bring your little sister, Annie."

"I'd better not," said Cynthia. "Annie still powders her nose in bed."

A three-year-old boy was having trouble unfastening the back button of his pajamas. He interrupted his mother's hot canasta session to ask: "Hey, Mom, how about opening my bathroom door?"

"Johnny," said his nervous mother, "if you have another helping of cake, you'll burst!"

"Good golly," Johnny replied thoughtfully, "everybody stand back!"

The father was scolding his young son for not doing his homework.

"If I had a computer, it would be so much easier," coaxed the son.

"You don't need a computer," replied the father. "When Abraham Lincoln was your age, he studied by candlelight in a log cabin."

"And when he was your age," the son replied, "he was President of the United States!"

Most kids are not so obstreperous as the little monster who crawled all over Tallulah Bankhead one afternoon. "Our little Philip is a heckuva problem," admitted the mother. "We don't know what to make of him."

Miss Bankhead seized a moment when Mama's head was turned the other way to give Philip a hearty cuff on the ear and suggest, "How about a nice rug?"

"When I was a boy," recalled Duke Ellington, "I put books inside my pants for padding when a good spanking was due me. Since then, I've known the value of a literary background."

Richard: "Can I have the wishbone, Mom?"

Mother: "Not until you've eaten your vegetables."

Richard: "But I want to use the wishbone, so I can wish I don't *have* to eat them!"

"I hear you've got another addition at your house—a big, grand baby."

"Nope! It's a big baby grand."

Yes, indeed, TV certainly has spoiled the entertainment appetite of children. Four-year-old Sally Hoopster was taken to the circus when it came to Boston.

Right in the middle of the lion act, when it seemed the lion tamer would be devoured by the lions, Sally nudged her mother: "I've seen this on TV before!" she whispered.

The eight-year-old son of an Indianapolis friend was fascinated by that TV commercial that shows a pretty girl going around blowing kisses on the cheek of all the boys in sight in the interest of selling a brand of toothpaste that promises to "give your mouth sex appeal." He persuaded his father to get him a tube of the stuff.

The kid could hardly wait to try it out. This toothpaste was extra frothy and had a biting taste. He filled his brush and began to scrub away. A few minutes later, he reported back to his father, his face covered with lather and his eyes watering.

"If this is sex appeal," he said, "I don't want any more of it!"

A Boston mom had been forced to correct her five-year-old daughter for something she had done. So the child made up her mind to the inevitable and ran away from home.

After a few minutes, she returned to ask a pertinent question.

"Mommy," she wondered, "If a person runs away from home, does she run up the street or down the street?"

A little girl and her mom walked up to the checkout counter in a supermarket.

The man ahead of them was huge, so much so that the girl couldn't take her eyes off him. He was wearing a pager on his belt.

As the man paid his bill, his pager began to beep. The little girl grabbed her mom's hand tighter and yelled: "Watch out! I think he's going to back up!"

A father and his son were watching a 1930s film on TV. As it ended with the usual 1930s romantic clinch and fade out, the teenager said, "Gosh, Pop, your movies ended where ours begin."

If your kids are anything like mine, they love to receive presents—but deeply hate having to write thank-you letters. My Bobby got around to thanking his Uncle Paul for a Christmas gift along about March 25. What he wrote was, "I'm sorry I didn't thank you for my present, and it would serve me right if you forgot about my birthday next Friday..."

A little girl, born and bred in Decatur, IL, had never seen the ocean and looked forward to seeing it in Florida. Arriving in Miami, her daddy took her hand and treated her to a first taste of the surf. She was squealing with joy when she rejoined her mother on the beach. "I sure do love the ocean, Mommy," she enthused, "except when it flushes."

Consider the case of a Tennessee mother who was certain her four-year-old son was a true prodigy because of the way he could repeat nursery rhymes. A friend stopped by the house and Mom called upon her child to perform for the company. The kid stood self-consciously in front of the visitor without uttering a word.

"Little Boy Blue, come blow...," the mother tried to get him started. When that failed, she tried again, "Little Boy Blue, come blow..."

"Little Boy Blue come blow...," the child started, then hesitated before saying: "Little Boy Blue come blow your nose!"

Say you don't have a clue as to how to cook that Thanksgiving bird? Or any of the other traditional T-Day dishes, liked mashed potatoes, gravy, pumpkin pie, etc.?

Then all you need is the new Thanksgiving Cook Book, full of original recipes contributed by students in Julie Ruskey's first- and second-grade class at Hazel Dell, School, Springfield, IL as printed in the Toby McDaniel column of the *State Journal-Register* of Springfield, IL

Among the recipes that will tempt your taste buds:

Turkey by Sherrell Meek

Get a turkey from outside in the cage. Pull the feathers off. Pull the wings off. Pull the little bitty hair off. Kill it.

Take it in the house and put the brown stuff around it. Put butter on top. Cook it in the oven for two minutes at three degrees.

Get a glove and feel if it's done. If it's kind of dried up, then it's done. Cut it up.

Get something to drink before you eat—like chocolate milk. Give everybody a piece. Say a prayer for your food. Sit down and eat it with that brown stuff and white bread.

Turkey by Erik Sanders

Kill a turkey. Get all the fat off of it. Try to get all the feathers off. Get all the stuff out of it, like the bones and blood and stuff like that.

Put it in a pan. Put some stuffings in it. Put some ketchup on top.

Cook it for half an hour. Take it out of the oven. Set it on the table. And then DIG IN!

Gravy by Willie LeSeure

Cut up meat into little pieces. Put some hot sauce on the little bitty pieces. Move it around with your hands. Put it in the oven for 20 seconds.

Take it out and move it around with a spoon. Mash it up with a knife. Put it in a little thing that has a thing right there that you can put your finger in and you can pour out of it.

Sprinkle some A-1 on top of the gravy. Pour it on the turkey and the mashed potatoes. That's all I know.

GASPIRTZ

"YOU'LL HEAR FROM MY LAWYER!"

Pumpkin Pie by TeAra Brown

Go to the store and get your ingredients. Buy them. Go home. Then you start making it.

First, you get the little pumpkin pie thing and you put it in the pan with water. Start stirring it up for about 19 hours. Sprinkle in a little bit of sugar. After that, you put it in the pan and then you make the crust.

After that, you start eating it. Eat it with green beans.

Turkey Bits

Students in Vallie Gould's third-grade class at Rochester were assigned to express their Thanksgiving turkey thoughts in rhyme. A sampling:

> A turkey went to play,
> And that was on Thanksgiving Day.
> The man who ate him,
> Said hooray!
>
> *Andy Shull*

> Terry Turkey touched the sun,
> Tingled and jingled and had some fun,
> But when he saw us,
> He wanted to run.
>
> *Ben Vehovic*

> The turkey had a date,
> He said he would be late,
> His date
> Was on a plate!
>
> *Chris Trammell*

The first-grade class at Beaver Dam in which Beth Ann McBride is enrolled had been talking about birds.

"Can anyone give a birdcall?" the teacher wondered.

"I can!" Beth Ann replied. "Here, birdy!"

From *Joe Creason's Kentucky*
Reprinted with permission of William S. Creason

One cloudy day, a bad storm started near Virginia, Illinois. There were repeated flashes of lightning and bad thunder and little Ben, only five years old, was frightened.

"Don't let it bother you, Ben," his mother reassured him. "It's just God's work."

"Well," the boy replied, "God better watch His step and quit foolin' around, or somebody's gonna get hurt around here."

Little Emaline had just lost a tooth and she and her mother were discussing the loss. "I think the tooth fairy'll leave a coin to kinda repay you for the tooth," her mother said.

"Just so she doesn't forget," the little girl responded.

"Don't worry about that...she won't," mother said.

"Well, she better remember the sales tax, too. Or else!"

A Columbus, Ohio mother was looking through an old box of photographs, family mementoes, when she was approached by her six-year-old. The lad picked up one snapshot and asked who it was.

"Oh, that's just me when I was a young girl," mother responded.

"Well, I'll be." the little guy remarked. "Why in heck didn't you keep the face you had back then?"

All mothers and fathers dread that fatal day when the inevitable question of babies, and where they come from, comes up in the family. So when little Albert rushed into the house to gasp, "Mama! Mama! Bobby, next door is going to have a new baby. Tell me...just where do babies come from?"

Mother sighed, sat down, took the boy on her knee and carefully, honestly explained the entire matter.

The little boy sat quietly for a time after she'd finished, then got off her lap, faced her and said, "Mom, you just gotta be kidding!" and ran off to resume play.

Our neighbor just recently retired with the rank of colonel, sometimes a rank referred to as "screaming eagle." We were glad to have him and his seven-year-old son as neighbors. One day, I needed to ask him a question and called him. His little boy answered the phone. "Let me talk to the screaming eagle," I jokingly said.

"Hey, Mom," the boy called loudly, "somebody wants to talk to you."

"Hey, Mother," the little boy said, "I just had a great ride with Daddy. We saw lotsa interesting things."

"Like what?" asked Mom.

"Like a couple of fools, a moron, and a whole bunch of jerks."

———————— 🏃 ————————

A little boy was viewing the ocean for the first time. He turned to his mother and exclaimed: "Look, Mama! It just keeps flushing and flushing!"

———————— 🏃 ————————

A child's definition of "impatience": waiting in a hurry.

———————— 🏃 ————————

Little boy reciting the Golden Rule: "Do unto others before they do unto you."

———————— 🏃 ————————

"Sally, you're prettier than your mother," a neighbor said to the little girl.

"Yeah, I know," Sally replied. "That's because I'm a later model."

———————— 🏃 ————————

"Hey, mister," the weeping little boy called to the floorwalker in the store, "have you seen a lady walkin' around in here without a boy who looks like me?"

———————— 🏃 ————————

Five-year-old's definition of nursery school: "A place where they teach children who hit, not to hit, and children who don't hit, to hit back."

———————— 🏃 ————————

After her parents had repeatedly ordered the little girl to eat a bit more, she replied: "I don't want to grow up to be strong and big...I just want to be pale and interesting!"

Just when a lad reaches the age where he realizes just how much he owes his parents, a girl comes along and takes over the indebtedness!

The little boy was petting the family's cat when he turned to tell his parents something: "Hey, Dad and Mom, I think Tabby must be talking to somebody...I can hear busy signals."

Little Charlie Hatcher had been fishing for over an hour and hadn't caught a thing. Finally, disgusted, he exclaimed, "Mama...I just can't seem to get waited on!"

Small boy to father: "Sure, I know the value of a dollar—that's why I asked for two."

The modern child, hearing the Cinderella story, inquires whether, when the pumpkin turns into a golden coach, it's straight income or capital gain.

The little girl was at a bagpipe concert and turned to her Mom to say: "Mommy, if they'd just quit squeezing those things, I bet they'd quit screaming."

Father: "Yes, my boy, I'm a self-made man."
Little Tommy: "Gee, Pop, that's what I admire about you—you never try to duck the blame."

The little boy came home from school and greeted his dad: "Hey, Pop, I've got great news for you!"
"Good. I could use some good news."
"Well, remember that twenty bucks you promised me if I passed in school?"

"Of course."
"Well, you don't have to spend it now."

Grandfather was staying the night at the home of his son. His little granddaughter watched him as he prepared for bed, removing his false teeth and then his wig.

"Do that again, Grandpa. I thought that was real funny."

So Grandpa put his teeth back in, replaced his wig, then removed them both just to amuse the little girl. "There, all's in order. What would you like me to do now?"

"Why don't you try to take off your nose, Grandpa!"

In a nearby home, there hangs a huge moose head. The young daughter of a visiting friend was fascinated by the hanging moose head and asked: "Can I go into the next room and see the rest of it?"

It was Elmer's first day ever in school, and when he came home his mother asked, "What did you learn in school today, Elmer?"

Elmer replied: "Not enough, Mom. I got to go back tomorrow."

An elderly lady was walking down the street when she heard a little boy crying and sobbing while he sat on his front porch steps.

She stopped and asked, "Dear little boy...what's the matter?"

"Oh, I want to go (sob) to the movies (sob), but my Dad and Mom won't take me (wail!)."

"But do you have to cry like that? Do you think that'll influence them to take you?" she asked.

"Sometimes they do, sometimes they don't. But it ain't no trouble to try!"

A visitor to the Brown home was making the customary comparisons between the baby and mother and father. The visitor said, "She certainly has the eyes of her father."

Daddy grinned proudly and then remarked: "Yes, and she certainly does have her mother's hair, thank the Lord."

Little Amos, who had heretofore received all the family attention, said: "I got to tell you somethin'...she has Grandpa's teeth."

A little girl got angry, just furious, with her parents, packed her clothes in a tiny bag and started out of the house. Her father asked, "Where you goin', little one?"

"That's the heck of it," she said, "I haven't decided."

A teen-ager was forever pestering his Dad for the family car. The father was tired of the constant use of the car by the boy and asked him: "Why do you suppose God gave you two feet, young man?"

"Well," replied the boy, "Y'see, one is for the brakes and the other is for the accelerator."

"WOULDN'T IT BE EASIER JUST to GIVE KIDS CHARGE PLATES AND LET THEM BUY WHAT THEY WANT?"

It was the end of the school year and Joey's mother asked: "And were the exam questions difficult?"

"They weren't bad at all," her son replied. "It was the answers that gave me all the trouble."

A twelve-year-old was leading a cow down the country road when he passed a neighbor's house. The neighbor called to him: "George, what are you doing out on this road with that cow?"

"I'm takin' her down to Mr. Moore's bull."

"But that's a dangerous job...a job for an adult. Shouldn't your father be doing that?"

"Naw...he ain't able to. This's a job for a *bull.*"

She was a modern little girl and when she asked her Mom as to how she came to be on earth, Mom replied: "God sent you."

"And did God send you, too, Mommy?"

"Yes, dear."

"Well, how about Grandma?"

"Yes, dear. Same."

"And Great-Grandma?"

"All of our family came from God."

"Mom, are you trying to tell me that there haven't been any sex relations in our family for over a hundred years?"

The babysitter was caring for a six-year-old girl who was normally very good and easy to handle. But one day, she was bad all day and the babysitter finally asked, "Edith, what happened to the halo you usually wear?"

The little girl shrugged and said: "I'll bet Mom forgot to pick it up from the cleaners!"

Little Tommy's dad attended a funeral where he was a pallbearer. When he got home, Tommy asked, "Poppa, where's your mask?"

"Mask? What mask? What do you mean?"

"Well, Mom told me you were off being a polar bear and I wondered what you looked like then."

A housewife answered the door to find the neighbor's little girl and her barely-able-to-walk younger brother standing on the porch. They were dressed in adult clothes and so heavily garbed with them that they could hardly stand. "I'm Mrs. Edit," the little girl said, "and this is my husband, Mr. Edit. We've come to call."

Highly amused, the woman invited the kids into the house, sat them down on the sofa and said, "Why don't we have tea. I'll go make some at once," and she left for the kitchen. When she came back, carrying milk and cookies, the kids were already heading for the door.

"Oh dear," said the lady. "Do you have to go so soon? I would so much like you to stay for tea."

The little girl shook her head. "So sorry, but we must go. Mr. Edit just wet his pants."

The lady was walking her little poodle when suddenly it started to rain hard. She picked up the puppy and put him inside her coat near her waist, allowing the dog to stick out his head at her waistline.

At the corner, they waited for the light to change. Suddenly a small boy walked up, saw the pup's head protruding and asked: "Lady...are you a kangaroo?"

Grandma and her little grandson were in the park picking up ripe walnuts on a beautiful fall day. "These are the kind of nuts your Daddy loves best," she said.

The little boy replied, "Maybe he likes these things best but the nuts I like are doughnuts!"

Holding tightly to her father's hand, a little girl peeked cautiously from the edge of the Grand Canyon into the deep abyss with its peaks and gorges. Pulling back, the youngster gasped: "Gee, Daddy, what went wrong here?"

On a school essay paper, a little girl wrote: "Most of us get our fathers and mothers when they are so old it's awful hard to change them."

The little girl ran into the room exclaiming, "Hey Mom! Do you remember that vase you were always so afraid I'd break?"

"Yes. What about it?"

"Well, now your worries are over."

Six-year-old Basil came downstairs, just crying hard as he could. "Basil, what's wrong?"

"Daddy was hanging pictures in your bedroom and he hit his thumb with the hammer."

"That shouldn't cause you to cry, Honey," his mother assured him. "Why didn't you just laugh?"

"I did," sobbed the little guy.

A Chicago father gave his ten-year-old daughter twenty dollars for her birthday so that she could open her first bank account. The little girl was filling out the application for the account when she came to a line that asked the name of the applicant's former bank. She wrote, "PIGGY."

The parents were able to send their son to a very reasonable camp that cost only $150 for two weeks. The lad had never been away from home before. About a week after he had left home, a letter came from the little guy: "Mama and Dad...Come and get me. You're wasting your money."

After surveying her daily delivery of junk mail, my daughter said she was going to move her trash basket out by the mailbox and put a "Direct Deposit" sign on it.

The little boy stood at the foot of the escalator, waiting and waiting. Finally, the floor manager asked him, "Something wrong, little fellow? Anything I can do to help?"

"Nope, my only trouble is my bubble gum is on the derned rail and I'm waiting for it to come back to me."

Of Course

The lost youngster was crying as though his little heart would break. "There, there, little man," said a woman shopper soothingly, "tell me your name and I will tell your mother."

The boy considered a moment, then started crying all over again.

"Come now, Dear," persisted the woman, "why don't you tell me your name so I can tell your mother?"

"That won't do any good," bawled the boy, "she already knows my name."

The minister was having dinner with the Eldridges when suddenly their little boy walked into the room, up to the preacher and held out his piggy bank.

"James!" his mother exclaimed, "What are you doing! We do not ask our guests for money! Go to your room!"

"But why not, Mom? We hafta give him some when we go to his place."

The little boy came running into the living room from the dining room, "Daddy," he said, "there's a big, black cat on the table in the dining room!"

"Don't worry, son," Dad replied, "black cats are lucky."

"Well, Dad, this one sure is...He's eating your dinner!"

"George, you shouldn't have thrown rocks at that neighbor boy just because he threw rocks at you. Why didn't you come and get me?"

"Heck, Ma, you couldn't have hit him any better than I did!"

Mother was explaining the denominations of coins to her daughter. She laid five pennies on the table, saying, "Five pennies make a nickel." Just then, the telephone rang and she left to answer it.

When Mother got back to the room and renewed her explanations of coins and their denominations, she found her little daughter staring intently at the pile of five pennies. "Tell me, Mama, when will the five pennies make a nickel?"

Several years ago while we were stopped at Customs going into Canada, the officer approached the passenger side of the car where my five-year-old sister was seated. He said, "Well, little miss, where were you born?" Looking directly at him without hesitation, she replied, "In the front bedroom."

Illinois Farm Bureau Almanac   March 1994
Barbara Hickam, Washington, IL

My son, Gregory, my husband and I were on an extended trip out to the far west. We finally came to a small town in Idaho and stopped at a steakhouse for lunch. Our little boy went to the restroom but came back almost immediately, asking, "Hey, Daddy, am I a bull or a heifer?"

When mother returned from shopping with a friend for tea, she noticed that the tea had already been strained.
"Did you find the tea strainer?" she asked her little daughter.
"No, Mom, I didn't, so I used the fly swatter," replied the little girl.
Her mother gasped and paled, so her little daughter added, "Don't get excited, Mom, I used the old one."

Teen-ager coming home from dance to mother: "Bobby was the life of the party—that tells how dull it was."

Our six-year-old son, Stanley, seemed given to lying at any and all occasions! We scolded him and punished him repeatedly but nothing seemed to deter him from those lies.
One day, exasperated beyond control, his father said, "Stanley, when I was your age I never...no, never told lies!" Stanley was quiet for a moment, then said, "Tell me, Dad, how old were you when you began?"

"TENT POLES? I THOUGHT THEY WERE FIREWOOD."

The head of the house asked his twelve-year-old son to make a list of the twelve greatest Americans and the lad took the paper and pencil and began.

Some minutes later, Dad asked: "How are you getting along with the list, Son?"

"I'm about done, Dad." the boy replied. "But I just can't make up my mind who to put down for quarterback."

The cow looked over the fence at the small family group from the city, then mooed. Then she swished her tail and mooed again.

"Hey, Mom!" cried the little girl. "She blew *both* of her horns!"

Recently, my husband and I took his five-year-old daughter, Jada, to see the movie, *Twister*. In one scene of the movie, it began to hail. Sada asked her dad what that was falling from the sky. He told her it was hail. She asked if it hurt, and he answered "When it hits you, it feels like being hit by rocks." She replied, "Oh! That must be why they say, 'hurts like hail'!"

Partner's Pearls
Rachelle Hollinshead, Effingham

Little Jimmy's mother heard screams coming from the bedroom and rushed in to see her three-year-old daughter pulling the hair of her older son, Jimmy. She carefully removed the little girl's hand from her son's hair, wiped away her son's tears and explained that little girls, like his sister, simply did not understand what they were doing.

Mom had scarcely left the bedroom when she heard more screaming. This time, it was the little girl!

She rushed back into the bedroom just as her son was leaving it. "She knows all about it now!" he said.

The mother stood her son on his feet in the bathtub and proceeded to dry him with a towel. She rubbed him from head to foot, vigorously. Finally, her son asked: "Mommy, do you really, truly love me?"

"Of course. Very much."

"Then why are you trying to erase me?"

I asked the six-year-old lad how many people were in his family.

"There are ten of us," he replied.

"Wow!" I gasped. "That must cost your folks a lot of money."

"Nope. We don't buy them. We raise them."

"Did God make you, Papa?"

"Yep! He certainly did."

"And did He make me, too?"

"Of course, He did."

"Well, He's certainly doing better as He goes along, isn't He?"

Little Emma returned from the birthday party and her mother asked: "Did you say 'thank you?'"

"Well, no," replied the little girl. "Y'see, the girl ahead of me thanked her and Leah, whose birthday it was, said, 'Don't mention it!' So I didn't."

When it comes to homework, Tod is as slow as a schoolhouse clock.

"Hey, Mom," a little boy said as he came running into the house from his kindergarten class, "I won a prize today. The teacher asked how many legs an elephant has and I answered 'three'."

"What! You said three and then won the prize? How could that be?"

"Well, y'see, I came the closest!"

───────── 🤸 ─────────

"I got to tell you, Tom, that mouth organ you gave me for my birthday is the best present I ever had."

"Well, well, I'm sure glad you like it."

"Yep! Mom gives me a quarter every week not to play it."

───────── 🤸 ─────────

"Dad?" the little boy asked, "who gave me that bicycle for Christmas?"

"Well, you should know that! Santa Clause gave it to you."

"Well, then, Santa was here this morning and said another installment is due."

───────── 🤸 ─────────

"Mary why did you kick your brother in the stomach!" exclaimed the angry mother.

"It was pure accident, Mama. He turned around."

───────── 🤸 ─────────

"Were you a good boy at school today?" the father asked his son.

"Yep! I was. How could I be anything else, standing in the corner all day!"

───────── 🤸 ─────────

There was a six-year-old boy who greeted his mother one night with these startling words, "Mom, I'm going to marry Clarissa tomorrow."

"That's nonsense. Why she's only six years old! What are you going to do about children?" And Mom restrained her laughter.

"Oh, Clarissa and I have talked it over," explained the boy. "Every time she lays an egg, we'll just step on it."

The family had a new baby and mother had to sleep separately with the baby. So she had their little daughter sleep with the father. That first night, the little girl snuggled up to her father, saying, "Papa, I'd a lot rather sleep with you than with our dog, Spiro."

"Mama, there's a man at the door," said little Charlotte. "He says he's collecting for senior citizens. Do you think maybe we oughta hide Grandpa?"

The family was going through an old family album holding photos of the family going back forty years. Mother pointed out one man, and their son asked: "Who's that handsome guy with the big muscles?"

Mother said, "Why that's your Daddy, Son."

"Then who the heck is he?" he asked, pointing to his father.

The family was watching television when a scene came on showing a woman talking on the telephone. My four-year-old daughter remarked: "I know that lady doesn't have any kids…She's talking away on the phone and doesn't have a finger stuck in her ear."

A lady stopped to talk to a little boy in a parked car near one of our local supermarkets. The lad was having a great time playing with a dog of uncertain heritage.

"What's your dog's name, little boy?" she asked.

"We call him Ben Hur," came the answer.

"My, what an unusual name for a dog. Did your daddy help you pick it out?"

"Nope. My dog was just plain Ben until he had a litter of pups."

We were stringing beans on the back porch, my four-year-old daughter and I , when she said, "Mama, I got to wash my hands."

"We'll be through in just a few minutes, wait 'til then."

"But Mom," she replied, "I really must…I got to…well, my thumb needs suckin'."

"Hey, Dad," the little boy said. "At school, they told me to tell you that there's a small PTA meeting tomorrow night at school."

"If it's just a small PTA meeting, I don't think I'll go."

"But you got to, Dad. It's just you and me and the principal!"

There was a sale of purebred hogs at the local sale barn and my wife and I and our little boy, Elmer, attended the sale. After all the pigs were sold, they ran in a series of sheep. My son remarked, "Looky there, Dad, they got their housecoats on!"

The little boy ran up to the policeman shouting, "Come quick, Mr. Policeman, some guy is fightin' my Pappy!"

The policeman ran around the corner and, sure enough, there were two guys fighting. "Which one of those guys is your Pappy?" asked the officer. The little boy stuttered and stammered, then said, "I don't rightly know. That's what they're fightin' about."

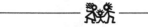

Elrod was a lively, bright little fellow of five years. One day, his Mom noticed him busily scratching his head. She asked: "What makes you scratch your head, Elrod?"

"Well, y'see, it's 'cause I'm the only one that knows it itches," he replied.

Our six-year-old daughter had learned to write all the letters in the alphabet and was very proud of her talent. So, one evening, she wrote a mix of letters and ran to her father, asking, "What did I write?"

Father studied the mixed letters and said, "I don't know, Honey."

"Daddy!" exploded our little one, "you're almost fifty years old and you can't read?"

The little boy stood looking at his grandpa. At last, he asked: "Grandpa, what position did you play on the football team?"

"Whatever in the world gave you the idea that I played football?"

"Well, I heard daddy say that *after you kicked off,* we were going to get a new house."

Rosalia listened attentively as her mother told her father about the new baby the Ellis's, down the street, had just had. The mother told of the lovely baby's eyes and complexion and lips and was loving in her description. Not once did she mention the Ellis's other child.

Rosalia listened only a moment more, then interrupted, asking, "And did they get a good allowance on the trade-in of the other kid?"

Five-year-old Elmer was explaining how nets were made: "You just take a bunch of holes, put them together, sew them up and you got it!"

The family had just had their third child, and Daddy called from the hospital to tell the other kids of the new arrival. The babysitter answered the phone and the father asked for Edith, the oldest child. Father said, "Edy, I just want to tell you, and then for you to tell Sammy, that you have a new brother. Brand new."

"Gee, that's just fine, Daddy. But have you told Mother yet?"

A father and his son went for a ride in a bus. The boy seemed to be completely absorbed in the passing landscape and his father, feeling a little mischievous, lifted the boy's cap from his head and pretended to throw it out the window. The boy began to cry so his father whistled and put the cap back on the boy's head. He made believe that he was able to bring back the cap merely by whistling for it.

The lad grinned happily. "That's great," he said. "Let's do it again." And he threw the cap out of the window.

Mom was preparing the two children for bed and was telling bedtime stories. She remarked that God made eyes to see and ears to hear and noses to smell and feet to run. The little girl sat up and said, "But, Momma, I guess God got kinda mixed up with Tom, here, 'cause Tom's nose runs and his feet smell!"

What has six legs, four ears and a tail?
A man on a horse.

Mary Ellen had never seen thin tea-sandwiches, so she picked one up and held it carefully, examining it.

"Hey, Mom, did you cut the bread for these sandwiches?" she asked.
"Yes. Every one of them."
"Well, it looks to me like you almost missed."

With a frown wrinkling his forehead, Little Elmer was working hard at his father's desk scratching a pen along a page of his paper. His mother asked, "Are you writing a letter to your little girlfriend, Son?"

"Nope," he grunted, "It's a letter to myself."
"Well," she smiled, "What are you going to write about?"
"How should I know?" he squeaked, "I haven't received it yet."

Little Aimee was away from home and visiting her Uncle Mathew. She had never been away from home before and after two or three days, she became homesick and began to cry.

"I'll bet you're homesick, that's what," her aunt said.

"No, I'm not home sick...I'm *here* sick!" the little girl replied, sobbing.

A man called his friend's house and a small voice greeted him.

"Is your Daddy there?" he asked.

"Yes."

"Could I speak with him?"

"He's busy," the little voice replied.

"Well, can I speak to your mother?"

"Nope! She's busy, too."

"Well then, let me talk with your brother."

"He's busy, too."

"For goodness sakes! What are they so busy doing?"

"They're looking for me!"

What can you put in your right hand but not your left?
Your left elbow.

The Accordion Dog

When I's a little boy, I had this dog my daddy gave me and I didn't want to go to school no more. I wanted to spend all my time playing with that dog. Everywhere I went he went and everywhere he went, I went. You couldn't separate us a-tall. Now when I started growing up, we went out huntin' together. And he's a pretty fast dog.

Well, we was comin' back in one Saturday afternoon, hit was raining' cats and dogs, and walking along the state road, I was about as wet as Noah during the forty-day rain. Well, this tourister came along driving a big black Cadillac and asked me if I'd like a ride. I told him I'd sure appreciate it. It was okay back in those days to take a ride with a stranger, but I wouldn't do it today. I got in and told my dog to come in with me. Now that tourister, he said, "I'll take you for a ride but I won't take your dog." So I told that tourister that was all right. My dog was fast and he could just run along outside.

So that tourister, he started up and he was going about thirty-five miles an hour and says, "How's your dog a-doing'?" And I told he's right out-side the window doin' fine. Well, he went up to fifty-five miles an hours, asked me. "How's your dog a-doin'?" And I told him he's right outside the window doin' fine.

Well, that man he slammed on the brakes, jumped out, and ran around to my side of the car to see if I was a liar. And he seen my dog there. Course he didn't much look like a dog, all folded up like an accordion with his tail stickin' out his mouth. He said, "What in tarnation?"

I told him, I said, "Mister, my dog is used to runnin' fast but he ain't used to stoppin' that quick!"

From *Laughter in Appalachia,* edited by Loyal
Jones and Billy Edd Wheeler (August House, 1987)
Copyright 1987 by Loyal Jones and Billy Edd
Wheeler. Reprinted by permission.

The first day of school had ended and little Johnny came home from first grade. "Tell me, Johnny, is your teacher pretty? Just what does she look like?" his father asked.

"Well, Daddy, she looks just like the kindergarten teacher only with a different head."

Six-year-old Henry had never met his cousin Peter, but he'd heard a lot about him from his parents. Then, one day, Peter arrived with his parents for a visit but when he walked in the door, Henry burst into tears.

"What's the matter, Dear?" his mother asked. "This is your cousin Peter about whom you've heard so much."

"We-e-el," Henry said, stopping to sniffle a few times. "I always thought he was a rabbit!"

Why do cows wear bells?
Their horns don't honk.

Ten-year-old Bobby found a woman's purse and waited at the checkout counter, fairly certain that she would return looking for it. Sure enough, after about ten minutes, the frantic woman ran in yelling, "Did anyone find my purse?"

"Yes, Ma'am, here it is," the boy said, handing her the purse. The lady gave the boy a big hug, saying, "Thanks a million, Sonny. Now let me take a look to see if everything is here."

She went through the contents and said, "It's all here, but I had a ten dollar bill. Now there are ten ones. How do you account for that?"

"I did that, Lady. The last purse I found didn't have any change in it for a reward!"

Back in the 1930s, a lad came to the small-town store and told the grocer: "Write down fifteen pounds of sugar at 30¢ a pound, then put down four pounds of butter at $1.00 a pound. Then add five pounds of coffee at 60¢ a pound and, finally, three cakes of soap at 40¢ each."

The grocer finished writing, then said, "I got all that down."

"Good," said the lad, "and how much does it come to?"

"It all comes to $12.70," said the grocer.

"Good. Now suppose I gave you a $20.00 bill, how much change would I get?"

The grocer responded, "$7.30. So just give me the $20.00 and I'll wrap up the groceries for you."

"You don't understand," the boy said. "I ain't buying nothin'. But you sure helped me with my arithmetic lesson tomorrow."

If we can overlook the fact that her pun was unintentional, Jenny Cornelius, Deerfield, IL, joins the growing ranks of kid-punsters. Read on:

Jenny's mother: "We're going to The Country Square for Easter Dinner."

Jenny: "Wonderful! Did you make a resurrection?"

Pun American Newsletter — Lila Bondy
Deerfield, IL

"Shirley, drink your milk!" ordered the child's mother. "It will make your teeth strong."

Shirley took a reluctant sip. "Mama, if it's so good for the teeth," she commented crossly, "why don't you give my share to Grandma?"

Excerpted from *The Best of American Jewish Humor,*
by Henry D. Spalding, Copyright © 1976.
Reprinted courtesy of Jonathan David Publishers,
Inc., Middle Village, NY 11379

"So, Thelma, what'll you do when you're as big as your Mom?"
Thelma: "Why, diet, of course!"

Amie's mother had been scolding her for sucking her thumb. "And if you don't stop it, you'll swell big as a watermelon and bust!" Amie had her mother's caution on her mind when a friend of her mother's came to visit. The woman was big with child and suddenly Amie recalled her mother's warning and blurted out, "I know what you've been doing!"

Johnnie Ebons, a freshman in high school, was in the hospital with a broken leg. Hearing about it, his father hurried to see the boy to find out what happened. Once there, Dad asked just that. "Well, I was doing the latest dance with my date," the boy said, "when her old man walked in and saw us. The old guy is totally deaf and couldn't hear the music. So he threw me out the window."

I fixed it so you can now get all your fingers in your bowling ball.

At the Metropolitan Museum of Art shop in New York, a little girl was trying to buy a piece of art for her mother. She rejected a print of yellow flowers, then blue flowers, then a print of the sea and children playing. Finally, the clerk said, "Tell me what kinds of things your mother does like."

The little girl replied: "Men!"

───────── 🧒🧒 ─────────

"Do you get an allowance, young man?"
"Nope. But I get a nickel every time I don't wet my bed."
"How much money do you make?"
"Last week I made a dime."

───────── 🧒🧒 ─────────

Grandma and Grandpa never gave a thought to it when they had to get up at five every morning to milk the cows...and their grandkids don't think much of it either.

───────── 🧒🧒 ─────────

Dad had to work later than usual, and he returned home after his wife and three children had had their dinner.

"Did you help Mom today?" he asked the kids.

"Yep, Papa," said Margaret. "I washed the dishes."

"And I dried," announced Mannie.

The father smiled. "And what did *you* do?" he asked, his youngest child, Carla.

"I help the betht," she said, hopping up and down and clapping her little hands. "I picked up all the pietheth!"

Excerpted from *The Best of American Jewish Humor,* by
Henry D. Spalding, Copyright © 1976.
Reprinted courtesy of Jonathan David Publishers,
Inc., Middle Village, NY 11379

───────── 🧒🧒 ─────────

The little boy was sobbing quietly and then he decided to go to the policeman standing on the corner. "Mr. Policeman?" he asked, "Did you see a lady go by without me?"

A little boy from the east side of New York City was at summer camp, his first experience with life in the woods. On the second day there, he watched a counselor bury a dead bird to demonstrate the importance of camp hygiene.

The counselor asked him: "Can you describe what I'm doing?"

"I ain't sure," the lad replied. "But whatever it is, I betcha it won't grow!"

––––––––––––– 🧒 –––––––––––––

A boy of eight was on a train nearing Los Angeles, and was constantly sniffing, to the growing discomfort of the other passengers. Finally, a lady sitting across the aisle from the boy said: "Little man, do you have a hand-kerchief?"

"Yes, Ma'am," he said, "but I'm not gonna lend it to strangers."

––––––––––––– 🧒 –––––––––––––

Two children, one eight years old and her brother who was five, walked down the street with the little girl holding the hand of her brother who kept his eyes shut.

A passerby asked: "Has your brother hurt his eyes or is he blind?"

"No, he sees just fine," the girl explained. "It's just that we're on our way to the movies and the sun is so bright that he keeps his eyes closed while I lead him. That way, once we're inside, he opens his eyes and finds the two of us a seat in the dark."

––––––––––––– 🧒 –––––––––––––

A prisoner escaped from incarceration by digging a deep, deep hole. When he'd climbed down the hole, he discovered himself in a private yard with a little girl nearby. "Hurrah, I'm free, I'm free," he yelled.

The little girl replied: "Well...I'm four. So there!"

––––––––––––– 🧒 –––––––––––––

Mother and tiny daughter were attending the municipal symphony con-cert where, during a crashing crescendo, the child whispered: "Mama, how come that man is so mad at those players? They're all playing just as fast as they can."

––––––––––––– 🧒 –––––––––––––

"Y'know something, Daddy?" the little girl said to her father. "Some people's voices are awful hard to extinguish over the telephone."

228

A salesman rapped on the screen door of a house where an eight-year-old was laboriously practicing the piano. "Young man," the salesman inquired, "is your mommy home?"

The boy looked up, grimaced and said, "Just what in hell do *you* think!"

The new family in the neighborhood had a little boy who was playing outside the house. A neighbor lady passed by and asked: "What's your name, little fellow?"

"My name's Abe," he replied.

"Wonderful! A very famous name. The same as our greatest president. Would you like to grow up to be another Lincoln?"

"Heck no! I don't want to be a tunnel!"

Uncle Joe: "Peter, what do you want to be when you grow up?"
Peter: "A parachute jumper."
Uncle Joe: "But supposing your parachute doesn't open, then what?"
Peter: "Well...hmm...gosh...Guess I'd have to holler for a ladder."

───────── 🎎 ─────────

It makes you wonder where Dad got all that information he tells his kids.

───────── 🎎 ─────────

My granddaughter, Sarah, had a sixth birthday and I sent her a savings bond for her present. She wrote back: "Thanks, Grandma, for that birthday present of a piece of paper that turns into money."

───────── 🎎 ─────────

Asked by Dad if he knew what happens to children who lie, the boy replied: "Of course, I know! They get to see the movie for half price!"

───────── 🎎 ─────────

Neighbor: "How many brothers and sisters do you have, young man?"
Billie: "I got three brothers and one sister."
Neighbor: "What do you think is the biggest problem growing up in a large family like yours?"

Billie: "We have the most fights over who gets first in line to take a bath. You see, the last one gets only cold water."

Neighbor: "I guess you like the hot bath, right?"

Billie: "I don't know. I never had any."

A little girl, just home from her first grade class, was asked to count to ten. And she did it perfectly.

"Very good!" her mother said, clapping approval. "Now do the same thing, only count backward this time."

The little girl turned, faced the wall and counted to ten again.

The Jenkins' were worried about their child at home with a new babysitter. So Dad went to the phone and called the house. His six-year-old answered, saying, "Speak very softly, Daddy, the babysitter is asleep."

Amy was watching her Grandma step on the scale to weigh herself. "And how much do you weigh, Grandma?" she asked.

"Too much!" was the reply.

"Well, fer gosh sakes...that's just what Mom says when she gets on the scale."

When my dad says he wants me to have everything he didn't have when he was a kid, he means...A's on my report card.

"Hey, Daddy, a kid in school today told me I looked just like you."

"Wasn't that a nice thing to say. And what did you say to him?"

"Not a derned thing. He was lots bigger than me."

Summer is that time of year when the kid is out of school and Mom is out of her mind!

The little boy walked into the house and handed his father his report card. "Here's my report card, Daddy...and one of yours I found in the attic."

Eddie: "Hey, Pop!" the small lad asked his dad, "Do you know why they call tiny birds humming birds?"

Pop: "I sure don't, Eddie. Do you know why?"

Eddie: "I guess it's because they don't remember the words of the song."

I really appreciate the first day of school. Y'know why? 'Cause it's the only day of the entire year when I'm not behind in my homework.

I can't figure how my mother manages to do it, but she even buys shoelaces that are out of style.

Cleaning your house while the kids are still growing is like shoveling the walk before it stops snowing.

　　　　　　　　　　　　　　　　　　　Phyllis Diller

Never lend your car to anyone to whom you have given birth.

　　　　　　　　　　　　　　　　　　　Erma Bombeck

Charlie was watching his new-born sister squirm and turn and scream in her crib. "Daddy, did my new sister come from Heaven?"

His father replied: "She did indeed, Charlie."

"I can sure understand why they let her go!"

"I give up!" the little boy said while kneeling in prayer beside his bed. "Art doesn't listen to me at all."

"Art? Art who?" asked his mother.

"Art in Heaven," said the boy who had been praying for a bicycle.

" SIR, I'D LIKE TO ASK FOR YOUR DAUGHTER'S HA...."

Mother was lecturing her youngest. She was explaining the Golden Rule. "You must always remember that we are here to help others."
The boy replied: "Good! But then what are the others here for?"

Little Hugo had been such a bad boy all Sunday that his mother made him sit at a small table in the corner of the dining room. That night at supper, the family said grace. Finished, they heard Hugo just finishing his prayer: "I thank thee, dear God, for preparing a table in the presence of mine enemies."

Dad: "Well, Mary, did you enjoy reading *Moby Dick?*"
Mary: "Not really, Daddy. I got seasick!"

"Does your Grandma or Grandpa give you lots of advice, Mary?"
"Grandma does. Just yesterday, she said, 'The best way to save face is to keep the lower half closed'."

Mother: "How do you like school, Susie?"
Susie: "Closed."

———————— 🧒 ————————

Pauline: "Tell me, Dad... can you write your name in the dark?"
Dad: "Yes, I think so."
Pauline: "Good. Then will you please turn out the lights and sign my report card?"

———————— 🧒 ————————

The pastor had come to the Martin home for Sunday night dinner. He made a brief prayer and then sat back. Amos, the six-year-old son, said, "Gosh, Pastor, you sure don't pray long when you're hungry!"

———————— 🧒 ————————

Mother: "Bobby, I hope you're not talking in class anymore since your teacher told me about your interrupting her class."
Bobby: "Nope. Not any more...but not any less, either!"

———————— 🧒 ————————

Question: Where do dates grow?
Answer: On calendar trees.

———————— 🧒 ————————

Teacher: "Charles, why is it so difficult for you to learn how to spell?"
Charles: "Because you keep changing the words on us!"

———————— 🧒 ————————

A little boy was watching his first ballet. Well into the first act, he turned to his mother and asked: "Mom, why don't they just get taller girls to do this?"

———————— 🧒 ————————

Father: "Tell me how school went today. How do you like it?"
Billy: "It's hard to like a place that's haunted, Dad."
Father: "Haunted! What are you talking about!"
Billy: "It's that new teacher of mine...she keeps talking about the school spirit!"

I was born in Australia because my mother wanted me to be near her.

Edward Varese

Dad: "Toby, your teacher called me and told me that you are at the bottom of your class! How did that come to be?"

Toby: "Dad, it really doesn't make any difference because we learn the same things at both ends."

Missy: "Mom, I got good news...you won't have to buy me any new schoolbooks next year."

Mom: "That's wonderful! And why not?"

Missy: "Well...y'see...hm-m-m...the teacher didn't pass me."

Larry: "Mom, teacher said my penmanship is real bad."

Mom: "Then why don't you practice more—make it better?"

Larry: "If I do that, she'll figure out I can't spell!"

A School Poem Almost as Old as School

The more we study, the more we know,
The more we know, the more we forget,
The more we forget, the less we know,
The less we know, the less we forget,
The less we forget, the more we know
So why...study?

My mom was fair. You never knew whether she was going to swing with her right or with her left.

Herb Caen

Father: "So tell me...how was school today?"

Son: "Not so bad. It's just that dumb teacher I've got..."

Father: "What do you mean?"

Son: "Well, Dad, all she does the whole day long is ask us silly questions."

Father: "I want you to know that I am spanking you because I love you."

Son: "Thanks a lot! I wish I was big enough to return your love."

————————　🧍🧍　————————

Parents are the bones on which children cut their teeth.

Peter Ustinov

————————　🧍🧍　————————

A boy was caught in the neighbor's swimming pool but without their permission. The neighbor saw him and yelled, "Get out! You can't swim here!"

The boy sputtered and yelled back: "I ain't swimmin'. I'm tryin' to keep from sinkin'."

————————　🧍🧍　————————

Question: What is it that gets longer the more you take off from each end?

Answer: A ditch.

————————　🧍🧍　————————

Definition of spanking: Stern punishment!

————————　🧍🧍　————————

Mother: "You got an F in arithmetic. What does *"F"* mean?"
Son: "It means I did good. *"F"* means fantastic."

————————　🧍🧍　————————

An old man and a boy were sitting on opposite benches in Fagan Park. They sat silently for half an hour and then the old man shouted, "It's no use your trying to talk to me—I'm deaf!"

"I ain't talking to you," the lad replied. "I'm chewing gum."

————————　🧍🧍　————————

What holds water yet is full of holes?
A sponge.

A little girl was skipping down the street when a kindly old lady stopped her and asked: "And do you go to school now?"

"No," was the answer. "I don't go. I'm sent!"

Teacher: "Jane, do you know about Good Friday?"
Jane: "Didn't he do all the housework for old Robinson Crusoe?"

Art Linkletter quotes a boy saying he wanted most of all to be a giraffe. Linkletter asked: "What's so great about that?"

The lad answered: "Then my sister couldn't slap me in the face without getting a stepladder."

Sarah, ten years old, had come home from spending the day with Grandma. "Did you have a good time with Granny?" her mother asked.

"Yes. Real nice. But y'know, Mom, I sure wish Grandma had better fitting skin."

Dad had just finished disciplining little Robert who stood up and said: "Just wait till I grow up, Mister, and you're a kid. You better watch out!"

Walking down the street, a man saw a boy running toward him fast as he could go. He stopped the kid, saying, "Slow it down. Why are you running like this?"

The kid replied: "I'm trying to stop two guys from fighting."

"Who are they?" the man asked.

"Peter and me."

Dad: "Son, if you tell me one more lie, I'll use my belt on your bottom."

Son: "You'd better not do that, Dad."

Dad: "And why not?"

Son: "Because your pants will fall off."

Mother had her daughter at the school psychologist's office to decide which grade she was best fitted for. The psychologist proceeded to give a series of tests, saying: "First off, tell me…are you a boy or a girl?"

"That's easy," she replied. "I'm a boy."

"You don't say!" murmured the psychologist. "And what are you going to be when you are an adult?"

"I'm going to be a father," she replied.

"Now, darling," her mother broke in to ask nervously, "You know better than that! Why do you say such foolish things to the doctor?"

"Well," she responded, "if he's gonna ask me foolish questions, I'm gonna give him back foolish answers!"

" DAD, TELL ME AGAIN HOW WHEN YOU WERE A KID YOU HAD TO WALK ALL THE WAY ACROSS THE ROOM TO CHANGE THE CHANNEL."

The teacher was testing the level of knowledge of her students, fourth graders. She asked: "Which month has twenty-eight days in it?"

She nodded to George. The lad bowed his head a moment in thought, then said, "all of 'em do."

Peter's mom had just given birth to a baby and he asked his pal, "Guess what she had?"

"I guess a...a...boy."

"Nope. Guess again."

"A girl."

"You got it! Who told you?"

When the Petefish's daughter, Jill, came home from her first year at college, her father looked at her with great interest. "You sure have put on weight," he said. "Aren't you a lot heavier than when you left us for school?"

"Yep, Dad, I am. I weigh one hundred and forty-five pounds stripped for 'gym'."

Dad looked at her horrified. "Who the heck is Jim?" he exploded.

Eddie walked into the house and handed his folks his report card. His mother took a look at it, frowned and said, "What is the meaning of these low grades. They...are...terrible!"

"Aw, Ma, you know how it is after the holidays. They mark everything down."

At a party with Cardinal Joseph Bernadin of Chicago, a friend mentioned that her daughter passed the Cardinal's house on the daily afternoon walk. The Cardinal suggested that she tell her little girl to stop by and see him on her soon-to-be "trick or treat" venture.

All the following week, the mother had her child practice saying, "Thank you, Your Eminence...thank you, Your Eminence."

One day the child did stop by the Cardinal's house, knocked on the door and the Cardinal came out and gave the child candy.

The little girl looked at the candy, then at the Cardinal, smiled and said, "Thank you, your M & M's."

An excited boy burst through the door and said, "It's your son, Mrs. Elder. Your son!"

"What about my son?" was the reply.

"The kids were playing a game to see who could lean farthest out the window and your son won!"

Because of their size, it may be difficult to properly discipline parents.

"Tommy, where did you learn all those dirty, nasty words?"

"From Santa Claus."

"Santa Claus?"

"Yep. When he stubbed his toe and hit his knee against a chair after leaving me all my presents."

"Golly gee, I wish I'd been born 500 years ago," little Mary whined.

"What good would that do?" her mother asked.

"I'd have a lot less history to learn, that's what!"

"How is school going, Bobby?" his worried father asked.

"All I can tell you, Dad, is that my grades are all wet."

"What kind of answer is that? What do you mean!"

"They're all below C-level."

The daughter was nutty over up-to-the-minute clothes but came home from school one day near tears. "One of the girls in my class has a dress exactly like mine," she sobbed.

"I guess the only thing to do is buy you another outfit," her father said.

"Well, Dad," daughter said, smiling, "you got to admit that's cheaper than moving."

"Students, I'd like to ask you to give me one benefit of the automotive age," the history teacher said.

"One thing for sure," offered said one student, "it sure as heck has eliminated horse-stealing."

Mr. Tysom was puzzled by his son's report card. It showed an E in conduct but an A in courtesy.

"How on earth can this be?" he asked his son.

"Well, Dad, every time I hit a kid, I apologized."

Peter and his mother were shopping when suddenly Peter tugged on his mother's sleeve and said, "Looky there, Mama. That guy over there hasn't a hair on his head." His mother bend down and whispered, "Be quiet! He'll hear you."

Peter said, "Well, fergoshsakes, doesn't he know it?"

Grandpa: "What's wrong, Albert?"

Albert: "My Dad won't play cowboys and Indians with me. Boo-hoo-hoo!"

Grandpa: "Don't let it worry you. I'll play the game with you."

Albert: "It won't work. You've already been scalped!"

Sammy came home from school mad as all get out!

"For goodness sakes, Sammy, what happened?" his mother asked.

"If that derned principal doesn't take back what he said to me, I ain't going back to school!"

"Heavens! What'd he say to you?"

"Don't come back to school!"

The next-door boy leaned over the fence and said to the neighbor: "I'm not busy now and if you've got any work you want me to do, I'm available."

"Good," said the lad's neighbor. "I need to have my porch painted. Here's the green paint and the brushes, go to it. I've got to go to work."

That night the neighbor came home from work and stopped at his neighbor's house and spoke to the lad: "Well, did you get my porch finished?"

"Sure did," the lad replied. "I enjoyed doing it. But there is one thing. How come you told me to paint the Porche when it was a Mercedes?"

———————————— ✿ ————————————

"A dream," the little boy said to his father, "is when God shows a movie."

———————————— ✿ ————————————

Elmira: "Mom, Danny busted my doll."
Mom: "How on earth did he do THAT?"
Elmira: "I hit him on the head with it."

———————————— ✿ ————————————

Mom: "Mary Ann, I thought that you were going to write 'Happy Birthday' on the cake."
Mary Ann: "I did plan it that way...but I couldn't get it into the type-writer!"

———————————— ✿ ————————————

On his birthday, Charlie was given a dictionary. When asked how he like it, he replied: "I couldn't follow the story very well, but it sure did explain each word as I read along."

———————————— ✿ ————————————

"This letter you are writing to your grandmother, Daniel, why is the handwriting so large?"
"Well...y'know, Granny's kinda deaf so I'm writing her very loud!"

———————————— ✿ ————————————

Twelve-year-old Stanley was riding down the street on his bicycle but the bike had no seat! At the stoplight, a man asked: "How do you ride on a bicycle with no seat on it?"
"Very carefully," Stan replied.

———————————— ✿ ————————————

Little girl to bride at the wedding reception: "You don't look at all tired as I thought you would."

Bride: "I don't, Honey? But why did you expect me to look tired?"

Little girl: "Well, I heard my Mom and Dad say that you'd been running after Sam Goodby for months and months!"

Little Elmer Jenkins came home from school and announced that he'd won second place in a spelling match in his class. First place was won by a girl.

"Elmer! How come you let a mere girl beat you?"

"Daddy," the boy replied, "girls aren't nearly as mere as they used to be."

Dinner guests were in the main room while the hosts finished preparing dinner in the kitchen. Their little girl sat with the guests and one of them said of her, "Not very p-r-e-t-t-y."

"No," the little girl said, "but she's very s-m-a-r-t."

It was Suzanne's first time at a circus. When she came home, her mother asked: "Well, Suzanne, how did you like the circus?"

Suzanne replied: "Golly gee, Mom, it was great! If you'd go yourself, just one time, you'd never go to church again as long as you lived!"

Dad: "Shame on you, Peter. Why did you hit your little sister?"

Peter: "Well, Daddy, we were playing Adam and Eve with the apple and all. Well, instead of tempting me with that apple, she ate the thing herself!"

A city lad spent his first night ever on a farm. Early in the morning, he awoke from all the activity going on outside his room. He raised himself on one elbow and said, "Man, it doesn't take long to sleep here all night, does it!"

Little Sally Brown walked into the living room and began to watch a wrestling match on TV. Soon she remarked to her mother: "That's terrible...two grown men fighting each other in their playpen!"

"LOOK, MOM! I MADE PEE SOUP?"

An example of enterprise in the American way: A ten-year-old was allowed to come to the party her parents were giving. She was asked to take care of the guest's outer garments. Altogether unobserved, the little girl went to the kitchen, got a saucer, put a quarter in it and left it on the table next to the coat closet. When the first guest arrived and saw the quarter, he put a dollar in the saucer.

After the party, the little girl's father and mother were overwhelmed when they saw the saucer and counted the money their daughter had raised...$40.00!

Our family finally got back after a month's vacation, just in time for school. Our son, Jacob, was getting all his gear together for class and said: "Well, Pop, it's time to be starting the old mouse race."

I said to him, "I think you mean 'rat' race, don't you?"

"No," he replied, "it's you who's in the rat race. I'm still little."

It's a wise child that owes his own father.
Carolyn Wells

My grandfather is one determined guy. He hates smoking! In fact, he has put in his will that he wants to be buried in a "NO SMOKING" zone.

Teacher: "Can anyone tell me what Paul Revere said when he completed his historic ride?"

A little boy held up his hand: "I can, Teacher."

"Fine. Please tell us."

He said, "Whoa!"

Little Sally was visiting in the house of a new friend. She glanced at the lovely library filled with books and said, "We get our books from the library, too. But we take ours back."

Tommy had his friend over to play and it was the day after the New Year's Eve celebration. Tommy explained the icebag on his father's head in this way: "My Mom told me that thing on my Daddy's head is a special hat he got at his college reunion."

Two kids came downstairs but without a stitch of clothing on. Their mother screamed: "Get back upstairs. How dare you come down without wearing your clothes!"

One kid turned to his sibling: "See...I told you Mom's vanishing cream wouldn't work."

A little girl, almost ten years old, told her mother that on the school bus, a boy had asked her if she were a boy or girl.

"And what did you tell him?" mother asked.

"I told him the truth...that I was a girl."

"And then what did the boy say?"

"He told me to prove it!"

"Really!" the mother exclaimed, breaking into a sweat, "and what did you say to that?"

"Why, I just showed him my Girl Scout card."

A little boy was asked which came first, the chicken or the egg. The kid answered: "The chicken, fur sure. 'Cause God couldn't lay an egg!"

Little Georgie was listening to his parents talk about the new baby and debating on whether they'd have to move. Georgie meant to help in the decision when he said, "Because he'll just follow us wherever we go."

The teen-age daughter, sobbing bitterly, ran to her mother and cried: "What'll I wear to the dance tonight, Mom? All my sweatshirts are in the wash!"

A child began his bedside prayer as follows: "Dear God, I sure do wish you'd arrange to put vitamins in candy and chocolate ice cream the same as you do in spinach and cauliflower."

Mary, a six-year-old, was devastated by a slight spanking her father had given her. She ran to her mother and sobbed: "Mom, oh Mom! We made a terrible mistake...we married the wrong husband."

Finally, after repeated efforts, the women members of the Clinton Parents and Teachers Association arranged to have girls as well as boys serve as street-crossing guards. But it was necessary for those girls selected to serve, to be at training sessions at school at 7:30 A.M.

Charlotte had been in training for a week when, one morning, her mother awakened—or tired to awaken Charlotte early, so as to be on time for guard instruction. It was an hour before the other kids were awakened.

At breakfast, poor Charlotte, very drowsy, shook her head, saying: "Y'know, Mom...lately I've been thinking that women's lib isn't an altogether good thing."

Little Joey Jenkins was something less than well-mannered at the table, and his father was trying to teach him good table manners. One evening, when Joey was wolfing down his supper, his father gave him a stern lecture on proper table manners: "And what's more," he ended the lecture, "you're nothing but a little pig. Do you know what a pig is?"

"I think so," Joey replied. "Isn't he a hog's little boy?"

The little boy was outside with his father. "Dad," the little guy asked, "is God in the moon up there?"

"Of course," Dad replied. "God is everywhere."

"Is He in my tummy?"

"You be He is."

"Well, then, God wants an apple!"

Little Jeremy had been incorrigible, so bad that his mother had to send him to his room. A bit later, as he was saying his prayers, he murmured, "Dear God, I'd appreciate it if you don't send Mom and Dad any more kids. They don't know how to treat the one they've got!"

The little boy came home from school with a black eye. "Darn it, Petey," his mother said, "didn't I tell you to count to fifty when you got mad before you did any fighting?"

"Yeah, you sure did, Mom. But the other kid only counted to twenty-five."

The mother rushed to the window upon hearing her daughter scream, "Mother! Mother!"

"What's wrong, Dear?" Mother asked.

"It's Elmer. He's takin' off all his clothes and he's barefoot all over!"

Here is a female opinion of men as voiced by a sixth grade girl. "Men are the things that women marry. They smoke and drink and swear.. They are more logical than women but they hardly ever go to church. They say they are more logical than women but also are more zoological. Both women and men came from monkeys, but women came further than men."

Father: "You say you were troubled with dyspepsia in school today?"
Son: "Oh, I didn't have it, Pop. I just had to spell it and couldn't."

A mother was teaching her five-year-old girl and pointed to an illustration in the book. "Tell me, Dear, what is that?" she asked.
"Gosh, Mom, don't you know?"
"Yes, I do, but I want to know if you know."
"I know, too."
"Then tell me about it."
"Well, if you know what it is and I know what it is, what's the use of saying anything more about it!"

"That problem you helped me with last night, Daddy, was all wrong."
"Really! Well, I sure am sorry, Son. Mighty sorry."
"Oh, don't let it bother you, Daddy. None of the other daddies got it right either."

One day after they came home from Sunday church services, little Elmo asked his mother: "Is it true that we are made of dust?"
"That's right, Dear," his mother replied.
"And after we die, we go back to being dust again?"
"Yes, that's right, too."
"Well, last night, before saying prayers, I looked under my bed and there are people there who are either coming or going."

Son: "Daddy, how would you define a good listener?"
Father: "Let's put it this way...a good listener is a fellow to whom it is impossible to tell a funny story without its reminding him of one of his own."

"How old are you, little fellow?" the visitor asked the young boy.
"I'm at what they call the 'awkward age,'" he replied.
"What do you mean by that?" he was asked.
"Too darned old to cry and too darned young to swear."

Dad and the kids are in the living room watching television while Mom is in the kitchen cleaning up the supper dishes. Suddenly there is a crash in the kitchen and the daughter says: "That sure must be Mom's fault."

Dad asked, "How can you be so sure?"

"Because she didn't say anything."

A little boy was visiting a farm for the first time. He asked the farmer: "Tell me, Sir...is a chicken big enough to eat when it is two weeks old?"

"Nope. Takes a lot longer than that," the farmer replied.

"Well, then, tell me," the kid asked. "How does it keep itself alive?"

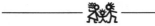

A little girl was standing at the perfume counter in the store and reading names like: "My Sin", "Ecstacy", and "Enticement." She asked the clerk: "Please, Ma'am, don't you have anything for a beginner?"

Georgie was always interfering with his sister and her boyfriend. One evening, the boyfriend said, "Georgie, go down to the corner and count every red hat that passes by. I'll give you a quarter for every one you count."

Surprisingly, the kid agreed and left. But in only a few minutes, he was back to tell them: "Man, oh man, my ship just came in. A Shriner's parade just passed me!"

The average little boy uses soap as if it were coming out of his allowance.

Dad walked into his six-year-old son's room to find the boy building with toy blocks. "What are you building, Terry?" he asked.

"A church," the lad replied. "Sh-h-h...be real quiet."

The father, trying to add to the boy's respect for church, asked: "Why should we be quiet in church, Terry?"

"Because everybody's asleep."

GASPIRTZ

"I MADE IT MYSELF!"

One of the most charming collections of childrens' sayings, observations, insights, is *Art Linketter's Kids Say the Darndest Things,* a collection of kids' comments made on his beloved television show. Here are a few of them:

Years ago, before the Pledge of Allegiance was changed, I heard a youngster solemnly repeat: "I pledge allegiance to the Flag of the United States, and to the Republic for which it stands. One naked individual with liberty and justice for all."

Five-year-old Liza came home from kindergarten all excited about somebody she had learned about. "He's a prisoner," she told her mother, "a wonderful prisoner who does things for people and he loves God."

"Who is he?" asked Mama.

"I can't remember," said Liza.

A few minutes later, she dashed in from the backyard where she had gone to play. "I remember now," she said. "He's Prisoner Eisenhower."

One of my all-time favorites is the boy who said: "My favorite song is 'I'm going to Alabama with a band-aid on my knee.'"

A little girl came to a costume party at the Linkletter house one day wearing a fancy colonial costume. "Who are you supposed to be?" I wondered.

"I'm George Washinton's wife. She saved her father's life by jumping on a horse and riding through the town yelling, 'The British are coming.'"

Listen carefully sometime to a group of youngsters singing a standard song, and you'll be convulsed by the phrases they unconsciously mangle. A small friend of ours when singing, "God Bless America" comes out with the logical lyrics: "Stand beside her, and guide her, with the light through the night from a bulb."

And here are some questions and the kids' answers while on Art's program:

What's matrimony?—
I think it's something to play with.
Is it something to eat?)
It's kind of medicine.
It's a big stage.

What's the prettiest thing you ever saw?
A bald-headed baby.

Ever tried to cook?
I tried to make some pancakes once.
What happened?
Nothing much.
Why not?
Because I left out the butter, milk and eggs.

What would you invent to help humanity?
I'd invent a cookie-cleaner-upper.
Do you like cookies?
Cookie's my parakeet.

What's your favorite slang expression?
He's real stiggy boom.
What does it mean?
It can mean you're a real cool, nice fellow, or else it can mean you're a bad guy.

What does "the pitter-patter of tiny feet above" mean?
It means there's a leak in the roof and the rain's coming in.

What do you think Politics are?—
Another name for a horse trader.
It's something you put in pillows.
It's a thick book that's hard to read.

It's kind of like a school where the teachers are real strict and there's bad boys in there.

Kids Say the Darndest Things by Art Linkletter
Prentice-Hall, Inc., Englewood Cliffs, NJ   1957
Reprinted with permission of Art Linkletter

The boy ran home and up to his grandfather who noticed the cuts and a black eye. "Fighting again!" his grandfather said, exasperated. "You mustn't fight; because every time you do, you make an enemy."

"Well, this time it was with Emil, my friend."

"He'll be your enemy from now on. And you'll have plenty of trouble with him, too. Take me for example, I never fight and I haven't got an enemy in the entire world."

"Well, Grandpa," the boy replied, "that's because you've outlived all of 'em ."

They were going on an overnight hike and the adult leader was checking bedrolls and knapsacks. He found an umbrella in one and asked the boy to explain. "Sir, did you ever have a mother?"

Victor Borge tells this story about his boyhood in Denmark.

"One time, my father came home and found me in front of a blazing fire. That made my father mad, very mad as we didn't have a fireplace."

––––––––– 🧍🧍 –––––––––

Kid with hiccups: "Hey, Mom, I'm percolating."

––––––––– 🧍🧍 –––––––––

Father (chiding his son for his low school grades): "How come your friend Tommy doesn't get C's and D's?"

Son: "That's because he's different. Y'see, he's got smart parents!"

––––––––– 🧍🧍 –––––––––

The second grade class was asked to make a drawing, subject to be their choice. So little Peter drew a picture of an airplane covered from nose to tail with bananas, oranges, apples, pears, that he titled: "AMERI-CA THE BEAUTIFUL." When the teacher asked him how he'd arrived at the title of the drawing, he replied: "Oh you know...The Fruited Plane..."

Little Albert had been having real problems and his Mom took him to a psychiatrist. After preliminaries were over, the psychiatrist asked: "Do you stir your cocoa with your left or your right hand?"
Albert replied: "I use a spoon."

Our six-year-old grandson had spent most of several afternoons out in the garden watching a mother robin hatch her eggs. After the chicks hatched, he asked what happened to the eggshell fragments. His Mom said, "Maybe the mother robin puts them out in the garden like I do."
"Oh, now I get it. That's where eggplants come from, huh?"

I was a bit disturbed by the unusual silence of my six-year-old grand-son who was sitting almost motionless by the door. "What are you doing, Teddy?" I asked.
"I'm thinking," he replied. "Do you know what thinking is?"
"Nope. Do you?"
"Yep. Thinking is when your head is talking but your mouth isn't."

Peter was kneeling beside his bed, saying his prayers while his mother waited for him to finish. Suddenly, Mom spoke up: "Peter! I can't hear you!"
Peter responded: "I'm not talkin' to you, Mom!"

Mother was busy in the kitchen preparing dinner for family and visitor, their pastor. She asked her daughter, Mary, to set the table.
When the pastor arrived, they all sat down at the table, said prayers and it was then that Mary's mother noticed that they had no silverware for the pastor. Terribly embarrassed, Mother asked Mary why she had not put silverware down for the pastor. "Because, Mama, Daddy says that he eats like a horse!"

"I'm not hungry, I ate with Skipper…"

The lad come home from Sunday services and announced to his mother and father that when he grew up he was going to be a minister.

"That's just dandy, Son," his father said. "But tell your mom and me just what happened to cause you to make your mind up."

"Well, since you take me to church every Sunday, I might just as well stand up there at the pulpit and shout and wave my arms as to sit still in the pew and listen!"

CHAPTER VII

Early American Humor

The Adventures of Little Audrey

Little Audrey is a folklore character about whom thousands of nonsensical short tales have been written.

One day, Little Audrey and her mother were driving along when all of a sudden the car door flew open and Little Audrey's mother fell out. Little Audrey just laughed and laughed, 'cause she knew all the time that her mother had on her light fall suit.

The nurse was going to take Little Audrey out for a walk; but the nurse was absent-minded, and she forgot until she was outside to take Little Audrey with her. So she called up to the cook and said, "Cook, throw Little Audrey out the window, and I'll catch her on the second bounce." The cook threw Little Audrey out the window and then she just laughed and laughed. She knew all the time that Little Audrey was not a rubber ball.

One day Little Audrey's mama went to town, and while she was gone, Little Audrey decided to bake a cake, 'cause she wanted to show her mama how smart she was. She got down the recipe book and mixed the cake according to directions. She sifted the flour, creamed the butter and sugar, beat the eggs, and stirred the ingredients together. Then she was ready to cook the cake; so she looked at the recipe book and it said: "Now set in the oven for thirty minutes." So Little Audrey crawled into the oven and closed the door.

By and by Little Audrey's mama came home. She looked everywhere for Little Audrey, but she couldn't find her. All of a sudden, she smelled something burning. She opened the oven door, and there was Little Audrey, burned to a crisp. Her mother just laughed and laughed. She didn't know that Little Audrey could read.

The next day, Little Audrey and her grandma were standing on their front porch watching the men pave their street. There was a cement mixer, a steam roller, and all kinds of things to watch. All of a sudden, grandma saw a quarter out there right in the middle of the street. She dashed right out to get it, but just as she picked it up, along came that old steam roller and rolled her out flatter than a sheet of theme paper. Little Audrey just laughed and laughed, 'cause she knew all the time it was only a dime.

One day Little Audrey was playing with matches. Mama said, "Ummm, you better not do that." But Little Audrey was awful hardheaded; she kept right on playing with matches, and after a while, she set the house on fire, and it burned right down to the ground. Mama and Little Audrey were looking at the ashes, and Mama said, "Uh huh, I told you so! Now, young lady, just wait until your papa comes home. You will catch it!" Little Audrey just laughed and laughed. She knew all the time that Papa had come home an hour early and gone to bed to take a nap.

The next night, Little Audrey and her date were sitting on the sofa when all of a sudden the lights went out. "Oh," said Little Audrey's boy friend, "it sure is dark in here. I can't even see my hand in front of me." Little Audrey just laughed and laughed, 'cause she knew all the time that his hand wasn't in front of him.

"The Adventures of Little Audrey" by
Cornelia Chambers, from *Straight Texas,*
Publication of the Texas Folklore Society No. XIII,
1937.

She Was Only a...

She was only a creditor's daughter, but she allowed no *advances.*

She is only a taxi driver's daughter, but you *auto meter...*

She was only a gravedigger's daughter, but you ought to see her lower the *beer.*

She was the village *belle,* so I gave her a *ring.*

She was only a plumber's daughter, but she had good *connections.*

She was only a milkman's daughter, but she was the *cream* of the crop.

She was only a film censor's daughter, but she knew when to *cut it out.*

She was only a surgeon's daughter, but oh what a *cut-up.*

She was only a photographer's daughter, but she was well *developed...*

She was only a hash-slinger's daughter, but how she could *dish it out...*

She was only a plumber's daughter, but oh, those *fixtures...*

She was only a blacksmith's daughter, but she knew how to *forge ahead.*

She was only a golfer's daughter, but her *form* was perfect...

He was only a garage man, but he had the *jack.*

The Pelican, pp. 151-152
California Humor Magazine

Personal Characteristics

Tallness. A boy has become so tall that hot soup freezes before it goes down his stomach. When he eats meat, he is obliged to get that which is just killed, or it will spoil before it reaches his gizzard.

There is a boy out west, who is growing so fast that his shadow can't keep up with him.

There is a chap in Albany so tall that he has to stand on a chair to button his shirt. This boy is a relative to the one mentioned in the San Francisco *Golden Era* in 1869: They are going to have at Wood's Museum, a boy so tall that he has to go down upon his knees to put his hands into his trouser pockets...

A man "out west" is so remarkably tall that he has to go up a ladder to comb his hair.

It is reported that there is a boy in Vermont who grows so fast that his clothes are too short for him before the tailor can get them made, and that lately he grew so fast in one day that his head was seen protruding three inches through the crown of his hat.

How do you spell *hard water* with only three letters?
I-C-E.

How do you spell *dry grass* with only three letters?
H-A-Y.

If you see twenty dogs running down the street, what time is it?
Nineteen after one.

My School Days

By Bill Nye, 1850-1899

Looking over my own school days, there are so many things that I would rather not tell, that it will take very little time and space for me to use in telling what I am willing that the carping public should know about my early history.

I began my educational career in a log school house. Finding that other great men had done that way, I began early to look around me for a log school house where I could begin in a small way to soak my system full of hard words and information.

For a time, I learned very rapidly. Learning came to me with very little effort at first. I would read my lesson over once or twice and then take my place in the class. It never bothered me to recite my lesson and so I stood at the heard of the class. I could stick my big toe through a knot-hole in the floor and work out the most difficult problem. This became at last a habit with me. With my knot-hole I was safe, without it, I would hesitate.

A large red-headed boy, with feet like a summer squash and eyes like those of a dead codfish, was my rival. He soon discovered that I was very dependent on that knot-hole, and so one night he stole into the school house and plugged up the knot-hole, so that I could not work my toe into it and thus refresh my memory.

Then the large red-headed boy, who had not formed the knot-hole habit, went to the head of the class and remained there.

After I grew larger, my parents sent me to a military school. That is where I got the fine military learning and stately carriage that I still wear.

My room was on the second floor, and it was very difficult for me to leave it at night, because the turnkey locked us up at 9 o'clock every evening. Still, I used to get out once in awhile and wander around in the starlight. I do not know yet why I did it, but I presume it was a kind of somnambulism. I would go to bed thinking so intently of my lessons that I would get up and wander away, sometimes for miles, in the solemn night.

One night, I awoke and found myself in a watermelon patch. I was never so ashamed in my life. It is a very serious thing to be awakened so rudely out of a sound sleep, by a bull dog, to find yourself in the watermelon vineyard of a man with whom you are not acquainted. I was not on terms of social intimacy with this man or his dog. They did not belong to our set. We had never been thrown together before.

After that I was called the great somnambulist and men who had watermelon conservatories shunned me. But it cured me of my somnambulism. I have never tried to somnambulate any more since that time.

There are other little incidents of my school days that come trooping up in my memory at this moment, but they were not startling in their nature. Mine is but the history of one who struggled on year after year, trying to do better, but most always failing to connect. The boys of Boston would do well to study carefully my record and then—do differently.

Bill Nye's Red Book by Bill Nye
Willey Book Co., New York   1891.

A Child's Faith

During a big thunder shower awhile ago, little Willie, who slept upstairs alone, got scared and called his mother, who came up and asked him what he was frightened about. Willie frankly admitted that the thunder was a little too much for a little boy who slept alone.

"Well, if you are afraid," said his mother, pushing back the curls from his forehead, "you should pray for courage."

"Well, all right," said Willie, an idea coming into his head; "suppose you stay up here and pray while I go down stairs and sleep with paw."

Forty Liars and Other Lies by Bill Nye
Bedford Clarke & Co., Chicago, IL   1884

Fatness... The "fat girl" on exhibition at the Museum is so large that the cab is obliged to go twice to transport her from her lodgings to the exhibition room, it being impossible to carry her in one load.

"Capital punishment," as the boy said when the mistress seated him with the girls.

What's the difference between:
A school-boy and a postage stamp?
One you *lick with a stick,* and the other *stick with a lick.*   1868

A postage stamp and a lady?
One is a *mail fee* and the other is a *female.*   1868

"Who says two heads are better than one?" exclaimed Jaggs, as he woke up the next morning and took a dose of bromo-soda.   1893

"I beg your pardon!" sang out the convict, as the governor passed by his cell.   1893

What is the difference between a pretty girl and a night-cap? One is *born to wed,* and the other is *worn to bed.*

What is the difference between accepted and rejected lovers? The accepted *kisses the misses*, and the rejected *misses the kisses*.

What is the difference between a gambler and a theatrical critic? One is a *player at poker*, and the other is a *poker at players*.

What is the difference between a schoolmaster and a railroad conductor? One *trains the mind* and the other *minds the train*. It might be added that the conductor *looks before* when the switch is used, and the schoolmaster *looks behind*.

What is the difference between:
A D.D. and an M.D.? One *preaches and does not practice,* and the other *practices and does not preach.*

Uncleanliness and *Cleanliness*...a lad, while bathing in the river discovered after an industrious scrub of five minutes, a pair of drawers he had lost two years before.

Ignorance. There is a lady in New York so ignorant of all domestic work that she cannot even knit her brows.

There is a man living in St. Louis who is so wooden-headed that he has to shave himself with a jack-plane.

Modesty. There is a young lady in Maine so very modest that she cannot speak the naked truth.

What is the difference between a photographer and the whooping cough? The one makes *facsimiles* and the other makes *sick families.*

What is the difference between a wealthy toper and a skillful miner? One turns his *gold into quarts,* and the other turns his *quartz into gold.*

Phrenological Wellerisms

Philoprogenitiveness—What blessings children are! As the clerk said when he took the fees for christening them.

Pals

"I don't think Skippy has a tongue," said the minister smilingly as he looked over his glasses.

"No, Doctor, I don't think Skippy has a tongue," and Mr. Skinner regarded his son seated next to him.

"Skippy left his tongue at school, I guess," added Mrs. Skinner.

"The installment man knocked on the door for two whole hours today," Skippy announced in a loud voice. "Two whole hours. An' he sez we don't give a break in the clinches."

"Well, it's certainly been a beautiful day—" began the minister.

"Yes, Sir! Two whole hours," Skippy continued.

"Leave the table!" exclaimed his father.

"And go to your room," Mrs. Skinner warned.

Skippy paused on the stairs then leaning over the banister, shouted, "Raise me up to be quaint an' I will be quaint—very quaint."

Hearing nothing further, he stomped to his room. Pacing up and down for some seconds, he pushed the door partly open. Thoughts of an unfinished dessert sent the blood rising to his cheeks.

"So! This is the break I get from my own flesh an' blood."

Fearing that this priceless shot passed unnoticed, he repeated, "I say, me own flesh an' blood."

Skippy listened for the effect and was mortified to hear conversation going on in modulated tones.

"If a divorce busts out in this house, don't come cryin' aroun' me. I never did like the house anyway. Besides, I think our neighbors are very elegant people. No wonder ya can't get along. Oh, our neighbors are just lovely people. Hurrah! for our—"

"What do you mean by this conduct?"

"Er—Er—What conduct?"

"Take that! And that! I'll teach you to act like a hoodlum of the streets."

Mr. Skinner started to return to the dining room only to pause as Skippy sobbed, "An'—I—I—t-thought y-you—were m-my pal."

The words came from the child's heart and the father's conscience troubled him. After all, he was a child.

"W—we'll—n-never—be f-friends again."

Mr. Skinner fingered a watch chain and glanced at the little figure sobbing on the bed.

"N—Never—n-no—m-more."

The father put his hand on Skippy's head and spoke tenderly.

"Come on, son, let's forget all this. Daddy's your pal—he wants to be—Skippy, Daddy wants to be. I'm going out and get you some nice chocolate ice cream."

"I—I—d-don't want any c-ch-chocolate ice c-cream."

"No chocolate ice cream?"

"N-No—g-get st-strawberry."

Always Be Littlin' by Percy Crosby.   1927
The Unicorn Press. NY.

Oh, Lord, give me strength to brush my teeth every night and if Thou canst not give me that strength, give me the strength not to worry about it.

George Wilbur Peck (1840-1916) had the astonishing distinction of being elected governor of Wisconsin on the Democratic ticket back in 1890, when one of his party had about as much chance as does a Republican in present-day Mississippi. One of his greatest accomplishments was the creation of "Peck's Bad Boy," a mischievous and ingenious urchin who made life miserable for his father as well as the groceryman, who was compelled to keep his eye peeled constantly to guard against the lad's bold appropriation of such loose edibles as were found abundantly loose in boxes and barrels before the chainstores neatly packaged everything into standard parcels. Peck, whose newspaper, *Peck's Sun* first published the "Bad Boy" sketches, sailed jauntily into the governor's office as a result of his popularity as a humorist but was defeated for reelection by lion-maned "Fighting Bob" LaFollette. Peck is best remembered as the author of *Peck's Bad Boy* and *Peck's Bad Boy and the Groceryman,* both published in 1883.

His Pa Fights Hornets

"Go away from here now," said the grocery man to the bad boy, as he came into the store and was going to draw some cider out of a barrel into a pint measure that had flies in it. "Get right out of this place, and don't let me see you around here until the health officer says your Pa has got over the small-pox. I saw him this morning and his face is all covered with pustules, and they will have him in the pest house before night. You git," and he picked up a butter tryer and went for the boy, who took refuge behind a barrel of onions, and held up his hands as though Jesse James had drawn a bead on him.

"O, you go and chase yourself. That is not small-pox Pa has got. He had a fight with a nest of hornets," said the boy.

"Hornets! Well, I'll be cussed," remarked the grocery man, as he put up the butter tryer, and handed the boy a slice of rotten muskmelon. "How in the world did he get into a nest of hornets? I hope you did not have anything to do with it."

The boy buried his face in the melon, until he looked as through a yellow gash had been cut from his mouth to his ears, and after swallowing the melon, he said, "Well, Pa says I was responsible, and he says that settles it, and I can go my way and he will go his. He said he was willing to overlook everything I had done to make his life unbearable, but steering him into a nest of hornets, and then getting drunk, was too much, and I can go."

"What, you haven't been drunk," says the grocery man. "Great heavens, that will kill your poor old father."

"Oh, I guess it won't kill him very much. He has been getting drunk for twenty years, and he says he is healthier today than he ever was, since his liver got to working again. You see, Monday was a regular Indian summer day, and Pa said he would take me and my chum out in the woods to gather hickory nuts, if we would be good. I said I would, and my chum said he would, and we got a couple of bags and went away out to Wauwatosa, in the woods. We clubbed the trees and got more nuts than anybody, and had a lunch, and Pa was just enjoying his religion first rate. While Pa was taking a nap under a tree, my chum and me looked around and found a hornets' nest on the lower limb of the tree we were sitting under, and my chum said it would be a good joke to get a pole and run it into the hornets' nest and then run. Honest, I didn't think about Pa being under the tree, and I went into the field and got a hop pole, and we put the small end of it into the nest, and gouged the nest a couple of times, and when the boss hornet came out of the hole, and looked sassy, and then looked back in the hole and whistled to the other hornets to come out and have a circus and they began to come out, my chum and me run and climbed over a fence and got behind a pile of hop poles that was stacked up. I guess the hornets saw my Pa just as quick as they got out of the nest, cause pretty soon we heard Pa call to 'Helen Damnation,' or some woman we didn't know, and then he took his coat that he had been using for a pillow, and whipped around, and he slapped hisself on the shoulders and then he picked up the lunch basket and pounded around like he was crazy, and bime-by he started on a run toward town, holding his pants up, cause his suspenders was hinging down on his hips and I never see a man run so, and fan himself with a basket. We could hear him yell, 'come on boys. Hell is out for noon' and he went over a hill, and we didn't see him any more. We waited till near dark because we was afraid to go after the bags of nuts till the hornets had gone to bed and then we came home. The bags were awful heavy and I think it was real mean in Pa to go off and leave us and not help carry the bags."

"I swear," says the grocery man, "you are too mean to live. But what about your getting drunk?"

"Oh, I was going to tell you. Pa had a bottle of liver medicine in his coat pocket and when he was whipping his hornets, the bottle dropped out and I picked it up to carry it home to him. My chum wanted to smell the liver medicine, so he took out the cork and it smelled just like in front of a liquor store on East Water Street, and my chum said his liver was bad, too, and took a swaller, and he said he should think it was enought to cut a feller's liver up in slices, but it was good, and then I had a peculiar feeling in my liver, and my chum said his liver felt better after he took a swaller, and so I took a swaller, and it was the offulest liver remedy I ever tasted. It scorched my throat just like the diphtheria, but it beats the diphtheria, or sore throat, all to pieces and my chum and me laughed we was so tickled. Did you ever take liver medicine? You know how it makes you feel as if your liver had got on top of your lights, and like you wanted to jump and holler. Well, Sir, honest that liver medicine made me dance a jig on the viaduct bridge, and an old soldier from the soldier's home came along and asked us what was the matter, and we showed him the bottle, and he said he sposed he had the worst liver in the world, and said the doctors at the home couldn't cure him. It's a mean boy that won't help an old veteran cure his liver, so I told him to try Pa's liver remedy and he took a regular cow swaller, and said, 'here's to your livers, boys.' He must have a liver bigger nor a cow's, and I guess it is better now."

"Then my liver begun to feel curious again, and my chum said his liver was getting torpid some more, and we both of us took another dose, and started home and we got generous and gave our nuts all away to some boys. Say, does liver medicine make a feller give away all he has got? We kept taking medicine every five blocks, and we locked arms and went down a back street and sung 'O it is a glorious thing to be a pirut kind,' and when we got home my head felt bigger nor a washtub and I though p'raps my liver had gone to my head, and Pa came to the door with his face tied up in towels, and some yellow stuff on the towels that smelled like anarchy, and I slapped him on the shoulder and shouted, 'Hello, Gov., how's your liver,' and gave him the bottle and it was empty, and he asked if we had been drinking that medicine and he said he was ruined, and I told him we could get some more down to the saloon, and he took hold of my collar and I lammed him in the ear, and he bounced me up the stairs, and then I turned pale, and had cramps and I didn't remember any more till I woke up and the doctor was with me, and Pa and Ma looked scared, and the Dock had a tin thing like you draw water out of a county cistern, only smaller, and Ma said if it hadn't been for the stomach pump, she wouldn't have had any little boy, and I looked at the knobs on Pa's face and I laffed and asked Pa if he got into the hornets, too. Then the Doc laffed and Ma cried and Pa swore and I groaned and got sick again and then they let me go to sleep again and this morning, I had the offulest headache and Pa's face looks like he had fallen on a picket fence. When I got out, I went to my chum's house to see if they had got him pumped out, and his Ma drove me out with a broom and she says I will ruin every boy in the neighborhood. Pa says I was drunk and kicked him in the groin when he fired me up stairs, and I asked him how I could be drunk just taking medicine for my liver, and he said to go to the devil, and I came over here. Say, give me a lemon to settle my stomach."

"But, look-a-here," says the grocery man, as he gave the boy a little dried up lemon, about as big as a prune, and told him he was a terror, "what is the matter with your eye winkers and your hair? They seem to be burned off."

"O, thunder, didn't Pa tell you about the comet exploding and burning us all? That was the worst thing since the flood, when Noar run the excursion boat from Kalamazoo to Mount Ararat. You see we had been reading about the comet, which is visible at four o'clock in the morning, and I heard Pa tell the hired girl to wake him and Ma up when she got up to set the pancakes and go to early mass so they could see the comet. The hired girl is a Cathlick, and she don't make no fuss about it, but she has got more good, square religion than a dozen like Pa. it makes a good deal of difference how religion affects different people, don't it? Now Pa's religion makes him wild, and he wants to kick my pants and pull my hair, but the hired girl's religion makes her want to hug me; if I am abused and she puts anarchy on my bruises, and gives me pie. Pa wouldn't get up at four o'clock in the morning to go to early mass, unless he could take a fish pole along and some angle worms. The hired girl prays when nobody sees her but God, but Pa wants to get a church full of sisterin', and pray loud, as though he was an auctioneer selling tin razors. Say, it beats all what a difference liver medicine has on two people, too. Now that hickory nut day, when me and my chum got full of Pa's liver medicine, I felt so good natured I gave my hickory nuts away to the children, and wanted to give my coat and pants to a poor tramp, but my chum, who ain't no bigger'n me, got on his ear and wanted to kick the socks off a little girl who was going home from school. It's queer, ain't it? Well, about the comet. When I heard Pa tell the hired girl to wake him and Ma up, I told her to wake me up about an hour before she waked Pa up, and then I got my chum to stay with me, and we made a comet to pay on Pa. You see my room is right over Pa's room, and I got two lengths of stove pipe and covered them all over with phosphorus, so they looked just as bright as a rocket, and we were going to touch off the Roman candles and the sky rocket just as Pa and Ma got to looking at the comet. I didn't know that a skyrocket would kick back, did you? Well, you'd a died to see that comet. We tied a piece of white rubber garden hose to the stove pipe for a tail and went to bed, and when the hired girl woke us up we laid for Pa and Ma. Pretty soon we heard Pa's window open, and I looked out, and Pa and Ma had their heads and half their bodies out of the window. They had their night shirts on and looked just like the picture of Millerites waiting for the world to come to an end. Pa looked and seed the stove pipe and he said:

"Hanner, for God's sake, look up there. That is the damnedest comet I ever see. It is as bright as day. See the tail of it. Now that is worth getting up to see."

Just then my chum lit the two Roman candles and I touched off the rocket, and that's where my eye winkers went. The rocket busted the joints of the stove pipe and they fell down on Pa but Ma got her head inside before the comet struck, and wasn't hurt, but one length of the stove pip struck Pa endways on the neck and almost cut a biscuit out of him, and the fire and sparks just poured down in his hair, and burned his night shirt. Pa was scart. He thought the world was coming to an end, and the window came down on his back and he began to sing, "Earth's but a desert drear, Heaven is my home." I see he was caught in the window, and I went down stairs to put out the fire on his night shirt, and put up the window to let him in, and he said: "My boy, your Ma and I are going to Heaven, but I fear you will go to the bad place," and I told him I would take my chances, and he better put on his pants if he was going anywhere where there would liable to be ladies present, and when he got his head in, Ma told him the world was not coming to an end, but somebody had been setting off fireworks, and she said she guessed it was their dear little boy, and when I saw Pa feeling under the bed for a bed slat, I got up the stairs pretty previous now, and don't you forget it, and Ma put cold cream on where the sparks burnt Pa's shirt, and Pa said another day wouldn't pass over his head before he had me in the Reform School. Well, if I go to Reform School, somebody's got to pay attention, you can bet your liver. A boy can't have fun these days without everybody thinks he is a heathen. What hurt did it do to play comet? It's a mean father that won't stand a little scorching in the interest of science."

The boy went out, scratching the place where his eye winkers were, and then the grocery man knew what it was that caused the fire engines to be out around at four o'clock in the morning, looking for a fire.

It's a truism that men believe in heredity, at least until their sons make asses of themselves.

Snow is white and coal is black,
If your pants are loose, pull in the slack.

When one child mocked another, the child mocked would say:
Mocking is catching,
Hanging is stretching.

Raccoon up a persimmon tree,
The possum on the ground;
He said you son of a gun,
Shake those simmons down.

Raccoon tail is ringed around,
Opossum tail is long and bare;
Rabbit has no tail.
Just a little bunch of hair.

Ring the bell to go to hell,
Climb the rod to go to God.

Tit for tat,
You kill my dog,
And I'll skin your cat.

Generations ago, children used to write rhymes such as the following in their textbooks:

I'm a little curly head,
My father is a preacher,
I love to go to Sunday school,
And listen to my teacher.

I'm a little Hindoo,
I do all I kindoo;
If my pants and shirt don't meet,
I'll make my little skindoo.

It is a sin,
To steal a pin;
It is greater,
To steal a potater *(potato)*.

I've got a rocket,
In my pocket,
I cannot stop to play.
Away she goes,
I've burnt my toes,
'Tis Independence Day.

I told Ma,
Ma told Pa;
Harry got a licking,
Ha! Ha! Ha!

Now don't get excited,
And don't be misled,
For Aunt Jemima went home
With a pain in her head.

Christmas is coming,
Turkeys are fat,
Please put a nickel
In grandpa's hat.

Comic Rhymes of Childhood

Amen,
Brother Ben,
Shot at a rooster,
Killed a hen.

Apple core,
Bite no more,
Point him out,
Hit him in the snout.

I beg your pardon, I'll grant your grace;
If that won't do, I'll spit in your face.

If you haven't a nickel,
A penny will do.
If you haven't that,
God bless you!

I should worry, I should care,
I should marry a millionaire.

I should worry, I should cry,
I should marry another guy.

Do you like beer?
A sock in the ear.

Do you like butter?
I'll punch you in the gutter.

Do you like jelly?
I'll punch you in the belly.

Do you like pie?
I'll punch you in the eye.

Do you want a nickel?
Suck a pickle.

Aunt Jemima ate cake,
Aunt Jemima ate jelly,

267

Aunt Jemima went home
With a pain in her—

I asked my mother for fifty cents,
To see an elephant jump the fence;
He jumped so high, he touched the sky,
And didn't get back till the fourth of July.

Josh Billings, 1818-1885 (Henry Wheeler Shaw), was one of the great comic geniuses of the 19th century. Of him, Abraham Lincoln said, "Next to William Shakespeare, Josh Billings is the greatest judge of human nature the world has ever seen."

Perhaps the best evaluation of this man was that of his hometown newspaper, writing at time of his death:

"In his quaint way, he preached the Ten Commandments; held up the follies of life that men might abandon them and live wisdom; gave advice marvelously sugar-coated with refined humor; scattered all over the world profound truths in two-line pearly paragraphs.

He has done his day and generation good."

Don't be discouraged by the phonetic spelling so popular in humor of the 1870s. It is fun to read!

Laughing

Laughing is strikly an amuzement, altho some folks make a bizzness ov it. It haz bin considered an index ov karakter, and thare iz sum, so close at reasoning, that they say, they kan tell what a man had for dinner, by seeing him laff. I never saw two laff alike. While thare are some, who dont make enny noise, thare are sum, who dont make ennything but noise; and sum agin, who hav musik in their laff, and others, who laff just az a rat duz, who haz caught a steel trap, with his tale. Thare is no mistake in the assershun, that it is a cumfert tew hear sum laffs, that cum rompin out ov a man's mouth, just like a distrik school ov yung girls, let out tew play. Then agin thare iz sum laffs, that are az kold and meaningless az a yester-day's bukwheat pancake,—that cum out ov the mouth twisted, and gritty, az a 2 inch auger, drawed out ov a hemlok board. One ov these kind ov laffs haz no more cumfert in it than the—stummak ake haz, and makes yu feel, when yu hear it, az though yu waz being shaved bi a dull razer, without the benefit ov soap, or klergy. Men who never laff may have good hearts, but they are deep seated,—like sum springs, they hav their inlet and outlet from below, and show no sparkling bubble on the brim. I don't like a gigler, this kind ov laff iz like the dandylion, a feeble yeller, and not a bit ov good smell about it. It iz true that enny kind ov a laff iz better than none,—but giv me the laff that looks out ov a man's eyes fust, to see if the coast is clear, then steals down into the dimple ov his cheek, and rides in an eddy thare awhile, then waltzes a spell, at the korners ov his mouth, like a thing ov life, then busts its bonds ov buty, and fills the air for a moment with a shower ov silvery tongued sparks, —then steals bak, with a smile, to its lair, in the harte, tew watch agin for its prey,—this it is the kind ov laff that I luv, and aint afrade ov.

Josh Billings.   1874

The Fust Baby

The fust baby has bekum one ov the fixed stars ov life; and ever since the fust one was born, on the rong side of the gardin ov Eden, down tew the little stranger ov yesterday, they hav never failed tew be a budget ov mutch joy—an event ov mutch gladness. Tew wake up some cheerful morning, and cee a pair ov soft eyes looking into yours—to wonder how so mutch buty could have been entrusted to you—tew sarch out the father, or the mother, in the sweet little fase, and then loze the survey, in an instant of buty, as a laffing Angel lays before you—tew pla with the golden hare, and sow fond kisses upon this little bird in yure nest—tiz this that makes the fust baby, the joy ov awl joys—a feast ov the harte. Tew find the pale Mother again bi yure side, more luvly than when she was wooed—tew see a new tenderness in her eye, and tew hear the chastened sweetness ov her laff, as she tells something new about Willie—tew luv her far more than ever, and tew find oftimes a prayer on yure lips—tiz this that makes the fust baby a fountain ov sparkling plezzure. Tew watch the bud on yure rosebush, tew ketch the fust notes ov yure song-bird, tew hear the warm praze ov kind frends, and tew giv up yure hours tew the trezzure—tiz this that makes the fust baby a gift that Angels hav brought yu. Tew look up the trak that life takes—tew see the sunshine and shower—tew plead for the best, and shrink from the wust—tew shudder when sikness steals on, and tew be chastened when death comes—tiz this—oh! tis this that makes the fust baby a hope upon arth, and a gem up in Heaven.

Tha tell me that femails are so skarse, in the far western county, that a grate menny married wimmin are alreaddy engaged tu their sekund and third husbands.

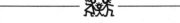

The Distrikt Skoolmaster

Thare iz one man in this basement world that I alwus look upon with mixt pheelings ov pitty and respekt.

Pitty and *respekt,* az a genral mixtur, don't mix well.

You will find them both traveling around amungst folks, but not growing on the same bush.

When they do hug each other, they mean sumthing.

Pitty, without respekt, hain't got much more oats in it than disgust haz.

I had rather a man would hit me on the side ov the hed than tew pitty me.

But thare iz one man in this world to whom I alwus take oph mi hat, and remain uncovered untill he gits safely by, and that iz the distrikt skoolmaster.

When I meet him, I look upon him az a martyr just returning from the stake or on hiz way thare tew be cooked.

He leads a more lonesum and single life than an old bachelor, and a more anxious one than an old maid.

He iz remembered jist about az long and affektionately az a gide board iz by a traveling pack pedlar.

If he undertakes tew make hiz skollars luv him, the changes are he will neglekt their larning; and if he don't lick them now and then pretty often, they will soon lick him.

The distrikt skoolmaster hain't got a friend on the flat side ov earth. The boys snow-ball him during recess; the girls put water in hiz hair die; and the skool committee make him work for haff the money a bartender gits, and board him around the naberhood, whare they give him rhy coffee, sweetened with mollassis, tew drink, and kodfish bawls 3 times a day for vittles.

And, with all this abuse, I never heard ov a distrikt skoolmaster swareing enny thing louder than—*Condem it.*

Don't talk tew me about the pashunce ov anshunt Job.

Job had pretty plenty ov biles all over him, no doubt, but they were all ov one breed.

Every yung one in a distrikt school iz a bile ov a diffrent breed, and each one needs a diffrent kind ov poultiss tew git a good head on them.

A distrikt skoolmaster, who duz a square job and takes hiz codfish bawls reverently, iz a better man to day tew hav lieing around loose than Soloman would be arrayed in all ov hiz glory.

Soloman waz better at writing proverbs and managing a large family, than he would be tew navigate a distrikt skool hous.

Enny man who haz kept a distrikt skool for ten years, and boarded around the naberhood, ought tew be made a mager gineral, and hav a penshun for the rest ov hiz natral days and a hoss and waggin tew do hiz going around in.

But, az a genral consequence, a distrikt skoolmaster hain't got any more warm friends than an old blind fox houn haz.

He iz jist about az welkum as a tax gatherer iz.

He is respekted a good deal az a man iz whom we owe a debt ov 50 dollars to and don't mean tew pay.

He goes through life on a backroad, az poor az a wood sled, and finally iz missed—but what ever bekums ov hiz remains, I kant tell.

Fortunately he iz not often a sensitive man; if he waz, he couldn't enny more keep a distrikt skool that he could file a kross kut saw.

Whi iz it that theze men and wimmen, who pashuntly and with crazed brain teach our remorseless brats the tejus meaning ov the alphabet, who take the fust welding heat on their destinys, who lay the stepping stones and enkurrage them tew mount upwards, who hav dun more hard and mean work than enny klass on the futstool, who have prayed over the reprobate, strengthened the timid, restrained the outrageous, and flattered the imbecile, who hav lived on kodfish and vile coffee, and haint been heard to sware—whi iz it that they are treated like a vagrant fiddler, danced to for a night, paid oph in the morning and eagerly forgotten?

I had rather burn a coal pit, or keep the flys out ov a butcher's shop in the month ov August, than meddle with the distrikt skool bizzness.

How to Pik Out a Wife

Find a girl that iz 19 years old last May, about the right hight, with a blue eye, and a dark-brown hair and white teeth.

Let the girl be good to look at, not too phond of musik, a firm disbeleaver in ghosts, and one ov six children in the same family.

Look well tew the karakter ov her father; see that he is not the member ov enny klub, don't bet on elekshuns, and gits shaved at least 3 times a week.

Find out all about her mother, see if she haz got a heap ov good common sense, studdy well her likes and dislikes, eat sum ov her hum-made bread and apple dumplins, notiss whether she abuzes all ov her nabors, and don't fail tew observe whether her dresses are last year's ones fixt over.

If you are satisfied that the mother would make the right kind ov a mother-in-law, yu kan safely konklude that the dauter would make the right kind of a wife.

After theze prelimenarys are all settled, and yu have done a reazonable amount ov sparking, ask the yung lady for her heart and hand, and if she refuses, yu kan konsider yourself euchered.

If on the contrary, she should say yes, git married at once, without any fuss and feathers, and proceed to take the chances.

I say take the chances for thare aint no resipee for a perfekt wife, enny more than thare iz for a perfekt husband.

Thare iz just, as menny good wifes az thare iz good husbands, and I never knew two people, married or single, who were determined tew make themselfs agreeable to each other, but what they suckceeded.

Name yure oldes boy sum good stout name, not after sum hero, but should the first boy be a girl, I ask it az a varour to me that yu kaul her Rebekker.

I do want sum ov them good, old-fashioned, tuff girl names revived and extended.

Babys

Babys I luv with all mi heart; they are mi sweetmeats, they warm up mi blood like a gin sling, they krawl into me and nestle by the side ov mi soul, like a kitten under a cook stove.

I hav raized babys miself, and kno what I am talking about.

I hav got grandchildren, and they are wuss than the fust krop tew riot amung the feelings.

If I could hav mi way, I would change all the human beings now on the face ov the earth back into babys at once, and keep them thare, and make this footstool one grand nussery; but what I should do for wet nusses I don't kno, nor don't care.

I would like tew have 15 babys now on mi lap, and mi lap ain't the handyest lap in the world for babys, neither.

My lap iz long enuff, but not the widest kind ov a lap.

I am a good deal ov a man, but I konsist ov length principally, and when I make a lap ov miself, it iz not a mattrass, but more like a couple ov rails with a jint in them.

I can hold more babys in mi lap at once, than any man in Amerika, without spilling one, but it hurts the babys.

I never saw a baby in mi life that I didn't want tew kiss; I am wuss than an old maid in this respekt.

I hav seen babys that i hav refused tew kiss untill they had been washt; but the baby want tew blame for this, neither waz I.

Thare are folks in this world who say they don't luv babys, but yu kan depend upon it, when they waz babys sumboddy loved them.

Babys luv me, too. I kan take them out ov their mothers' arms just az eazy as I kan an unfleged bird out ov his nest. They luv me bekauze I luv them.

And here let me say, for the comfort and consolashun ov all mothers, that whenever they see me on the cars or on the steambote, out ov a job they needn't hesitate a minnit tew drop a clean, fat baby into mi lap; I will hold it, and kiss it, and be thankful besides.

Perhaps thare iz people who don't envy me all this, but it is iz one ov the sharp-cut, well-defined joys ov mi life, mi love for babys and their love for me.

Perhaps thare iz people who will call it a weakness, I don't.

Female Eddikashun

Thare iz so mutch ced about the importanze ov female eddikashun, now a daze, that a near-sighted person wud suppoze that wimmin, was running tu waist. The more that wimmin ar elevated, the more men ar histed up too, so tha sa, and them who maik this statement, ain't fur from out ov the wa fur men hav bin clus after the wimmin, ever sinse humin beins waz perpetrated. Dear reader, dear, don't be maid a fool uv, by beleaving for the space ov a half-grown seckond, that Josh Billings, (more properly Joshua Billings, Esq.,) don't love, respeck, adore, and worship the sex, and ain't willing tu fite, even with the belly-ake onto him, two hundred pounds ov any kind ov man, in behalf ov enny vartuous, and worthy, or even good-looking woman.

I beleave in femail eddikashun, clear up tu the handle, provided the woman hankers for it, but if she don't hanker for it, I kant see why she shud be histed up into a posishun, where men has got to cease luving her, just in proposhun az tha are asked to wonder at her. Tha tell us that thare ain't enny posishun that man kan fill, but what wimmin kan fill it tu; but iz that enny reson why it iz best to prove it. I haven't enny doubt, that you could eddicate wimmin so muchly, that tha wouldn't kno enny more about getting dinner, than sum ministers ov the gospil kno about preaching, and while tha mite translate one ov Virgils ecklogs tu a spot, tha couldn't translate a baby out ov a kradle, without letting it cum apart.

I hold that natur haz its laws and programmy, all the wa down, for the biling over ov a volkano tu the wiggle ov a lam's tale. Suppose you shud take 100 yung injuns and eddikate them tu the highest pint, and then turn them luce! 95 ov them wud throw a blanket outu their shoulders, bid fairwell tu civilizashun, and dive intu the wildnerness; the uther 5 wud wander about among the pail faces, az far from hum az a Bufferlo wud be among a herd ov short tailed durhams. I believe in femail eddikashun, but I had ruther a woman cud beet me nussing a baby than tu feel that she cud beet me or enny other man in a stump speech, or a lektur on veteranara praktiss.

If Billings understands human natur, and he thinks he duz, thare aint nothing that a true woman luvs more than the hole ov a man's harte; and, in order tu git this, she haz got tu know less than he duz, or maik him think so. I thank the Lord that thare aint menny wimmin in the world who want tu know evry thing. I kalkerlate that 9 out ov evry 10 ov the wimmin who luv their huzbands and glory in their children, will sa that tha had ruther be looked down upon in luving tenderniss than tu be looked up tu in silent aw.

If Josh Billings haz ced a wurd, in what he haz now rit, wich iz kalku-lated tu damp the arder ov one single aspirin' woman, he iz reddy tu shed tears, but I hav alwus thort that the very highly eddikated wimmin work best in single harniss. In konklusion, I sa, elevate the wimmin, but if their heds and their hartes bekum antagonicks in the operashun, I shall contin-ner tu think that luv, swapped for wizdom, iz a doutful gain to the wimmin and a pozatif loss to us poor mail-claid devils. Mi christian friends, ajew!

I hav finally kum to the konklusion, that a good reliable sett ov bowels, iz wurth more tu a man, than enny quantity ov brains.

Man was kreated a little lower than the angells and has bin gittin a lit-tle lower ever sinse.

When a feller gits a goin down hil, it dus seem as tho evry thing had bin greased for the okashun.

The Henpecked Man

The henpecked man iz most generally married; but thare are instances on reckord of single men being harrassed by the pullets.

Yu kan alwus tell one ov theze kind ov men, espeshily if they are in the company ov their wives. They look az humble and resighned tew their fate as a hen turkey in a wet day.

Thare ain't nothing that will take the starch out ov a man like being pecked by a woman. It is wuss than a seven months' turn ov the fever and agy.

The wives ov hen-pecked husbands most alwus out liv their viktims, and I hav known them tew git married agin, and git hold ov a man that time *(thank the Lord!)* who understood all the hen-peck dodges.

One ov these kind ov husbands iz an honor tew his sex.

The hen-pecked man, when he gits out amungst men, puts on an air ov bravery and defiance, and once in a while will git a leetle drunk, and then go home with a firm resolve that he will be captain ov his household; but the old woman soon takes the glory out ov him, and handles him just az she would a haff-grown chicken, who had fell into the swill barrel, and had tew be jerked out dredful quick.

When yu korte a widder, yu want tu du it with spurs on.

Thar iz 2 things in this life for which we are never fully prepared, and that iz twins.

Tu git wrongs out ov yure child's head—comb it often.

Better leave yure children virtew, than money, but this is a sekret known only tu a few.

In youth we run intu difficultkys, in old age difficultkys run intu us.

Josh Billings - *Hiz Book*
Carleton   1867

Up at the Horsepital

"A month ago today—or was it yesterday, I was given up for dead," sighed Skippy. "Yes Sir—all the undertakers fighting over me, only we know the doctor a long time."

"Aw, that's a lot o' balloon soup, cause last week it was a month ago—no matter when I see ya it's always a month ago—wake ya up in the middle o' the night an' it's a month ago."

"Nice way to talk, ain't it—an me near wearin' a granite hat."

"Well, I must say granite is very becomin' an' so slippery," and Sooky turned—"Then again, ya mustn't forget the choir 'd turn out in a body."

"Yeh—cause they get ten cents extra for corpse singin'."

"What d'ya want for ten cents—a player piano?"

"Well, what would they sing for ten cents?"

"'Now the day is over—'."

"Let's bat out a little harmony an' see how it sounds."

"Now—the day is ooo-vur—night is drawing nigh—ii—"

"Ya flat."

"Your flat."

"I ain't—an' besides, I don't want no flat singin' over me."

"Ya was sayin' somethin' about the horsepital—"

"Yeh—I got some insides took off me."

"What insides?"

"Tonsils."

"Them ain't kidneys, are they?"

"No—they're just downstairs from the Adam's apple."

"Oh, yes—o'course—Was there many bozos in the horsepital?"

"Oh some—we had it filled all the time. Ya see it's different than a roomin' hause, cause they don't wait for customers to come in—they go out an' look for them. They got a conductor in a white suit an' make believe he don't bring in business."

"S'pose ya don't want to go to the horsepital?"

"Ya gotta go—'cause the cops are in with them."

"Is them all what goes there?"

"No—people who have a change of underwear and' a suit o' pajamas don't wait to be took in—they breeze in any time."

"Fancy?"

"One guy come in with a satchel an' took the room next to me an' he no sooner took a bath an' put on a wall paper suit than zingo!—dead."

"Gee! He died then, huh?"

"Like that—powie!" and Skippy's fingers snapped.

"Maybe it was the bath what did it."

"It was a very sad bust for a new horsepital an' besides everybody filled up cause the guy had a new suit with extra pants."

"Oh! Isn't that a shame."

"An' that ain't all—he had a dozen handkerchifs an' three shirts just done up."

"Tst! Tst!"

"The nurse told me somethin' else I didn't know—He had a set o' false teeth, but she says they looked like a picket fence in his face.

Always Belittlin' by Percy Crosby
Unicorn Press, New York　　1927

―――――――― 🧒🧒 ――――――――

Vesey Street Theology

"Who started this World?" inquired the Belittler.

"A very lovely man—and smart too," Skippy replied. "Why, what's the matter with it?"

"Well, to begin with—I don't like the way toitles is made."

"What's wrong with 'em ?"

"Their bellies don't fit right 'cause their heads is always fallin' in."

"So! That's the credit God gets, huh, after he stayed up nights tryin' to think up a toitle?"

"Why didn't he look in the zoo?"

"This was away before zoos—before everything even. Why he owns everything."

"Oh, Real Estate."

"No, before that—he just began on air."

"I got cha—insurance."

"No! No! Air! Don't ya know what they put in noses? That's what he put holes in ya for."

"Do ya call that lovely—putting' holes in a guy?"

"Ya have to have air don't ya?"

"I push it right back."

"Squeezin' me up the vestibule, ain't cha, but I ain't to be took in by belittlin'; if you're so hot why don't you think up a world?" and Skippy added, as if to ward off the possibility, "An' don't be comin' around unless ya got the stars to go with it."

"Ya mustn't forget I make me own kites."

"You're going' to listen to how this world was made if I have to give ya a sock in the nose."

When assured of the other's silence, Skippy began: "God just had to snap his fingers an' a flock o' angels'd bring an ocean. 'Put it here,' he'd say, and ZINGO! There's an ocean."

"I know it's a lot o' bother, usen't we have gold fish."

"An' if it didn't fit, he just had it moved over 'cause he had to make room for a beach, maybe—I dunno, Bible lessons aint very clear on that."

"Maybe he wanted to make room for a ferris wheel."

"No! That all came later; do ya think angels flew aroun' eatin' frankfurters an' gettin' mustard all over their wings? No, Sir! God was too very refined for any such goin's on."

"What did angels get for settin' up an ocean?"

"Angels is very lovely people—just beautiful! All they did was play aroun' with harps."

"Oh! then they was in with the cops."

"G'wan, ya little goose fly—always belittlin'!"

Always Belittlin by Percy Crosby
Unicorn Press, New York   1927

Grandma and Grandpa had unique ways of expressing themselves. And their sayings and descriptions were not only funny but were accurate in their analysis of the person or situation. Here are some old-timers that are as adequate today as back then.

Description of a very fat woman: She's easier to step over than to go around.

Confused person: He don't know c'mere from sic 'em.

He lies so much he has to have his wife call the dog.

If brains were dynamite...he couldn't blow his nose.

That's about as useless as ten buggies in a one-horse town.

(That out-of-place feeling): I feel like the bastard at a family picnic.

(Rejected woman): He told me he wouldn't take me to a dog fight—even if I had a chance to win.

Mr. Evans' trumpet pupils had a recital last night and it was noisier than two skeletons making love on a tin roof.

I'm just too busy now to help you. I'm busier than a one-legged man at an ass-kicking.

(To close a meeting): It's time to call the dog, piss on the fire and holler "let's go!"

We live so far back in the woods, we got to pack in our sunshine.

We're out in the country so far, we don't get Grand Ol' Opry till Wednesday.

That Ebenezer Scrooge...he's so tight he only has one shoe half-soled at a time.

He's really a nice boy. You can tell he's been corn-fed and hand-spanked.

To describe someone lacking brains: His elevator don't go all the way to the top. Or...his lights are on but nobody's home.

A good sermon: That preacher was shootin' rockets right thru them pearly gates.

I feel like a bar of homemade soap after a hard wash day...just like I've been chewed up and spit out.

Jerry was in the outhouse when brains was passed out.

I'm so excited about my new job, I gotta walk wideways to keep from flyin'.

They done give me a job that was harder'n tryin' to push a wheelbar-row with rope handles.

What a rough, coarse voice! He sounded like a buzz saw sawin' cast iron.

> *Granny Had a Word for it* by Tom Ludwig
> Rose Publishing Co., Little Rock, AR 1985

———————— 🧍🧍 ————————

Little Arbie met a bear,
And the bear met Arbie.
The bear was bulgy,
The bulge was Arbie.

———————— 🧍🧍 ————————

Why was the lettuce embarrassed?
Because it saw the salad dressing.

———————— 🧍🧍 ————————

Child at a magic show: "Where is that lady you sawed in half the last time you were in this town?"

"Well, I'll tell you...half of her is in New York and the other half is living in Los Angeles."

———————— 🧍🧍 ————————

Nurse: "The doctor told you to take your medicine after you were through taking your bath. Did you?"

Dickie: "After I finished all that bath water, there wasn't no room for the medicine!"

———————— 🧍🧍 ————————

The following are old-fashioned sayings from the little books, *How to Talk Dirty Like Grandad,* by Tom Ludwig and published by Rose Publishing Co., Little Rock, AR. This is the way our grandfathers talked while they built the country.

My wife made coffee so weak you could stand in a barrel full and still see your toes.

My wife don't git excited about nothin'. She wouldn't walk a mile to see a piss ant eat a bale of hay.

She's scarce-hipped. (Thin)

Is he fat? Well, I guess! He's two axe handles wide!

Conceit: Her nose was stuck so high in the air, she'd drown if she got caught in the rain.

He's so ugly when he lays on the beach, the tide won't come in.

He's so bucktoothed, he could eat sweet corn through a picket fence.

That man is useless as tits on a boar hog. (Male pig)

He's so crooked, they'll have to screw him in the ground when they bury him.

Your idea has about as much chance of succeedin' as a butterfly in a cement mixer.

When that blonde walked away, her rear end reminded me of two tom-cats fightin' in a gunny sack.

He didn't have no more chance of succeedin' than a grasshopper in a hen house.

They say she can carry a ton. Maybe so. But God help us when she delivers it.

On out-of-wedlock babies: They planted a garden before they had a fence around it. Or: They ate supper before they said grace.

An impossible job: Doin' that's like tryin' to scratch your ear with your elbow.

It ain't no disgrace to be poor...but it's mighty unhandy.

About a loud talker: If hot air was music, that feller'd be a brass band.

I feel so tired, like I done ironed all day with a cold iron.

I'm so unlucky! If I was to throw an apple up with one hand, I'd catch horse manure coming' down.

Is he a good salesman? Well, I guess! He could sell chastity belts to the whores in the St. Louis red-light district.

(About a womanizer) If I wore tin pants that feller'd be after me with a tin can opener.

Gettin' him to change his mind is like trying to nail jelly to the wall.

He's so old, he looks like he wouldn't last more'n one more clean shirt.

She's as nervous as a long-tailed cat in a room full of rockers.

That feller's got more money than a porcupine has quills.

That old gal sure wears tight pants. She had a dime in her back pocket the other day And I could see the head of it pressing out.

That dress is about as sexy as socks on a rooster.

That ol' boy is older than dirt.

He's so thin, you gotta shake the sheets to find him.

He's so skinny, he's got to walk by twicet to make a shadow.

She drove her ducks to a poor market. (She made a bad marriage.)
She's been eating 'taters and they all settled in one place!
He can carry a tune but Lord help us when he delivers it.
Marriage: When a man churches a woman.
It's no disgrace to be poor, but it's mighty unhandy!
Describing a long-married couple: They've been together so long, they're on their second bottle of Tabasco.
That guy is so useless, he couldn't drive nails in a snowbank.
To describe a person wearing shorts: He jumped into his britches too far.

———————— 🧑‍🤝‍🧑 ————————

What's your name?
John Brown.
Ask me again,
And I'll knock you down.

———————— 🧑‍🤝‍🧑 ————————

What's your name?
Pudding and tame.
Ask me again and
I'll tell you the same.

———————— 🧑‍🤝‍🧑 ————————

Where do you live?
Down the lane.
What's your number?
Cucumber.

———————— 🧑‍🤝‍🧑 ————————

Do you carrot all for me?
My heart beets for you,
With your turnip nose,
And your radish hose;

———————— 🧑‍🤝‍🧑 ————————

You are a peach.
If we cantaloupe,
Lettuce marry;
Weed make a swell pear.

Our School Days

Dear reader, in the midst of the hurry and the distraction of business do you ever look far out across the purple hills, with misty vision, and think of the days, now held in the sacred silence of your memory, when you trudged through the June sunlight to the little log school house, with bare feet and happy heart?

Do the pleasant memories come thronging back to you now of those hallowed years in your history when you bowed your head above your spelling lesson, and, while filling your mind with useful knowledge, you also filled your system full of doughnuts and thought?

How sweetly come back to us to-day, like an almost forgotten fragrance of honeysuckle and wood violets, the recollections of the school-room, the busy hum of a score of industrious scholars, and, above all, the half-repressed sob of the freckled youth who thoughtlessly hovered o'er the bent pin for a brief, transitory moment. Oh! who can give us back the hallowed joys of childhood, when we ostensibly sought out the whereabouts of Timbuctoo in our geography while we slid a vigorous wasp into the pants pocket of our seat mate.

Our common schools are the foundations of America's free institutions. They are bulwarks of our liberty and the glory and pride of a great republic. It is there that the youth of our land learn the rudiments of greatness and how to throw a paper wad with unerring precision.

Do you remember when you had no dreams of statesmanship and when the holy ambition to be a paragrapher had never fired your young blood? Do you remember when you had no ambition except to be the boy who could tell the most plausible lie? Do you still remember with what wonderful discretion you sought out and imposed upon the boy you thought you could lick? And do you still call to mind the thrill of glad surprise that came over you when you made a slight error and the meek-eyed victim arose in his wrath and left you a lonesome ruin?

Do you ever stop to think of those glorious holidays you took without the teacher's consent? How you rambled in the wildwood all day and gathered nuts, and crab apples, and wood ticks, and watermelons and mosquito bites? Have you returned tired and hungry at night and felt that your parents wouldn't be so tickled to see you as they might be?

Do you know of the day when you rashly resolved to lick your father, and he persuaded you to change your mind and let him lick you?

Who would rob us of these green memories of other days? Who would snatch from us the joy we still experience in bringing up those pictures of careless childhood when we bathed in the clear, calm waters of the smooth flowing river, or pelted each other with mud or dead frogs while the town people drove by and wondered why the authorities didn't take some measures to prevent boys from bathing in public places.

   People come into The Boomerang office every day and see us writing out checks and raking in the scads and think that we must be happy, but we'd give all these gaudy trappings of wealth and luxuriant ease for one week of those schooldays, when we had less wealth but more appetite.

   It might not look dignified for a man upon whom the eye of the nation rests, to descend to the sports of youth, but every little while an almost irresistible spell comes o'er us to lay aside our white vests and costly gems, while we don a gingham shirt, a pair of top boots and some other finery, and make a raid on the watermelon trees of Wyoming.

Forty Liars, and Other Lies by Bill Nye
Bedford Clark & Co., Chicago & New York.   1884

Those Wicked, Wicked Boys!

Boys' wit and blunder are so different from girls'!

   Girls are sweet and confiding, while boys are robust and sometimes cruel in their answers. The fact is, boys are boys, and girls are girls. Sometimes I think our little Johnnie, Ethel's brother, is positively wicked.

   One evening when Johnnie was saying his prayers he broke out:

   "Oh, I do so wish I had a little pug dog!"

   "Had a what, Johnnie?" exclaimed his mother.

   "Why, a little pug dog, Mamma. I do want one so much."

   "Why, what does Mamma's darling want one of those ugly brutes for? Why could you want it, Johnnie?"

   "I want it because I know where I could sell his skin for fifteen dollars to a dog-stuffer, by ginger!"

   Where Johnnie got that "by ginger" we never knew, but after his mother had scolded him a little about using such words, she suggested that he finish his evening prayer, which he did, praying:

   "Oh, Lord, bless the baby and make him so he can't cry. Bless brother Bill and make him as good a boy as I am. Good-by, Lord. I'm going to the circus in the morning. Amen." Then, as if he had forgotten something, Charley hollered out: "Oh, Lord, don't forget Bill."

   The boy comes out the strongest in the youth on the possession of the first pair of boots or pants with big pockets in them. It's the pockets that make a boy jump from a boy to a man in an hour. When Johnnie put on his first trousers, he was very proud. He strutted up and down in front of his mother almost crazy with delight. Then he burst out:

   "Oh, mamma, pants makes me feel so grand! Didn't it make you feel grand when—" But an awful consciousness came over him that this bliss had never been shared by his mother, and he laid his wee, chubby hand pityingly against her cheek, saying pathetically:

"Poor mamma! Poor mamma!"

The question is often asked what makes our dear little baby boy so rude? I can answer that the boy's uncle is generally to blame. It amuses the uncle and he does not think that he is really spoiling the boy.

Now our little Johnnie was especially beloved by his Uncle William. Still his uncle used to tease him a good deal and teach him all kinds of nonsense rhymes just to plague his mother. One day I was telling the children about Satan. I told them that Satan was a wicked tempter and that is why our Saviour said, "Get thee behind me, Satan."

"Now," said I, "can any of you children tell me anything about Satan?"

"Johnnie can," said Ethel.

"Well, Johnnie," I said, "you can stand up and tell us what you know about Satan."

Then Johnnie arose proudly and repeated in a boyish key:

Now I lay me down to sleep,

I pray the Lord my soul to keep;

If I die before I wake,

It'll puzzle Satan to pull me straight.

"Why, Johnnie," I said in amazement, "did your mother teach you that?"

"No, but Uncle William did; and he taught me 'by ginger,' too!"

Oh, this wicked, wicked Uncle William.

Boys are usually shrewder than girls. They will show deep diplomacy in order to gain a point. One morning Johnnie climbed up into his grandmother's lap and showed great affection.

"Gran'ma," he said, as he twined his arm lovingly around her neck, "how old are you?"

"About sixty-six," said the grandmother.

"You'll die soon, won't you, gran'ma?"

"Yes, dear, I expect to."

"And when I die, gran'ma, can I be buried 'side of you?"

"Yes, dear," said she, as her heart warmed toward the little one, whom she folded closer in her arms.

"Gran'ma," softly whispered the little rogue, "gimme ten cents."

One day Johnnie was sliding down the banisters and making a great noise in the hall when his grandmother came to the head of the stairs and said:

"Boys, boys! I wouldn't slide down those banisters—I would not do it."

"Why, gran'ma, you can't," said little Charley disdainfully, as he picked himself up from the hall floor.

Yes, Johnnie is a sweet child, and loved his mother, but the boy in him was always breaking out. When his mother got sick, he came and stood by the bed, his great big eyes all full of tears, and said:

"Oh, dear mamma, I hope 'ou won't die till the circus comes!"

Johnnie's sister Ethel had been cautioned when they went up to their grandmother not to take the last egg, the nest egg, out of the nest. One morning, however, Ethel got it, and Johnnie came into a parlor full of company screaming, in a high ten voice:

"Oh, grandma! Ethel's got the egg the old hen measures by!"

Children often stumble into an exceedingly good joke. I think this is the best one I know of. The teacher was questioning the arithmetic class.

"Boys," he said, "before slates were in use, how did the people multiply?"

"I know, thir," said Johnnie, "I read it in my gog'fry this morning; they 'multiplied on the face of the earth.'"

"Right, Johnnie," said the teacher. "And now, Joseph," he added, addressing another boy, "why is it that Johnnie can multiply so much quicker than you?"

"Because 'fools multiply very rapidly,' thir."

Johnnie's first composition on dogs ran as follows: One time there was a feller bot a dog of a man in the market, and the dog it was a biter.

After it had bit the feller four or five times he threw a clothesline over its neck and led it back

to the dog man in the market, and he said to the dog man, the feller did, "Ole man, dident

you use to have this dog?" The dog man he luked at the dog, and then he thot awhile and

then he said, "Well, yes, I had him about haf the time and the other haf he had me." Then

the feller he was fewrious mad, and he said, "Wat did you sell me such a dog as thisn for?"

And the old man he spoke up and sed, "For four dollars and seventy 5 cents, loffle money." Then the feller he guessed he wude go home if the dog was willing.

Eli Perkins - Thirty Years of Wit
Melvine D. Landon.   1891

ACKNOWLEDGMENTS

Always Be Littlin!, Bill Nye. 1884. Bedford Clarke & Co., Chicago, IL.

Bill Nye's Redbook, Bill Nye. 1891. Wiley Book Co., NY.

Children's Letters to God, Stewart Hemple and Eric Marshall. Workman Publishing Co., NY.

Eli Perkins - Thirty Years of Wit. 1891. Melvine D. Landon.

Forty Liars and Other Lies, by Bill Nye. 1884. Bedford Clarke & Co., Chicago, IL

Granny Had a Word for It, Tom Ladwig. 1985. Rose Publishing Co., Little Rock, AR

How to Talk Dirty Like Grandad, Tom Ladwig. 1988. Rose Publishing Co., Little Rock, AR

Illinois Farm Bureau Almanac, Bloomington, IL

Joe Creason's Kentucky, by Joe Creason. The Louisville Courier. 1972. Reprinted by permission of Bill Creason.

Joker Number One, Cadumus Press. 1910. Galesburg, IL

Josh Billings - Hiz Book, by Josh Billings. 1867. Carleton.

Just for the Fun of It by Carl Goerch. 1954. Edwards & Broughton Co., Raleigh, NC.

Justin Wilson's Cajun Humor, by Justin Wilson and Howard Jacobs. 1974. Pelican Publishing Company, Gretna, LA.

Kids Say the Darndest Things, Art Linkletter. 1962. Bernard Geis Associates, New York, NY.

Laughter in Appalachia, by Loyal Jones and Billy Edd Wheeler. 1987. August House, Little Rock, AR.

New England Joke Book, by Arthur G. Crandall. 1922. F.A. Davis Company, Publishers, Philadelphia, PA

Partner's Pearls, Bloomington, IL.

Pun American Newsletter, Lila Bondy. Deerfield, IL.

State Journal-Register, Toby McDaniel. 1996. Springfield, IL

Straight Texas, by Cornelia Chambers. Texas Folklore Society No. XIII, 1937. Nacogdoches, TX.

Tar Heel Laughter, Richard Walser, Editor. 1974. University of North Carolina Press, Chapel Hill, NC.

That Darned Minister's Son, by Haydn S. Pearson. 1950. Doubleday & Company, Inc., Garden City, NY.

The Best of American Jewish Humor, Henry D. Spalding. 1976. Jonathan David Publishers, Inc. Middle Village, NY.

The Cornbread Chronicles, Ludlow Porch. 1983. Peachtree Publishers, Ltd., Atlanta, GA.

Trails Plowed Under, by Charles M. Russell. 1927. Bantam Doubleday Dell Publishing Group, Inc., New York, NY.

When It's Laughter You're After, Stewart Harral. 1969. University of Oklahoma Press, Norman, OK.

Cartoons:

Bucella, Martin — Cheektowaga, NY.

Carpenter, Dave — Emmetsburg, PA.

Epstein, Benita — Cardiff, CA.

Gaspirtz, Oliver — Brooklyn, NY.

Hawkins, Jonny — Sherwood, MI.

Henderickson, Walter — Rockford, IL.

Hayes, John — Lenexa, KS.

Linkert, Lo — Mission, B.C., Canada

Masters Agency, George Crenshaw — Capitola, CA.

Schwadron, Harley — Ann Arbor, MI.

The Saturday Evening Post Society — Indianapolis, IN.

Also available from Lincoln-Herndon Press:

*Grandpa's Rib-Ticklers and Knee-Slappers ....$ 8.95
*Josh Billings—America's Phunniest Phellow ....$ 7.95
Davy Crockett—Legendary Frontier Hero...$ 7.95
Cowboy Life on the Sidetrack ....$ 7.95
A Treasury of Science Jokes...$ 9.95
The Great American Liar—Tall Tales...$ 9.95
The Cowboy Humor of A.H. Lewis ....$ 9.95
The Fat Mascot—22 Funny Baseball Stories and More ....$ 7.95
A Treasury of Farm and Ranch Humor ....$ 10.95
Mr. Dooley—We Need Him Now!..$ 8.95
A Treasury of Military Humor ....$ 10.95
Here's Charley Weaver, Mamma and Mt. Idy ....$ 9.95
A Treasury of Hunting and Fishing Humor ....$ 10.95
A Treasury of Senior Humor...$ 10.95
A Treasury of Medical Humor...$ 10.95
A Treasury of Husband and Wife Humor ....$ 10.95
A Treasury of Religious Humor ....$ 10.95
A Treasury of Farm Women's Humor...$ 12.95
A Treasury of Office Humor..$ 10.95
A Treasury of Cocktail Humor ....$ 10.95
A Treasury of Business Humor ....$ 12.95
A Treasury of Mom, Pop & Kids' Humor ....$ 12.95
The Humorous Musings of a School Principal..$ 12.95
A Treasury of Police Humor ....$ 12.95
A Treasury of Veterinary Humor ....$ 12.95

*Available in hardback

The humor in these books will delight you, brighten your conversation, make your life more fun, and healthier, because "Laughter is the Best Medicine."

Order from:
The Lincoln-Herndon Press, Inc.
818 South Dirksen Parkway
Springfield, IL 62703
(217) 522-2732
FAX (217) 544-8738